Apples for Jam

Apples for Jam

A COLORFUL COOKBOOK

-TESSA KIROS-

PHOTOGRAPHY: MANOS CHATZIKONSTANTIS
STYLING: MICHAIL TOUROS   ART DIRECTION: LISA GREENBERG
ILLUSTRATIONS BY THE MICE

Andrews McMeel
Publishing, LLC

Kansas City

FIRST PUBLISHED IN 2006 BY MURDOCH BOOKS PTY LIMITED
PIER 8/9, 23 HICKSON ROAD, MILLERS POINT NSW 2000

APPLES FOR JAM COPYRIGHT © 2006 BY MURDOCH BOOKS PTY LIMITED. TEXT COPYRIGHT © 2006 BY TESSA KIROS. PHOTOGRAPHS COPYRIGHT © 2006 BY MANOS CHATZIKONSTANTIS.

07 08 09 10 11 TEN 10 9 8 7 6 5 4 3 2 1

ISBN-13: 978-0-7407-6971-9

ISBN-10: 0-7407-6971-5

LIBRARY OF CONGRESS CONTROL NUMBER: 2007928063

WWW.ANDREWSMCMEEL.COM

PHOTOGRAPHY: MANOS CHATZIKONSTANTIS
STYLING: MICHAIL TOUROS
ART DIRECTION: LISA GREENBERG
EDITOR: JANE PRICE
DESIGNER: SARAH ODGERS
FOOD EDITOR: JO GLYNN
PRODUCTION: MEGAN ALSOP
ILLUSTRATIONS BY THE MICE
CHIEF EXECUTIVE: JULIET ROGERS
PUBLISHER: KAY SCARLETT

ATTENTION: SCHOOLS AND BUSINESSES

ANDREWS MCMEEL BOOKS ARE AVAILABLE AT QUANTITY DISCOUNTS WITH BULK PURCHASE FOR EDUCATIONAL, BUSINESS, OR SALES PROMOTIONAL USE. FOR INFORMATION, PLEASE WRITE TO: SPECIAL SALES DEPARTMENT, ANDREWS MCMEEL PUBLISHING, LLC, 4520 MAIN STREET, KANSAS CITY, MISSOURI 64111.

- FOR THE MAMMAS -

FOR GIOVANNI WHO HELPED ME MAKE THE MICE,

AND FOR YASMINE, CASSIA, ANAIS, AND DANIEL,

THE FOUR FAIRIES I KNOW BEST

- contents -

recipes for life

I have collected these recipes over the years. This
is food for families, for young people, for old people,
for children, for the child in all . . . for life. Some are
recipes I remember from my own childhood, others
are the food I want to cook now for my family.

I have looked in the hide-and-seek places of children and tried to find four-
leaf clovers; dug through the coloring boxes of summer and winter and
found many treasures. This is about whispering advice to a sister,
swapping recipes over fences, sharing crumbs on a train with a stranger.
I am passing on those things that I wish to know from people—the very
stuff that makes me smile and puts a twinkle in my eye. The things that
we hold, together with emergency cookies, in our apron pockets—that we
take to bed with us at night. The knowing and unknowing at that moment
just before we close our eyes, when we wonder what we did all day and if
what we did do was right.

Feeding a family is about stitching all the bits together on a steady
thread—between the school cafeteria, your knowledge of nutrition, your
own family's tastes, your capacity, and how much you can give—and still
leaving some space for spontaneity and the will of nature. And all this
should still have the grace and honesty of a daisy chain.

Daisy chains, circuses, ice cream cones, fishing nets, dressing-up in
mamma's clothes . . . we dreamed of reaching the stars. We knew it all,
had solutions for everything, and never got tired until they forced us to
bed and we fell, exhausted, not wanting to miss a drop of anything. We
had such dare in our glare, such things to get done, ideas that sprouted

nonstop into our fertile minds, while our parents were trimming and weeding, and, I am sure, at moments wishing the blossoms would stay still forever.

I love the collage of it all—a little bit like dancing together—the mixing of a child's soul and tastes with your own, and adding a squeeze of lemon and a dash of creativity. Step one, miss one, step one, miss one, don't step on that line or you'll marry a snake. And nod at every pillar on the way home from school.

As a child, I wanted orange soda and special sandwiches held together with mystery. I wanted tiny colored cakes and other things that I'd read about that impressed me—tubs of purity lying amongst fresh flowers in a field and wondering what the next password would be in our tiny club house. These are the things I want my children to have now—now, as I watch them lying in the grass hugging only this moment, while my mind is spinning with the washing machine and wondering what school lunch should be tomorrow.

For a lot of the time, I feel as if we are in a relay race, swapping batons just in the nick of time, trying to get it all going a little smoother. But children are just so now, I try to take lessons from them—they want it now, to eat what they want now, to have fun now. No borrowing. No point.

I will not force them to like the smell of boiled cauliflower, but I will paint better pictures in their bowls, let them make their own sandwiches, have apple bread when they come home from school, ratty and ravenous, and tell stories while we eat, and love them all the same whether they like meat or not. I will try to compliment them on their differences and insight and hold them up to the light of other moons, and maybe hand-sew their marble sacks if they will have them in florals—just like the dresses I wanted to sew for my dolls, while I made mud pies and dreamed of being part of the circus. I wanted to somersault my way through life and fly gracefully through the air, all glittery and well-composed. I wanted to be confided in by the other girls, wanted the teacher to love me, wanted to eat home-churned butter and cream and have my sandwiches made from farmy things. And I wanted braces on my teeth—just like all the others had—so that I could blend in and be part of the flock.

And now I carefully weave things into lunch pails so that they, too, can belong in the flock. I give them chocolate bread with butter, fish pie, and bright-colored fruit salad, roast chicken, and pancakes, all with an air of no fuss and no importance, as if they just happened to be there. I will give them the things I dreamed about on my walks with my brother and sister. It is what I can give them from the depth of me . . . because I want to give them my best. My BEST chocolate cake.

I want to wash their sheets so they smell of tumbling hills and blossoms, roll out crisp beautiful pastries, and boil up bright floral and strawberry jams. Wrap their dreams up beautifully and set them down on stable stones—with some big whole wheat bread crumbs dropped down in case they lose their way.

Let me forget and just giggle with them, and leave apples lying around the house with just a couple of bites taken out, and fly with the winds of now as I collect the pearls that spill from their mouths. Let me scatter some inspiration onto them and hope to see it in their drawings—hope their suns are smiling and that I am always drawn next to them. Let me sprinkle more cinnamon sugar on their paths and hold hands as we collect apples and bright berries and watch them all joining together in the pan for jam.

Have I added to their building blocks, shoring them up with strength and their own magnificence? Have I shown them enough color? Did I let them have enough ice cream and leave them alone enough without my anxieties? How can we know which is the right way? We have to go with our inner instincts and the feeling in our bones. But I can contribute to their growing cells, show them some foods that are better than others, walk with them, and encourage their own tastes. I can teach them to love and appreciate food, help them treat their bodies like gold, listen to them wanting more or less. The rest I have to trust.

May I just get to the end of my road and say, I have done this important thing in my life, and I have done it well.

So here are some of my recipes to add to yours. Leave out the wine and use unsweetened grape juice, if you like. Grind pepper over whoever's plate will appreciate it, and add your own favorite ingredients, or just use them as they are.

Tessa

red

Cranberry syrup
Vermicelli soup with tomato and basil
Vermicelli soup with lemon and butter
Penne with tomato, eggplant, and ricotta
Pasta with tuna, tomato, and olives
Spaghetti with meatballs
Pasta with prosciutto, tomato, and oregano
Pasta with tomato sauce
Tomato lasagne
Meat lasagne
Tomato risotto
Fried risotto balls
Rice and vegetable pilaf
Chicken casserole
Chicken cutlets with tomatoes and capers
Veal involtini
Hamburger patties
Sautéed tomatoes in olive oil and rosemary
Ripe tomato salad
Cannellini beans in tomato
Eggs in tomato
La pizza rossa
Raspberry sauce
Berry and buttermilk cake
Chocolate and cranberry cookies
Strawberry sorbet
A colored fruit salad
Meringue with strawberries and chocolate
Rosehip jam
Rosehip semolina puddings
Strawberry jam
Quince jam
Jam shortbread

- memory -

I am scrambling everything into a basket for a picnic, wondering what should go with the red peppers on the sandwiches and if we have enough drinks and paper towels. They are bickering about which toys to take and how many books. The wonder of it all. I'd like to keep them this way—just hopping, scar-free, from one moment to the next.

I remember those moments, too, when long playful days skipped onto rainbow-streaked colors through the sky, as if a flutter of fairies had just danced across, and we could smell the night air beginning to settle. But we still had some adventure left in us, so we carried it into the dark and shone flashlights to illuminate it. We fell asleep to the colors of pompoms, still counting out the numbers of our badly drawn hopscotch. Every day was like a holiday. We fell into our clothes after leap-frogging out of bed and marched our way through the house, demanding early morning answers to our curiosities.

I would love a moment of that back—that excitement at being allowed to leave the table, just to fly through a field of long grass and find a nest.

1 1/2 CUPS CRANBERRIES
2/3 CUP SUPERFINE SUGAR OR
    VANILLA SUPERFINE SUGAR
1/2 CUP BOILING WATER

Cranberry syrup

Here are two ways to make a cranberry syrup: one for drinking with ice and the other for drizzling over vanilla or mango ice cream. This second version is also good drizzled over pancakes or waffles, with some whipped cream or vanilla ice cream. I love starting from scratch with this type of thing—it really makes me feel as if I am doing something special. Add more or less sugar according to your personal taste, and you can use fresh or frozen cranberries. I like to use vanilla-infused superfine sugar if I have some in the cupboard.

Rinse the cranberries well. Put them in a deep nonaluminum bowl, sprinkle the sugar over the top and squish it through your fingers to break up the cranberries (children might like to help you with this). Pour in 1/2 cup of just-boiled water and leave it to mingle for a bit. Crush the cranberries more now with a wooden spoon (or a potato masher works well). Strain through a sieve that is fine enough to eliminate all the seeds and skins, pressing down with your wooden spoon to extract all the juice. Cool completely, then chill.

Pour into glasses and top up with as much sparkling or still water as you like and a few ice cubes, or even just ice cubes, depending on how strong you like it.

For a thicker syrup to serve over ice cream, put the cranberry syrup into a small pan and simmer over medium heat until it reduces and thickens. If necessary, skim the surface with a slotted spoon to remove any foam. The syrup will turn ruby red and cling a little to the spoon. Cool completely.

Makes 1 1/2 cups of drinking syrup or a scant
1 cup of pouring syrup

7 CUPS WATER OR BROTH
1 TABLESPOON CANNED TOMATO SAUCE
4 BASIL LEAVES
1 1/2 TEASPOONS SALT (OPTIONAL)
1/4 (16-OUNCE) PACKAGE VERMICELLI OR
    ANGEL HAIR PASTA, BROKEN UP
OLIVE OIL, TO SERVE
GRATED PARMESAN CHEESE, TO SERVE

Vermicelli soup with tomato and basil

This is very simple, quick, and memorable when it's properly cooked. It really is my crisis-saver. If you use vegetable or chicken broth, your soup will have a stronger taste—but with just plain water like this, it is quick and beautiful and means you can present a meal in no time. Serve this immediately or the pasta just swells in the soup. If you're not feeling fantastic, or are feeling miserable with a bit of a cold, this is the thing to lift your spirits.

Put the water, tomato sauce, and basil leaves in a pan and add 1 1/2 teaspoons of salt (this shouldn't be necessary if you're using broth). Bring to a boil, then simmer over low heat for 6 to 7 minutes before adding the pasta. Cook the pasta until a few seconds before the package says it should be ready (it will continue cooking in the hot broth) and then immediately remove the pan from the heat. Ladle out into bowls, diving to the bottom of the pot each time to make sure everyone has a fair helping of pasta and broth. Drizzle a little olive oil over each bowl if you like, but definitely give a good sprinkling of Parmesan (about 1 very heaping tablespoon for each bowl). Serve immediately.

Serves 4 to 6

7 CUPS WATER OR BROTH
JUICE OF HALF A LEMON
2 TO 3 TABLESPOONS BUTTER
1 1/2 TEASPOONS SALT (OPTIONAL)
1/4 (16-OUNCE) PACKAGE VERMICELLI OR
    ANGEL HAIR PASTA, BROKEN UP
FINELY GRATED HALOUMI OR PARMESAN CHEESE,
    TO SERVE
BLACK PEPPER, TO SERVE
3 TO 4 MINT LEAVES, TORN (OR A LITTLE CRUSHED
    DRIED MINT), TO SERVE

Vermicelli soup with lemon and butter

Here is a version of vermicelli soup that they tend to make in Greece and Cyprus. If you have a light chicken, fish, or meat stock, then use that, but I love this even just with water . . . a soup in moments. You can leave out the mint, if you'd prefer.

Put the water, lemon juice, and butter in a pan and add 1 1/2 teaspoons of salt (this shouldn't be necessary if you're using broth). Bring to a boil, then simmer over low heat for 6 to 7 minutes before adding the pasta. Cook the pasta until a few seconds before the package says it should be ready (it will continue cooking in the hot broth) and then immediately remove the pan from the heat. Ladle out into bowls, sprinkle with haloumi or Parmesan, and give a good grinding of pepper and a scattering of mint for those who'd like it. Serve immediately.

Serves 4 to 6

The thing that every Italian person, in Tuscany at least, has told me when I ask what they remember from their childhood is a piece of white bread, rustic country bread, quite thickly cut, hand-splashed with red wine and then scattered with white sugar. Served just like that to the waiting children. They all remember it well.

1 SMALL EGGPLANT
SALT AND FRESHLY GROUND PEPPER
5 TABLESPOONS OLIVE OIL
1 LARGE CLOVE GARLIC, PEELED AND SQUASHED
  A BIT
1 (14-OUNCE) CAN DICED TOMATOES,
  OR 1 (14-OUNCE) CAN TOMATO SAUCE
3/4 (16-OUNCE) PACKAGE PENNE
1/4 CUP SALTED MATURE RICOTTA
  OR FINELY GRATED PARMESAN CHEESE
3 TABLESPOONS CHOPPED FRESH PARSLEY

Penne with tomato, eggplant, and ricotta

This has just a dash of eggplant, but you could add more if you like. A nice, mild, and still very Italian pasta.

Cut the eggplant into slices about 1/4 inch thick and about 1 inch across. Toss them into a colander, sprinkle with a teaspoon of salt, and leave them for about 30 minutes to drain off any bitter juices.

Heat half the olive oil with the garlic clove in a smallish pan over medium-low heat until you can just smell the garlic. Add the tomatoes and season with some salt and pepper. When it comes to a boil, lower the heat and simmer uncovered for 15 to 20 minutes, until it all melts into a sauce. Break up any bits of tomato with a wooden spoon as you stir. Keep warm.

Rinse and drain the eggplant pieces and pat them dry with paper towels. Heat the remaining oil in a nonstick frying pan and sauté the eggplant over medium heat until it is crusty and golden in places on the outside but still soft inside.

Meanwhile, cook the penne in a large pan of boiling salted water, following the package instructions. Drain, keeping a cupful of the water.

Put the pasta in a large serving bowl. Add the eggplant, the tomato sauce, cheese, and parsley and mix together thoroughly, adding some of the pasta cooking water if the pasta seems dry. Serve immediately.

Serves 4

My Greek friends remember coming home from school to a piece of white bread, lightly broiled and splashed with olive oil, then sprinkled with some beautiful oregano, crushed between their mamma's fingers.

2½ TABLESPOONS OLIVE OIL
2 CLOVES GARLIC, PEELED AND SQUASHED A BIT
1 SMALL LEAFY CELERY STALK, FINELY CHOPPED
1 (14-OUNCE) CAN DICED TOMATOES
SALT AND FRESHLY GROUND BLACK PEPPER
1 (6-OUNCE) CAN TUNA IN OIL, DRAINED
4 TABLESPOONS HOT WATER
3 BASIL LEAVES, TORN
2 TABLESPOONS FINELY CHOPPED FRESH
   PARSLEY
8 PITTED KALAMATA OLIVES, HALVED
16-OUNCE PACKAGE PASTA (PENNE, FARFALLE,
   OR SPAGHETTI)
OLIVE OIL, TO SERVE

Pasta with tuna, tomato, and olives

Olives may or may not be appreciated by young ones, so I just add a few, leaving them in big chunks so the grown-ups can remove them. I like to use penne, farfalle, or spaghetti with this sauce. Adults can also sprinkle a little chopped chile or chile oil over theirs.

Heat the oil and garlic in a wide saucepan. When you can smell the garlic, add the celery and sauté over gentle heat until it softens and turns pale gold. Add the tomatoes, season with salt and a twist of pepper and simmer for 10 to 15 minutes, breaking up the tomatoes with a wooden spoon. Add the tuna, breaking up the chunks with your wooden spoon. Add 4 tablespoons of hot water, let it come to a boil, and then stir in the basil, parsley, and olives. Simmer for a few minutes before removing from the heat. The sauce should not be too dry, so add a few more drops of water if necessary.

   Cook the pasta in a large pan of salted water, following the package instructions. Drain, keeping a cupful of the cooking water. Toss the pasta with the sauce, adding a little cooking water if necessary to help the sauce coat the pasta. Serve immediately, with a drizzle of olive oil and a little black pepper for the adults.

Serves 4

MEATBALLS:
1½ SLICES SOFT CRUSTLESS WHITE BREAD,
   TORN INTO CHUNKS
5 TABLESPOONS MILK
14 OUNCES GROUND PORK AND VEAL
3 TABLESPOONS CHOPPED FRESH PARSLEY
½ TEASPOON GROUND CINNAMON
½ TEASPOON GROUND CUMIN
½ TEASPOON SALT
½ SMALL RED ONION
ABOUT 5 TABLESPOONS LIGHT OLIVE OIL, FOR FRYING

SAUCE:
2½ TABLESPOONS OLIVE OIL
2 CLOVES GARLIC, PEELED AND SQUASHED A BIT
1 (14-OUNCE) CAN DICED TOMATOES
SALT
3 OR 4 BASIL LEAVES, TORN
1 CUP WATER

¾ (16-OUNCE) PACKAGE SPAGHETTI
2 TABLESPOONS BUTTER
GRATED PARMESAN CHEESE, TO SERVE

Spaghetti with meatballs

If you're organized, you could make the meatballs in tomato sauce the day before and just heat them up while you're cooking the pasta. Once you have fried the meatballs, you will have some nice tasty oil with meaty bits in the saucepan. I like to sauté some just-parboiled spinach or even potatoes in this until they have mingled with the pan oil and drunk up the flavor. Serve the spinach as a side dish, and then all you need is a couple of small scoops of ice cream for dessert and you're settled.

For the meatballs, soak the bread in the milk in a small bowl, squishing it through your fingers so that it breaks up completely.

Put the ground meat in a large bowl with the parsley, cinnamon, cumin, the bread mixture, and ½ teaspoon of salt. Grate in the onion (it is easier to do this holding the whole onion and then keeping the unused half for another time). Mix everything together thoroughly, kneading it with your hands as though it were a bread dough. Form about 25 small meatballs the size of large cherry tomatoes, rolling them between your palms so they are compact and smooth. Keep the made ones on a plate while you finish rolling the rest. Depending on their age, kids might like to help you with the rolling.

Heat the light olive oil in a nonstick frying pan and fry the meatballs in batches, making sure they are golden before you turn them. You should be able to shuffle them by holding the handle of the pan and giving a good flick with your wrist. If not, use tongs to turn them.

Meanwhile, make the sauce. Heat the oil in a large saucepan that will eventually also hold the meatballs. Add the garlic cloves and, when you can smell them, add the tomato. Season with salt, add the basil, and simmer for 10 minutes or so. Break up the tomatoes with a wooden spoon as you stir from time to time.

When all the meatballs have been fried, add them to the tomato sauce and stir in about 1 cup of water. Simmer uncovered for another 20 to 25 minutes, until the meatballs are soft and there is a fair amount of thickened sauce to toss into your pasta. Taste for salt, adjusting if necessary.

Cook the spaghetti in boiling salted water, following the package instructions. Drain, return to the cooking pan, and gently but thoroughly toss the butter through. Serve the pasta in individual bowls with a good ladleful of the tomato sauce, a few meatballs, and a scattering of Parmesan on top.

Serves 4

----

5 TABLESPOONS OLIVE OIL
2 CLOVES GARLIC, FINELY CHOPPED
1 (14-OUNCE) CAN DICED TOMATOES
1 TEASPOON DRIED OREGANO, CRUSHED BETWEEN
  YOUR FINGERS
SALT
3/4 (16-OUNCE) PACKAGE SPAGHETTI
6 TO 7 SLICES PROSCIUTTO CRUDO (RAW
  PROSCIUTTO), CUT INTO STRIPS
GRATED PARMESAN CHEESE, TO SERVE
CHOPPED FRESH CHILE (OPTIONAL)

Pasta with prosciutto, tomato, and oregano

This is my friend Mariella's spaghetti—it is so easy and a good variation on tomato pasta. I sometimes use ham and sometimes prosciutto crudo, and for adults I scatter in a bit of chopped chile at the last minute.

Heat half the oil in a saucepan and sauté the garlic over medium-low heat until you start to smell it. Add the tomatoes, oregano, and some salt, lower the heat a little and simmer for 15 to 20 minutes, crushing up the tomatoes with your wooden spoon every now and then as you stir so that it all melts into a sauce.

Meanwhile, bring a large pan of salted water to a boil and cook the spaghetti, following the package instructions. When both the sauce and the pasta are ready, add the prosciutto to the sauce and cook briefly to heat through. Drain the spaghetti, return it to its pan, and add the sauce and the rest of the oil. Toss lightly to coat the spaghetti.

Spoon into bowls and serve with grated Parmesan all round, and some chopped chile for those who like it.

Serves 4

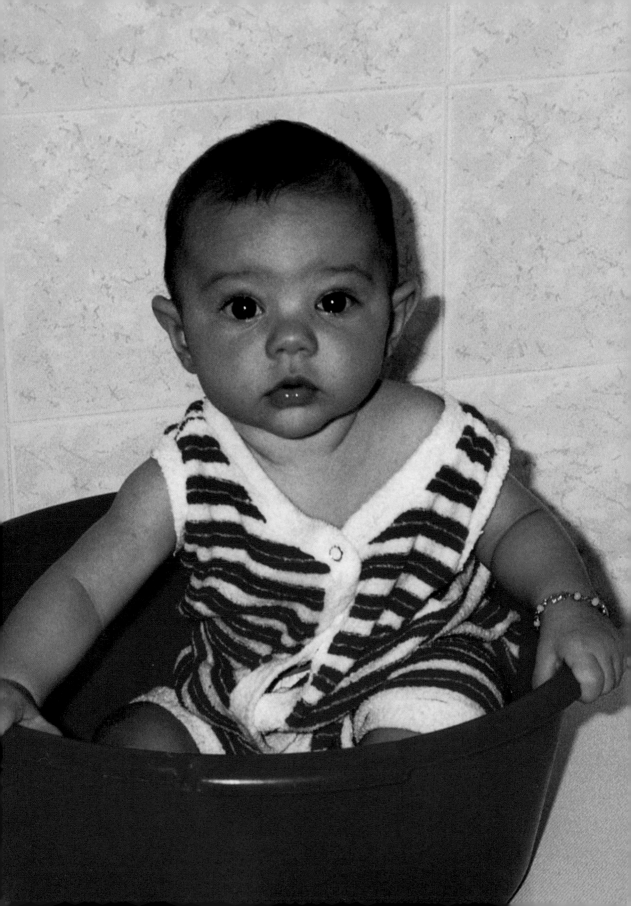

2½ TABLESPOONS OLIVE OIL
1 CLOVE GARLIC, PEELED BUT LEFT WHOLE
1 (14-OUNCE) CAN DICED TOMATOES
SALT AND FRESHLY GROUND BLACK PEPPER
ABOUT 4 BASIL LEAVES, TORN
¾ (16-OUNCE) PACKAGE SPAGHETTI, OR YOUR
    FAVORITE PASTA
OLIVE OIL, TO SERVE
FRESHLY GRATED PARMESAN CHEESE, TO SERVE

Pasta with tomato sauce

My family loves tomato sauce on pasta. Of course, other ingredients can be added, but this is a quick basic sauce to make. If you prefer a totally smooth sauce, then you can quickly whiz it with a handheld blender. If you aren't going to use the sauce immediately, let it cool completely and then freeze it. Otherwise, keep it in a glass jar in the fridge, completely covered by a layer of olive oil.

Put the oil and garlic in a saucepan over medium heat. When you can smell the garlic and it has flavored the oil, add the tomatoes. Add a good pinch of salt and some pepper and bring to a boil. Lower the heat and cook uncovered for about 15 to 20 minutes, until the tomatoes have all merged with the oil into a sauce. Add the basil and a few drops of hot water toward the end of the cooking time if it looks as if it needs it. If you like, purée the sauce until smooth, taking out the garlic clove first.

Meanwhile, cook the pasta in boiling salted water, following the package instructions. Drain the pasta and stir through most of the sauce. Divide among four serving bowls and spoon the rest of the sauce on top. Drizzle with a little olive oil, if you like, and serve with grated Parmesan.

Serves 4

TOMATO SAUCE:
1/2 CUP OLIVE OIL
3 CLOVES GARLIC, PEELED BUT LEFT WHOLE
SALT
3 (14-OUNCE) CANS DICED TOMATOES
ABOUT 12 BASIL LEAVES, TORN
1 CUP HOT WATER

BÉCHAMEL SAUCE:
1/4 POUND PLUS 1/2 TABLESPOON BUTTER
2/3 CUP ALL-PURPOSE FLOUR
4 CUPS MILK, WARMED
SALT AND FRESHLY GROUND BLACK PEPPER
FRESHLY GRATED NUTMEG

3/4 (16-OUNCE) PACKAGE LASAGNE NOODLES
1 CUP GRATED PARMESAN CHEESE

Tomato lasagne

This is a straightforward recipe to which you can add a few blobs of goat's cheese, some dollops of pesto, a little cooked spinach, or broiled long slices of zucchini between the layers. This is just lasagne noodles, a good tomato sauce, and béchamel, and my children love it. The easiest thing is to buy dried "no-boil" pasta noodles that can be put directly into your dish, but they do absorb quite a lot of liquid so you need to keep your sauces fairly runny. If you prefer, use the noodles that require boiling first.

For the tomato sauce, heat the oil and garlic in a large pan. When you begin to smell the garlic, add the tomatoes and a good pinch of salt and bring to a boil. Lower the heat and cook uncovered for about 20 to 25 minutes, until it has all merged into a sauce. Add the basil and 1 cup of hot water toward the end of the cooking time. Purée until smooth, minus the garlic if you'd prefer.

To make the béchamel, melt the butter in a small saucepan over low heat. Whisk in the flour and cook for a few minutes, stirring constantly, then begin adding the warm milk. It will be immediately absorbed, so work quickly, whisking with one hand while adding ladlefuls of milk with the other. When the sauce seems to be smooth and not too stiff, add salt, pepper, and a grating of nutmeg and continue cooking, even after it comes to a boil, for 5 minutes or so, mixing all the time. It should be a very thick and smooth sauce.

Preheat the oven to 350°F and grease a deep 8 1/2 by 12-inch baking dish. Drizzle some béchamel over the bottom of the dish to cover it very thinly. Put a slightly overlapping layer of lasagne noodles on top. Dollop a thin layer of tomato sauce over that, spreading it with the back of the ladle. Add about two ladlefuls of béchamel in long drizzles and then cover with a sprinkling of Parmesan. Add another layer of lasagne noodles, then tomato, béchamel, and Parmesan as before, and then repeat the layers one more time. You should have about 4 tablespoons of tomato sauce and a good amount of béchamel left. Make a final layer of lasagne noodles and cover with all the remaining béchamel. Dollop the tomato sauce here and there and sprinkle with any remaining Parmesan. Bake for about 30 minutes, or until it is bubbling and golden on top.

Serves 6 to 8

MEAT SAUCE:
1/2 CUP OLIVE OIL
3 ONIONS, CHOPPED
2 CLOVES GARLIC, FINELY CHOPPED
2 1/4 POUNDS GROUND BEEF
2 BAY LEAVES
1 CINNAMON STICK
2 1/2 TABLESPOONS WORCESTERSHIRE SAUCE
1 TEASPOON DRIED MINT
2 TEASPOONS SWEET PAPRIKA
1 1/2 CUPS WHITE WINE
2 (14-OUNCE) CANS DICED TOMATOES
SALT
3 CUPS WATER
1 SMALL BUNCH PARSLEY, CHOPPED

BECHAMEL SAUCE:
1/4 POUND PLUS 1/2 TABLESPOON BUTTER
2/3 CUP ALL-PURPOSE FLOUR
4 CUPS MILK, WARMED
SALT AND FRESHLY GROUND BLACK PEPPER
FRESHLY GRATED NUTMEG

3/4 (16-OUNCE) PACKAGE LASAGNE NOODLES
1 CUP GRATED PARMESAN CHEESE

Meat lasagne

My mother makes a good lasagne—and she isn't Italian. She mostly uses the dried "no-boil" noodles and sometimes adds chopped celery, bell peppers, and mushrooms to the meat sauce. The no-boil noodles do absorb quite a lot of liquid, so it's important to keep your sauces fairly runny. If you prefer, just use the noodles that need boiling beforehand. The meat sauce and béchamel can be made in advance. I often make huge pans of the ground meat sauce and freeze it; then when I want to make lasagne, it doesn't seem much of a job at all.

For the meat sauce, heat the olive oil in a large saucepan and sauté the onions over medium heat until they are quite golden. Stir in the garlic and then add the meat, bay leaves, cinnamon stick, Worcestershire sauce, mint, and paprika. Sauté over high heat for 8 to 10 minutes until the meat starts to brown, stirring often to prevent sticking. Add the wine and cook for 5 minutes or so, until it evaporates. Add the tomatoes, cook for a few minutes, and then add 3 cups of water. Season with salt. Bring to a boil, lower the heat and simmer uncovered for 1 hour. Add the parsley for the last 10 minutes.

To make the béchamel, melt the butter in a small saucepan over low heat. Whisk in the flour and cook for a few minutes, stirring constantly, then begin adding the warm milk. It will be immediately absorbed, so work quickly, whisking with one hand while adding ladlefuls of milk with the other. When the sauce seems to be smooth and not too stiff, add salt, pepper, and a grating of nutmeg and continue cooking, even after it comes to a boil, for 5 minutes or so, mixing all the time. It should be a very thick and smooth sauce.

Preheat the oven to 350°F and grease a deep 8½ by 12-inch baking dish. Drizzle some béchamel over the bottom of the dish and rock it from side to side so that the béchamel more or less covers the bottom very thinly. Put a slightly overlapping layer of lasagne noodles on top. Ladle on a thin layer of meat sauce, spreading it with the back of the ladle. Add about two ladlefuls of béchamel in long drizzles and then cover with a sprinkling of grated Parmesan cheese.

Add another layer of lasagne noodles, then meat sauce, béchamel, and Parmesan, as before, and repeat this layering twice more. Use up all the meat sauce in a last layer, then top this with a final layer of pasta. Scrape out the last of the béchamel to thinly cover the lasagne noodles and sprinkle the top with any remaining Parmesan. Put in the oven with a pan underneath to catch the drips and bake for 30 to 40 minutes, until it is crusty in parts, golden, and bubbling.

Serves 6 to 8

I watch them playing in the moment. I think about their stickers—the ones I save in the drawer for when they are exceptional and lay out on the rug for them to choose. They take the first one that grabs their young and cheerful eyes and don't give it another thought. They stick it in their book, askew, in whatever way it lands, and that's that. Then they flip their books shut and lie back and think of what to do next. If I said "let's go and live in China," they'd believe me and pack with the most enthusiasm I'd ever seen, and tag along, not even wanting any big details, until we got all the way to China—as long as they had one or two toys to play with.

BROTH:
1/2 RED ONION, PEELED
1 SMALL CARROT, PEELED
1/2 LEAFY CELERY STALK
3 PARSLEY STALKS
1/2 SMALL TOMATO
5 CUPS WATER
SALT

4 TABLESPOONS OLIVE OIL
1/2 RED ONION, FINELY CHOPPED
2 CLOVES GARLIC, PEELED BUT LEFT WHOLE
PINCH OF DRIED CHILE FLAKES (OPTIONAL)
1 CUP RISOTTO RICE
1 CUP CANNED TOMATOES, PUREED
2 LARGE BASIL LEAVES, TORN
1/4 CUP GRATED PARMESAN CHEESE
2/3 CUP 1/2-INCH BLOCKS FRESH MOZZARELLA
    CHEESE
2 1/2 TABLESPOONS OLIVE OIL, TO SERVE
GRATED PARMESAN CHEESE, TO SERVE
FRESHLY GROUND BLACK PEPPER, TO SERVE

Tomato risotto

This is lovely with the little cubes of mozzarella stirred through near the end, but if you think you're going to have some left over to make fried risotto balls (opposite), put that to one side before you add the mozzarella. Leave out the chile when you're feeding youngsters. Use arborio or carnaroli rice.

For the broth, put the onion, carrot, celery, parsley, and tomato in a pan with 5 cups of water. Add salt and bring to a boil. Reduce the heat to low and simmer for 30 minutes, then turn down the heat as low as it will go and leave the pan over the heat.

Heat the olive oil in a wide heavy-bottomed pan. Sauté the onion and garlic over low-medium heat for about 5 minutes, or until lightly golden. Stir in the chile flakes and rice, and cook for another minute. Add half the tomato purée, half the basil, and 1 1/2 cups of the hot broth.

Reduce the heat to low and simmer for 10 minutes, stirring now and then. Add the rest of the tomato purée and the remaining broth, and simmer for 10 minutes, or until the risotto is cooked (if it needs another few minutes or a little more liquid, just use hot water). Remove the garlic cloves and throw them away. Stir in the Parmesan, mozzarella, and remaining basil. Serve as soon as the mozzarella starts to melt, drizzled with olive oil and with a good grating of black pepper for the adults. Pass around the extra Parmesan.

Serves 3

ABOUT 3 CUPS COLD RISOTTO
  (½ BATCH TOMATO RISOTTO, OPPOSITE)
4 TABLESPOONS GRATED PARMESAN CHEESE
2 EGGS
½ CUP SMALL CUBES FRESH MOZZARELLA CHEESE
1 ½ CUPS DRY BREAD CRUMBS
OLIVE OIL, FOR FRYING
LEMON WEDGES, TO SERVE

Fried risotto balls

My kids love these. You can use any leftover risotto, but they are particularly good made with the tomato risotto (opposite).

Mix the risotto and Parmesan together in a bowl. Lightly beat one of the eggs and gradually stir into the risotto, stopping when the risotto is damp but still firm enough to be shaped. Moisten your hands with a little water, take a heaping tablespoon of the mixture, and roll it into a ball. Make a tunnel into the center with your finger and push a mozzarella cube into it. Squeeze the ball to close the opening and seal in the mozzarella. Do this with the rest of the mixture.

Lightly beat the other egg in a flat bowl. Put the bread crumbs on a plate. Roll the balls in the egg and then the bread crumbs and put on a cookie sheet or large plate. Chill for at least 30 minutes.

Pour about 1 inch of olive oil into a frying pan and heat until hot but not smoking. Fry the balls in batches, gently moving them around in the oil and turning them often so that they brown evenly. Each batch will take about 2 minutes, then you can lift them out onto a plate lined with paper towels to absorb the excess oil. Fried risotto balls are best served warm with a squeeze of lemon juice but are also fine eaten at room temperature.

Makes about 36 balls

2 TABLESPOONS BUTTER
2½ TABLESPOONS OLIVE OIL
1 SMALL RED ONION, CHOPPED
1 TEASPOON SWEET PAPRIKA
2 CLOVES GARLIC, CHOPPED
1 SMALL RED BELL PEPPER, DICED
1 SMALL LEAFY CELERY STALK, DICED
1⅔ CUPS DICED BUTTON MUSHROOMS
5 TABLESPOONS CHOPPED PARSLEY
2½ TABLESPOONS WORCESTERSHIRE SAUCE
2½ TABLESPOONS SOY SAUCE
1 (9-OUNCE) CAN DICED TOMATOES
1½ CUPS LONG-GRAIN RICE
3 CUPS HOT WATER

Rice and vegetable pilaf

Adults can add a few shakes of Tabasco sauce to this tasty rice. It can be made in advance and served warm or at room temperature, alone or with a dollop of thick, plain yogurt. This could nicely accompany a broiled chicken dish, or fish. Once all the vegetables are chopped up finely, no one will be at all suspicious of them, but if you think you won't get away with serving these to your children, then leave out the mushrooms and peppers.

Heat the butter and oil in a heavy-bottomed pan. Sauté the onion over low heat for a few minutes, until it is softened and golden. Add the paprika, sauté for half a minute or so and then add the garlic, pepper, celery, and mushrooms. Increase the heat and continue cooking and stirring until all the juice has evaporated and the vegetables become soft and golden and look almost gooey. This is important so that they don't taste steamed at the end. Add the parsley, Worcestershire sauce, and soy sauce. Let it bubble up and then pour in the tomatoes. After a few minutes, when the tomatoes surrender and collapse, add the rice, stirring to coat it well. Season with salt (remembering you have added soy sauce already) and pepper, then cover with 3 cups of hot water.

 Bring to a boil and cook for a couple of minutes to get it going. Give it a stir, cover the pan, and lower the heat to an absolute minimum. Cook for 15 minutes or so, until holes appear on the surface and the rice is cooked. Take care not to burn it, but it's fine to have a few nice crusty patches on the bottom. Remove from the heat and fluff it up a bit with a fork. Cover with a dish towel, replace the lid, and leave to steam for 10 minutes or so before serving.

Serves 6 as a side dish, or 4 as a main meal

4 TABLESPOONS OLIVE OIL
1 LARGE CHICKEN, CUT INTO 8 PORTIONS
SALT
1 RED ONION, CHOPPED
1 SMALL LEAFY CELERY STALK, CHOPPED
3 CLOVES GARLIC, FINELY CHOPPED
2 TEASPOONS SWEET PAPRIKA
1 (14-OUNCE) CAN DICED TOMATOES
FRESHLY GROUND BLACK PEPPER
2 CUPS HOT WATER
2 LARGE ROSEMARY SPRIGS

Chicken casserole

This is a simple casserole to which you can add any other vegetables that you like. I sometimes get a small cauliflower, break it up into florets, and boil them in lightly salted water for a few minutes, just to soften. I pat them dry, sauté in olive oil over high heat until golden, and add them to the casserole just toward the end so they don't collapse—they go well with the tomato. Zucchini and carrot chunks, or mushrooms can also be added here. Serve with bread, brown rice, or boiled potatoes with parsley (page 233).

Preheat the oven to 350°F. Heat the oil in a large flameproof casserole. Fry the chicken in batches over medium-high heat so that it is golden all over. Lift the pieces out onto a plate as they are done and sprinkle them with salt.

Add the onion to the casserole, reduce the heat, and sauté until quite golden. Add the celery and continue cooking until it is all a bit sticky looking and well cooked. Stir in the garlic and paprika and, when you can smell the garlic, add the tomatoes. Season with salt and pepper. Let it bubble up for a bit then add 2 cups of hot water and the rosemary and return the chicken to the casserole. Bring to a boil.

Cover the casserole and move it to the oven. Bake for an hour, then take off the lid and spoon the juices over any exposed bits of chicken. Cook uncovered for another 30 minutes so that the sauce reduces and the chicken pieces brown a bit. Put the lid back on, turn the oven off, and leave the casserole in the oven until you are ready to eat. If that is a long time off, then you can gently reheat the casserole on the stovetop.

Serves 4

ABOUT 5 TABLESPOONS OLIVE OIL
2 CLOVES GARLIC, PEELED AND
   SQUASHED A BIT
1 CUP CHERRY TOMATOES, HALVED
SALT
4 CHICKEN CUTLETS
ALL-PURPOSE FLOUR, FOR DUSTING
2 SAGE SPRIGS
4 TABLESPOONS WHITE WINE OR WATER
1 1/2 TABLESPOONS DRAINED CAPERS
   OR CAPERBERRIES IN VINEGAR, RINSED
1 1/2 TABLESPOONS CHOPPED PARSLEY

Chicken cutlets with tomatoes and capers

This is the kind of dish my mother-in-law has taught me to make—she is such an inspiration. You can add a couple of olives or anything else you think might be appreciated. I like to serve this with some pan-fried potatoes with rosemary and sage (page 245) or even just my favorite bread. Buy chicken cutlets from your butcher, or buy one chicken breast and thinly slice it horizontally into four thin slices.

Heat half the oil with the garlic in a large nonstick frying pan. Add the tomatoes with a little salt, and fry over high heat until they are just starting to pucker. Lift them out onto a plate.

    Add the remaining oil to the pan. Lightly dust the chicken with flour on both sides. Put into the pan, add the sage, and fry over medium-high heat until the underside is golden. Turn over and season with salt. Put the garlic cloves on top of the chicken if they look in danger of burning. Cook until the new underside is golden brown, then turn the chicken again and season with salt. Add the wine, put the tomatoes on top of the chicken cutlets, and throw in the capers and parsley. Let it bubble up and evaporate a bit, then put on the lid and leave for a couple of minutes before serving.

Serves 2

TOMATO SAUCE:
2½ TABLESPOONS OLIVE OIL
1 CLOVE GARLIC, PEELED AND SQUASHED
   A BIT
1 (14-OUNCE) CAN DICED TOMATOES
1 TEASPOON SALT
3 BASIL LEAVES, TORN

8 THIN VEAL SCALOPPINI, ABOUT
   $\frac{1}{16}$ INCH THICK
8 THIN SLICES HAM, ROUGHLY THE SAME SIZE
   AS THE VEAL
4½ OUNCES FRESH MOZZARELLA CHEESE,
   CUT INTO 8 THIN SLICES
½ CUP GRATED PARMESAN CHEESE
5 TABLESPOONS ALL-PURPOSE FLOUR
4 TABLESPOONS OLIVE OIL
SALT

Veal
involtini

The veal for this should always be best quality. I usually ask the butcher for four long slices that each weigh about 3 ounces, then cut them in two and bash them out even thinner.

For the tomato sauce, heat the oil in a pan with the garlic. When you can smell the garlic, add the tomatoes and 1 teaspoon of salt. Mash up a little with a wooden spoon and simmer for about 15 minutes, or until the tomatoes and oil have melted into each other. Add the basil leaves and simmer for another couple of minutes.

Meanwhile, put the veal slices flat on a board. Lay a piece of ham on top of each one, then a slice of mozzarella over the ham. Scatter a teaspoon of Parmesan over each one and roll up securely. Secure them closed with toothpicks, so that the toothpicks lie flat and don't stick up. Don't worry if they all look different. Put the flour on a plate and lightly roll the involtini in it to coat them on all sides. Shake off the excess flour.

Heat the oil in a large frying pan and fry the involtini for just a few minutes, turning them often so that they are golden brown all over. Scatter them with a little salt when they are done, remembering that the tomato sauce is well salted. Leave them in the pan and add the tomato sauce, making sure they are coated. Cover with a lid and simmer for a minute or so. The mozzarella will have softened and started to melt. Remove from the heat but leave the lid on for a minute longer to cook the meat all the way through. Serve immediately, whole or sliced, with extra toothpicks to use as forks.

Serves 4

4 SLICES WHITE BREAD
ABOUT ½ CUP MILK
1¼ POUNDS GROUND PORK AND VEAL
2½ TABLESPOONS CHOPPED FRESH PARSLEY
SALT
2½ TABLESPOONS OLIVE OIL
JUICE OF 1 LEMON

Hamburger patties

These are my friend Didi's. Her mom, Helen, often made these for us when we went to their house after school. This will make about eight delicious soft patties. I like mine more oval-ish than round and love them with the sautéed tomatoes (page 46) and some bread, although fries are good, too. You can easily add some extra spices to the mixture—cumin, ground coriander, or paprika would be nice. And you could make these all beef, if you prefer. The patties can also be eaten on a roll with a few slices of ripe and sweet tomato, a bit of lettuce, cheese, or other fillings. You will need a good nonstick frying pan as no oil is used for the cooking here.

Tear the bread into pieces and put it in a small bowl. Add the milk and leave it to soak for a while, turning the bread over a few times with a spoon until it has completely collapsed.

Put the meat and parsley in a bowl and season well with salt. Add the bread and milk mixture, and then knead and squish the mixture through your fingers until it is completely smooth. Divide into 8 portions and shape into balls or ovals (your mixture might be quite soft and wobbly to shape but that's what makes the cooked patties so good).

Heat a nonstick frying pan on the stovetop. Put the patties into the hot pan and flatten them to about ½ inch thick. Fry them over medium heat until they are deep golden brown and crusty underneath, then gently flip them over with a spatula. Cook until the new underside is crusty and deep golden brown, then check that the inside is cooked through. Lift out onto a serving plate.

Mix the oil and lemon juice together, add some salt, and pour over the patties while they are still warm.

Makes 8

ABOUT 6 RIPE AND FIRM BUT JUICY
   MEDIUM TOMATOES
4 TABLESPOONS OLIVE OIL
2 CLOVES GARLIC, PEELED AND SQUASHED
   A BIT
2 SMALL ROSEMARY SPRIGS
SALT AND FRESHLY GROUND BLACK
   PEPPER (OPTIONAL)

Sautéed tomatoes in olive oil and rosemary

These are simple and good and are great on toasted bread (particularly olive bread) or served with a main course such as hamburger patties (page 44) or any other broiled meat or fish. You can also dress a pasta with them. I prefer to use tomatoes that are slightly longer than they are round. Whatever shape you use, your tomatoes must be ripe and juicy to make the finished dish sticky, sweet, and tasty rather than watery. Try to keep the tomatoes more or less in their shape and not too collapsed. You might like to add some anchovies and capers to the pan.

Cut the tomatoes into quarters from top to bottom. Heat the oil in a large nonstick frying pan and add the tomatoes, garlic, and rosemary sprigs. Cook over quite high heat at first, until the undersides of the tomatoes are deep golden. Turn them gently. The skins may be loosening a bit, which doesn't matter—just try to keep them as intact as possible. Sprinkle with some salt and pepper if you like. Lower the heat and cook for about 10 minutes, or until the juice from the tomatoes mingles with the oil and makes a syrup in the bottom of the pan. If the garlic cloves seem to be getting too dark, just sit them on top of one of the tomatoes. Cook until the tomatoes have a lovely color and look roasted rather than boiled. Serve warm or even at room temperature.

Serves 5

2 TO 4 VERY RIPE BUT FIRM MEDIUM TOMATOES
1 CLOVE GARLIC, PEELED AND SQUASHED A BIT
4 TABLESPOONS OLIVE OIL
SALT
½ TEASPOON DRIED OREGANO

Ripe
tomato salad

You need the best and sweetest tomatoes (cherry tomatoes are also good).
Make this in advance so the flavors have time to mingle (later on you can
dip bread into the juice that collects at the bottom of the tomato bowl). If
you're feeding adults, this is wonderful with a chopped fresh red chile
tossed through just before serving. Or you could tear up a few basil leaves
and toss them in. It is sometimes just the simplest of things that you need
to accompany a meal like hamburger patties, but this is also perfect for
lunch with bread and a good piece of cheese (I like mozzarella or feta).

Cut the tomatoes into chunks and put them in a serving bowl. Add the garlic, olive
oil, and salt to taste. Crush the oregano between your fingers and add to the bowl.
Toss together gently and then leave to marinate for an hour or so before serving.

Serves 5

2½ CUPS DRIED CANNELLINI BEANS, SOAKED
IN COLD WATER OVERNIGHT
1 SAGE SPRIG
1 BAY LEAF
SALT
5 TABLESPOONS OLIVE OIL
1 SMALL RED ONION, FINELY CHOPPED
2½ TABLESPOONS CHOPPED FRESH PARSLEY
1 TABLESPOON CHOPPED CELERY LEAVES
2 CLOVES GARLIC, FINELY CHOPPED
1 TEASPOON SWEET PAPRIKA
1½ (14-OUNCE) CANS DICED TOMATOES
FRESHLY GROUND BLACK PEPPER
2 CUPS HOT WATER

Cannellini beans in tomato

My family seems to like any version of white beans in tomato sauce. I make quite a lot so that we can have it over two days. I like the beans soft and creamy. Serve them with broiled sausages or another meat, or just on their own on toast with a great heap of grated parmesan on top. These are cooked first on the stovetop for an hour and then finished in a casserole dish in the oven for another hour or so. Leftovers are great for throwing into a soup.

Put the beans in a large pan, cover with plenty of cold water, and bring to a boil. Skim the surface, lower the heat, and add the sage sprig and bay leaf. If the bay leaf is fresh, add it toward the end of cooking. High simmer for about an hour, uncovered, topping up with hot water if it seems necessary. Add about a teaspoon of salt toward the end. Preheat the oven to 350°F.

Meanwhile, heat the olive oil in a large casserole dish over medium heat. Sauté the onion for a few minutes until it is golden and a bit sticky. Add the parsley and celery leaves, cook for a few moments, and then stir in the garlic and paprika. When you can smell the garlic, add the tomatoes and simmer for about 15 minutes or until they melt into a sauce. From time to time, stir and squash them with your wooden spoon. Season well with salt and a couple of grinds of pepper. Drain the beans and add to the casserole with 2 cups of hot water. Bring to a fast boil and boil for a few minutes. Put the dish, uncovered, in the oven for about 45 minutes, or until it looks golden on the top. It's not necessary to stir, but check a couple of times that nothing is sticking. Turn down the heat to 300°F, add a little hot water if it looks too dry, and bake for 15 to 20 minutes more. Taste for salt, put the lid back on, and turn off the oven. Leave the beans in the oven to cool down a bit before serving.

Serves 8

2½ TABLESPOONS OLIVE OIL
1 CLOVE GARLIC, PEELED AND SQUASHED A BIT
½ (14-OUNCE) CAN DICED TOMATOES
SALT
2 BASIL LEAVES, TORN UP
2 EGGS
FRESHLY GROUND BLACK PEPPER (OPTIONAL)

Eggs in tomato

You can also make this in individual egg pans, if you like, and take them straight to the table. If your children are old enough to cope with the heat, that's a lovely way to serve them—mine enjoy dipping the bread into their own pan. If not, use a bigger frying pan and cook the two eggs together, as in this recipe. You could easily pop another egg into the larger pan, too. Take the eggs out of the fridge a while before you cook them. Serve with thick slices of rustic white bread, toasted and cut into dipping triangles.

Heat the olive oil and garlic in an 8-inch frying pan. When it begins to sizzle and you can smell the garlic, add the tomatoes. Season with salt, add the basil, and cook for a few minutes over medium heat, until the tomatoes start to melt together.

Reduce the heat and carefully break the eggs into the pan, leaving a little space between them. Cook until the whites just start to set, then make sure the bottoms aren't sticking to the pan. Cover the pan with a lid and cook for about half a minute until the whites are milky-set. Sprinkle a little salt over the soft yolks. Adults will probably need a little freshly ground black pepper as well. Leave the eggs slightly undercooked and take the pan to the table with the lid on, rather than risk having the eggs hard and overcooked, as you need to be able to dunk your bread in the yolks.

Serves 2

DOUGH:
1 ³/4 CUPS WARM (COMFORTABLE TO YOUR FINGERS) WATER
1 (³/4-OUNCE) CAKE FRESH YEAST, CRUMBLED, OR 1 (¹/4-OUNCE)
   PACKAGE ACTIVE DRY YEAST
1 TEASPOON HONEY
1 ¹/2 TABLESPOONS OLIVE OIL
4 ³/4 CUPS ALL-PURPOSE FLOUR
1 ¹/2 TEASPOONS SALT

TOMATO TOPPING:
5 TABLESPOONS OLIVE OIL
1 LARGE CLOVE GARLIC, PEELED AND SQUASHED A BIT
2 (14-OUNCE) CANS DICED TOMATOES
1 TEASPOON SALT
3 BASIL LEAVES, TORN

La pizza rossa

Many times we have this plain, but if you like, you could add 1 ¹/2 cups coarsely grated mozzarella cheese and scatter it here and there over the pizza about 10 minutes before the end of the cooking time. Often I do half red and the other half with mozzarella. You could also scatter a few thin slices of ham or salami over the top. The dough must be sticky (this is what gives a nice texture to the cooked pizza), so don't feel you've done something wrong or be tempted to add any more flour. Mine is impossible to knead on the table, so I just punch it around and bash it in the bowl until it is smooth. It takes about 5 minutes to get the dough unstuck from my hands and find my ring. It gets a bit easier to work with after the rising. There should be quite an abundant amount of tomato sauce, which is the way I like it. If you prefer, you can set a few spoonfuls aside to dress pasta later or use for eggs in tomato (page 49).

Put the water, yeast, honey, olive oil, and 3 fistfuls of the flour in a bowl. Mix with an electric beater until smooth. Cover the bowl and leave for 20 to 30 minutes, until the mixture froths up and looks foamy on top. Mix in the rest of the flour and 1 ¹/2 teaspoons of salt. The dough will be very soft and sticky—don't be tempted to add more flour. Now, using a dough hook, mix for about 4 to 5 minutes so everything is completely incorporated. If you don't have a dough hook, just mix it with your hands, slapping it from one side of the bowl to the other as it will be too soft to knead. Cover the bowl with a couple of cloths and leave it in a warm and draft-free place for about 1 ¹/2 hours, or until the dough has puffed up well.

   Very lightly oil an 11 by 15 by 1 ¹/2-inch baking pan. Punch down the dough with one firm blow to the center. Spread the dough gently onto the pan, right out to the edges, working it with your palms to stretch it along the pan. If it won't stretch easily, leave it to relax for another 5 minutes and then gently stretch out the dough, starting from the center and flicking your palms across it. Make sure the dough doesn't break anywhere and that it is more or less evenly spread. Put it in a warm draft-free place. Arrange four glasses around the pan and drape a couple of dish towels or a towel over them like a tent to completely cover the sheet (so that the dough doesn't stick to the cloth as it rises). Leave for 45 minutes or so, until the dough has puffed up.

For the tomato topping, heat the oil with the garlic in a saucepan and, when you begin to smell the garlic, add the tomatoes, basil, and 1 teaspoon of salt. Cook for about 15 minutes over fairly strong heat, until the sauce loses its wateriness and starts to look thick and bubbly. If you like, you can whiz it a couple of times with a handheld blender to make it a little smoother, but still keep some chunks. Meanwhile, preheat the oven to 450°F.

Dimple the top of the dough here and there with your fingers so that the tomato has some nests to settle into (take care not to deflate your dough, though). Scatter the tomato sauce over the top and gently spread it out with the back of the ladle. It may seem like a lot of sauce, but it keeps the pizza lovely and moist. Put the pan in the oven and bake for about 20 minutes (depending on the strength of your oven) until the pizza is golden and a bit crusty here and there. Check that the bottom is crusty and crisp, too, and cook for longer if you need to. Cut up into squares to serve. I think this is best warm, but it can also be served at room temperature, or reheated.

Cuts up into 12 to 15 pieces

2½ TABLESPOONS SUPERFINE SUGAR
JUICE OF HALF A LEMON
½ CUP WATER
2 CUPS FRESH OR FROZEN RASPBERRIES

Raspberry sauce

This is perfect for making sundaes, and it's also lovely drizzled over a dollop of Greek-style yogurt or a bowl of apricot ice cream. Spoon some into a glass before pouring in your milkshakes or smoothies, or serve it with cream over crepes, pancakes, and waffles. Or you could use about ½ cup of sugar and only 4 tablespoons of water and add the berries to the pan at the start to make a fruit syrup. Pour a little into a glass and top it up with sparkling or still water. You can use any berries you like— blueberries, cherries, cranberries . . .

Put the sugar and lemon juice in a saucepan with ½ cup water. Bring to a boil, then reduce the heat and simmer for 5 to 10 minutes until slightly thickened. Put the raspberries in a processor or blender, pour the hot syrup over the top, and purée until smooth. Strain the sauce through a fine sieve.

Makes about ⅔ cup

2½ CUPS ALL-PURPOSE FLOUR
1 TABLESPOON BAKING POWDER
SCANT ½ CUP SUPERFINE SUGAR
FRESHLY GROUND NUTMEG
2 EGGS
1 CUP BUTTERMILK
4 TABLESPOONS BUTTER, MELTED
1 TEASPOON GRATED LEMON ZEST
1 CUP FRESH BLUEBERRIES
2½ TABLESPOONS RAW SUGAR

Berry and buttermilk cake

I use blueberries here, but fresh strawberries, hulled and halved, work very nicely, too. Try to choose firm berries that look perfect; frozen berries are a bit too mushy and will collapse. This is my new friend Jo's recipe, and it is lovely with a cup of tea or coffee, or even for breakfast or supper with a big cup of milk.

Preheat the oven to 400°F. Grease and flour a 12 by 8-inch pan with sides at least 2 inches high. Sift the flour and baking powder into a large bowl and add the sugar and a few good grinds of nutmeg. Put the eggs in a bowl and whisk until light and fluffy. Add the buttermilk, butter, and lemon zest, and beat together well. Pour into the dry ingredients and mix gently with a wooden spoon just until everything is combined. If you beat too hard, the cake will be tough.

Spoon the mixture into the pan, spreading it thinly to reach all four sides. Scatter the blueberries over the top and sprinkle these with raw sugar. Put in the oven and bake for about 25 minutes, or until a skewer poked into the center of the cake comes out clean. Leave to cool in the pan before cutting into squares. This keeps well in a sealed container for up to a week.

Makes 12 to 15 squares

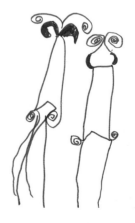

5 1/2 TABLESPOONS BUTTER, SOFTENED
1/4 CUP FIRMLY PACKED SOFT BROWN
     SUGAR
1/4 CUP SUPERFINE SUGAR
1 EGG
A FEW DROPS OF VANILLA EXTRACT
1 1/3 CUPS ALL-PURPOSE FLOUR
1/2 TEASPOON BAKING POWDER
SALT
3/4 CUP COARSELY CHOPPED SEMISWEET
     CHOCOLATE
1/2 CUP DRIED CRANBERRIES

Chocolate and cranberry cookies

These I learned from my American friend Sue. When I first made them my children said they were the best ever and I must definitely put the recipe in this book—so here it is. I also love them with dried strawberries instead of cranberries, and sometimes my girls prefer them without the cranberries, just chocolate. I like these small so I make them no bigger than a good teaspoon of dough, but you might like to make them larger. I also like to take them as a gift, packed in a lovely box and tied with a ribbon. Unless you have a huge oven, you will need to bake these in batches, so have the two cookie sheets ready.

Preheat the oven to 375°F and line two cookie sheets with parchment paper. Mash up the butter and sugar with a wooden spoon until well mixed, then whisk with an electric beater until smooth. Mix in the egg and vanilla. Sift in the flour and baking powder, and add a small pinch of salt. Beat with the wooden spoon to make a soft sandy mixture. Stir in the chocolate and cranberries.

Lightly moisten your hands and roll teaspoons of the mixture into balls. Arrange them on the sheets, leaving a fair space between for flattening and spreading. Bake for about 12 to 15 minutes, or until the cookies are golden and darkening around the edges. Remove from the oven, but leave them on the sheet to cool and firm up. These will keep in a cookie jar for a couple of days.

Makes 30 cookies

3½ CUPS FRESH STRAWBERRIES, HULLED
ABOUT 1 CUP SUGAR
JUICE OF HALF A LEMON
ONE LONGISH STRIP OF LEMON PEEL WITH NO PITH
1½ CUPS COLD WATER
5 TABLESPOONS MILK

Strawberry sorbet

This is fresh, soothing, easy, and just lovely for that time of year when strawberries show up. It works well both by hand or in an ice cream machine, but if do you use a machine, you'll get a particularly smooth sorbet with no icy granules. I like this served with a small dollop of fresh cream or totally alone.

Purée the strawberries in a blender or processor until they are completely smooth, then tip them into a medium-size bowl or container that has a lid.

Put the sugar, lemon juice, and lemon peel in a pan with 1½ cups of cold water. Bring to a boil and cook, stirring, for just long enough to dissolve the sugar. Remove from the heat and leave to cool for 10 minutes or so.

Remove the lemon peel and pour the syrup into the strawberry purée. Add the milk and mix well, then put the lid on and put in the fridge until completely cooled. Now put the bowl in the freezer. After an hour, give the mixture an energetic whisk with a hand whisk or an electric mixer. Put it back in the freezer and then whisk again after another couple of hours. When the sorbet is nearly firm, give one last whisk and put it back in the freezer to set.

Alternatively, pour into your ice cream machine and churn, following the manufacturer's instructions.

Serves 5 to 6

We wanted sleepovers and midnight feasts and would insist on setting the alarm for five to midnight. My father would sit on the terrace those nights, quite silent in his robe, until we had just about finished.

ABOUT 4 CUPS WATERMELON CHUNKS
1 1/3 CUPS FRESH CHERRIES, PITTED
1 1/3 CUPS SMALL STRAWBERRIES, HULLED
2 SMOOTH-SKINNED PEACHES OR
  NECTARINES, PITTED AND SLICED
1 POMEGRANATE
JUICE OF 1 ORANGE
2 1/2 TABLESPOONS SUPERFINE SUGAR

A colored
fruit salad

I love serving bowls of color. You could use all green fruits: say, kiwi,
honeydew melon, and green apples with some berries for contrast. Or
golden mangoes, pineapples, and oranges with a handful of strawberries
thrown in. Figs are also lovely in here—you can add anything you like as
long as you use beautiful juicy sweet fruit that smells gorgeous and is the
freshest of the fresh. Serve this on its own or with a scoop of strawberry
sorbet (page 59) or vanilla ice cream (page 374).

Remove any seeds from the watermelon chunks. Put in a bowl with the cherries,
strawberries, and peaches. Halve the pomegranate and squeeze the juice from one
half into the bowl. Carefully pick out the seeds from the other half, making sure
there is no white pith attached, and add to the bowl. Add the orange juice and
sugar, and mix together gently but thoroughly.

Serves 5

MERINGUE:
4 EGG WHITES
3/4 CUP SUPERFINE SUGAR
1 TEASPOON VANILLA EXTRACT
2 TEASPOONS APPLE CIDER VINEGAR
1/2 CUP FINELY CHOPPED WALNUTS OR
   HAZELNUTS
1/2 CUP FINELY CRUSHED UNSALTED CRACKERS

TOPPING:
1 CUP CHOPPED SEMISWEET CHOCOLATE
1 CUP HEAVY WHIPPING CREAM
1 TEASPOON VANILLA EXTRACT
1 CUP STRAWBERRIES
CONFECITONERS' SUGAR, TO SERVE

Meringue with strawberries and chocolate

This is my friend Sue's meringue. It's well-dressed, showy—quite over-the-top—and easy to make. You can add a little confectioners' sugar to your cream as you whip it, if you like your sweet things very sweet. I whip it without and just shake a little sugar over the top of the cake to serve. This is lovely with strawberries, blackberries, or raspberries, served in slices with a big cup of milky tea.

Preheat the oven to 250°F. Cover the bottom of a 9 1/2-inch springform cake pan with a sheet of parchment paper before clipping the side in place. The paper will stick out of the side, making it easier to remove the meringue later. Grease the side of the pan.

Whisk the egg whites in a bowl until they lose their foaminess and look like very thick, stiff shaving cream. Whisk in the sugar bit by bit until it is all incorporated, then whisk in the vanilla and the vinegar. Gently but thoroughly fold in the nuts and crackers. Spoon into the pan and level the surface, making a slight indent in the middle.

Bake for about 1 1/4 to 1 1/2 hours, until the meringue is lightly golden and coming away from the side of the pan. Turn off the oven, prop the door just slightly ajar, and leave the meringue inside until it is completely cool. Take the meringue out of the pan and put it on a serving plate, removing the paper.

Melt the semisweet chocolate in the top of a double boiler, making sure that the water doesn't touch the bottom of the bowl. Drizzle over the meringue in a criss-cross pattern and then leave to harden completely.

Whip the cream with the vanilla until it holds thickly on the beaters. Dollop onto the meringue, leaving a small border to show off the chocolate. Dot the berries on top and cover with a gentle shake of confectioners' sugar to serve.

Serves 8

APPLES FOR SAM

ABOUT $^{1}/_{2}$ POUND ROSEHIPS
2 CUPS WARM WATER
ABOUT 1 $^{1}/_{3}$ CUPS SUGAR
JUICE OF HALF A LEMON

Rosehip jam

I love the deep red color of this jam. Aunt Paola taught me the recipe and makes it every year. Rosehips must be fully ripe and ideally should be picked just after the first frosts, which soften them enough for jam making. Aunt Paola says we should pick the berries and freeze them in a plastic bag until we are ready to make the jam, because if you wait too long, they will spoil on the bush, and if you pick them and leave them lying about in your kitchen, they dry and harden. This is slightly thinner than most jams, but still very easy to spread, and chock-a-block full of vitamin C.

Cut the black tips off the rosehips. If they are large, remove the tuft on the end. Smaller ones may not have them, and the tiny ones can be left whole (the jam is later passed through a sieve that will catch any bits). Halve the rosehips lengthwise and scoop out all the seeds and hairy bits (throw these away). Put the rosehips in a saucepan and cover with 1 $^{1}/_{2}$ cups of warm water. Put a lid on and leave to soak overnight.

Sterilize your jars for when the hot jam is ready to bottle. It is always best to use several small jars, rather than one or two big ones. Wash the jars and lids in hot soapy water, or in the dishwasher, and rinse well in hot water. Then put the jars (and the lids) on a baking sheet and leave in a 250°F oven for at least 20 minutes, or until you are ready to use them. (Don't use a dish towel to dry them—they should dry thoroughly in the oven.)

Bring the pan of rosehips to a boil, then lower the heat, cover the pan, and simmer for 30 minutes. Add another $^{1}/_{2}$ cup of hot water and purée thoroughly. Return to the cleaned pan. Add the sugar and lemon juice, and bring the mixture to a boil to melt the sugar. Remove from the heat and pour through a sieve to collect any seeds.

Put the jam back in the pan and bring it back to a boil. Lower the heat and simmer uncovered for about 8 minutes, stirring constantly so that nothing sticks—the jam will start glooping a bit on the surface and look a bit syrupy. Test if the jam is ready by dropping a heaping teaspoonful onto a plate. When you slightly tilt the plate, the jam should not run off, but cling and slowly glide down (it will thicken a little when it cools). If the jam seems too thick already, add a bit more water and simmer for another moment. If it doesn't seem thick enough, carry on simmering for a while longer.

Spoon into the warm sterilized jars and close the lids tightly. Turn the jars upside down, cover with a dish towel, and leave to cool (this creates a vacuum that can be seen on the lid). Turn upright and store in a cool dark place. The jam will keep for about 6 weeks before it is opened. After opening, keep it in the fridge.

Makes about 1 $^{3}/4$ cups

ABOUT 1/3 CUP DRIED ROSEHIPS
5 ROSEHIP TEA BAGS
6 CUPS WATER
1/4 CUP PEELED PISTACHIOS
3/4 CUP SUPERFINE SUGAR
2/3 CUP FINE SEMOLINA
2 CUPS MILK
1 TEASPOON VANILLA EXTRACT
1 1/2 TABLESPOONS BUTTER
1 EGG, LIGHTLY BEATEN

Rosehip semolina puddings

Fresh rosehips are best, but this version is just as delicious when they are out of season. Rosehip tea bags give a lovely color and their flavor is good. Using all tea bags (use 10 instead of five) also makes good puddings with a lovely color and subtle flavor.

Preheat the oven to 350°F and grease six 1/2-cup pudding molds. Put the rosehips and tea bags in a saucepan with 6 cups of water and bring to a boil. Simmer over low heat for 20 minutes, or until it is a good rich color and flavor. Leave to cool.

Meanwhile, spread the pistachios on a baking sheet and toss with 1/2 teaspoon of the sugar. Roast in the oven for about 5 to 10 minutes until they are crisp, then let them cool before coarsely chopping them.

Strain the rosehip liquid into a bowl and throw away the solids. You should have about 3 cups of liquid. Put 1 cup of it in a heavy-bottomed saucepan over medium heat. Just before it comes to a boil, add the semolina in a fine steady stream, whisking constantly so that no lumps form. As it starts to thicken, stir in the milk, vanilla, and 1/2 cup of the sugar. Lower the heat and simmer for about 10 minutes, whisking almost continuously, until thickened and smooth. Take the pan off the heat and stir in the butter. Sit the pan in a sink of cold water, stirring a few times to help it cool. Whisk in the egg.

Meanwhile, put 1 1/2 cups of the cooking liquid and the remaining sugar in a small saucepan and bring to a boil, stirring until the sugar has dissolved. Lower the heat and simmer for 15 to 20 minutes, stirring occasionally, until the syrup has thickened. Keep on one side.

Divide the semolina among the molds (they won't be completely full). Cover each one with a circle of parchment paper and put the molds in a roasting pan. Pour hot water into the pan to come halfway up the sides of the molds. Carefully move the pan to the oven and bake for about 30 minutes, until the puddings are puffed, set, and slightly pulling away from the sides of the molds. Remove from the oven and the water bath and leave to cool a little (they will lose a bit of their height). Peel off the parchment paper and unmold them onto serving plates. Drizzle with the syrup and scatter some pistachios on top. Serve warm or at room temperature.

Serves 6

3½ CUPS STRAWBERRIES, HULLED
1 CUP SUPERFINE SUGAR
JUICE OF 1 LEMON

Strawberry jam

I like this with some bits of strawberry in, but you can easily decide that you want it all smooth. It is also incredibly easy to make with just this small amount of strawberries; it's not necessary to make a supply for the whole year and the whole neighborhood—although wouldn't that be nice? This is great dolloped onto pancakes or homemade white or brown bread and can also be used to sandwich together a simple sponge. I love it spooned into tiny sweet tart shells with another miniature dollop of whipped cream on the top. I always try to find small strawberries, which I think have more flavor than those large ones. You can make raspberry jam like this, too (and pass it through a fine sieve to get rid of the seeds).

Quarter the strawberries, or cut them up even smaller if they are large. Put them in a nonaluminum bowl and add the sugar and lemon juice. Toss them around to distribute everything evenly. Cover and leave them overnight in the fridge to draw out the juices.

Sterilize your jars for when you have a panful of hot jam ready to bottle. It is always best to use several small jars, rather than one or two big ones. Wash the jars and lids in hot soapy water, or in the dishwasher, and rinse well in hot water. Then put the jars (and the lids) on a baking sheet and leave in a 250°F oven for at least 20 minutes, or until you are ready to use them. (Don't use a dish towel to dry them—they should dry thoroughly in the oven.)

Drain off all the liquid from the strawberries into a large heavy-bottomed jam pan. Add half the strawberries and bring to a boil. Lower the heat and simmer gently for about 15 minutes, until thickened. Purée until smooth, then add the rest of the strawberries and bring back to a boil. Simmer over low heat for 10 to 15 minutes more, and then test if the jam is ready by dropping a heaping teaspoonful onto a plate. When you slightly tilt the plate, the jam should not run off, but cling and slowly glide down. If the jam isn't ready, put it back on the heat for a while. It should be a lovely red and look quite sticky.

Spoon into the warm sterilized jars and close the lids tightly. Turn the jars upside down, cover with a dish towel, and leave to completely cool (this creates a vacuum that can be seen on the lid). Turn upright and store in a cool dark place. The jam will keep for about 6 weeks before it is opened. After opening, you need to keep it in the fridge and use it up fairly quickly.

Makes 1½ cups

ABOUT 6 MEDIUM-SIZE QUINCES
JUICE OF 1 LEMON
ABOUT 3^1/4 CUPS SUGAR

Quince jam

My mother-in-law taught me a love of this jam. I like having a few jars of this in the house to see us through those early cooler months just after the quinces have made their brief appearance.

Rinse the quinces, rubbing their skins well. Put into a saucepan with enough cold water to just cover them, and add the lemon juice. Boil for 30 minutes. Remove from the heat and leave the quinces in the liquid overnight.

Drain the fruit, keeping the liquid. Peel and core the quinces and then cut them into chunks. Put them in a large heavy-bottomed pan and add the sugar. Measure the cooking liquid and top up with water until you have 10 cups, then add this to the quinces. Bring to a boil and, when the sugar has dissolved, turn the heat to low and simmer for 1^1/2 to 2 hours until the quinces have turned deep purple-red and blended with the syrup.

Meanwhile, sterilize your jars for when you have a panful of hot jam ready to bottle. It is always best to use several small jars, rather than one or two big ones. Wash the jars and lids in hot soapy water, or in the dishwasher, and rinse well in hot water. Then put the jars (and the lids) on a baking sheet and leave in a 250°F oven for at least 20 minutes, or until you are ready to use them. (Don't use a dish towel to dry them—they should dry thoroughly in the oven.)

Test that the jam is ready by dropping a heaping teaspoonful onto a plate. When you slightly tilt the plate, the jam should not run off, but cling and slowly glide down. If the jam isn't ready, put it back on the heat for a while.

When the jam is ready, remove it from the heat. If you like your jam smooth, mash it with a potato masher or purée with a handheld blender. Spoon into the warm sterilized jars and close the lids tightly. Turn the jars upside down, cover with a dish towel, and leave to completely cool (this creates a vacuum that can be seen on the lid). Turn upright and store in a cool dark place. The jam will keep for 10 to 12 months before opening. After opening, you need to keep it in the fridge.

Makes 6 cups

7 TABLESPOONS BUTTER, SOFTENED
1/2 CUP SUPERFINE SUGAR
1 2/3 CUPS ALL-PURPOSE FLOUR
1/2 TEASPOON BAKING POWDER
1 EGG, LIGHTLY BEATEN
A FEW DROPS OF VANILLA EXTRACT
ABOUT 2/3 CUP OF YOUR FAVORITE JAM

Jam shortbread

This is Jem's jam shortbread. I loved it straightaway: It's so simple and so good. I love it with any jam that's not too sweet, but I usually use strawberry, raspberry, or plum (it's very special with fig jam, too). It's my children's favorite kind of thing—a bit like those cookies sandwiched together with raspberry jam that shows through the round window in front. You can use more jam if you like a lot.

Preheat the oven to 325°F. Have a 12 by 16-inch baking pan ready—you can line it if you like, to help you lift out the shortbread when it's cooked, but it's not absolutely necessary.

Put the butter and sugar in a good-sized bowl and work them together by hand or with a wooden spoon until combined. Add the flour and baking powder and work them in. Add the egg and vanilla and knead them in until it is all compact and smooth. Cover with plastic wrap and leave in the fridge for at least half an hour until the dough is firm enough to roll out.

Divide the dough in half. Roll out one half on a lightly floured surface so that it will fit into your pan. It should be about 1/8 inch thick. Fit it into your baking pan, making sure that it is a fairly even thickness all over. Spread the jam over the top, as if you were spreading it over a slice of toast. Roll out the other half of the dough and fit it as exactly as possible over the bottom one. If it is difficult to lift, roll it loosely over your rolling pin and carry it that way. It isn't essential that all your edges are exact; you can break off a bit from here and patchwork it in there. It will taste the same.

Bake for about 15 minutes, or until the shortbread is golden in places. The edges will start to turn golden brown first, followed by the top. Remove from the oven and cool for 5 minutes in the pan. Lift out of the pan, using the paper.

Cut into shapes with a cookie cutter, or just into squares or diamonds. Or you can leave it in one piece and keep cutting chunks out of it as you go past. It will keep in a sealed container for 5 or 6 days.

Makes 12 to 15 pieces, depending on the size you cut them

orange

Cream of winter squash soup
Sausage and potato goulash
Chicken drumsticks and wings with orange-tomato glaze
Winter squash pizza
Roast veal with oranges and lemons
Turkey breast with dried apricots and pancetta
Roast rack of pork with fennel and honey
Cabbage salad with oranges and lemons
Beef stew with carrots
Sage and rosemary mashed potatoes
Carrot purée
Creamy carrots
Baked butternut with butter and sugar
Winter squash fritters
Orange juice and olive oil cake with pine nuts
Greek yogurt with condensed milk and oranges
Whole wheat apricot and apple pie
Mandarin orange jam
Apricot sauce
Mango sorbet

- memory -

At preschool, there was a long winding cobbly hill with a witch's house on the side. This hill gave us so many scratches and bruised knees. The wall outside had jagged, unfriendly bits of glass cemented on to keep away our swallows. The witch's house was very very dark and spidery inside, with old velvety wine-colored curtains. We used to peep through where the window had a great big crack in it—the only place where you could see through the dust. The table was always a mess: Plates used and piled up from ages ago, it seemed. We knew that a witch lived there, so we would creep up in groups of three or four and hover around as long as the scare in us could keep us there. The bravest would go right up and press their noses against the unbroken window pane. Sometimes we would even throw our orange peels through the crack and then, with adrenaline fizzing through our arms and legs, we would fly back down the cobbles, down the higgledy-piggledy drive, our small hearts beating much faster than the clock that announced our break was over.

2 LARGE CHICKEN WINGS
9 CUPS COLD WATER
1 CARROT, PEELED AND HALVED
1 SMALL LEEK, TRIMMED AND HALVED
2 CLOVES GARLIC, PEELED BUT LEFT WHOLE
SMALL BUNCH OF PARSLEY
3 THYME SPRIGS
7 PEPPERCORNS
SALT
ABOUT 2³/4 POUNDS WINTER SQUASH
1¹/2 TABLESPOONS BUTTER
²/3 CUP HEAVY WHIPPING CREAM

Cream of winter squash soup

This is a full-bodied soup on account of the chicken broth base. I use beautiful deep red-orange winter squash. Serve with or without cream—it's nice both ways, although my kids like to see the swirls of cream through the orange soup. When you scoop out the seeds, rinse them and bake them in the oven with a scattering of salt—they make a great snack.

Put the chicken in a large saucepan with 9 cups of cold water and bring to a boil. Skim the surface well, then add the carrot, leek, garlic, parsley, thyme, and peppercorns and season with salt. Bring back to a boil, skimming off any more froth that comes to the surface. Lower the heat, cover the pan, and simmer for about an hour.

Strain the broth into a clean pan. (You won't need any of the solids here, but some chicken can be picked off and the vegetables can be chopped up, stirred through some rice, and served with parmesan.)

Peel and deseed the winter squash, then cut it up into smallish pieces. You should have about 5 cups. Heat the butter in a large nonstick frying pan and sauté the squash over fairly high heat so that it turns quite golden in places and starts to get a little soft inside. Tip it into the broth and simmer over low heat for about 20 minutes until it is soft all the way through. Purée with a handheld blender until it is completely smooth, and taste for salt. Add the cream, whisking it in a bit, and heat through, or swirl a little cream through each bowl. Serve with some brown bread and butter, and adults could add a small scattering of ground chili powder if they want.

Serves 6

1³/4 POUNDS GOOD-QUALITY SAUSAGES
2¹/2 TABLESPOONS OLIVE OIL
2 TABLESPOONS BUTTER
1 LARGE RED ONION, FINELY CHOPPED
1 TO 2 TEASPOONS SWEET PAPRIKA
5 TO 6 MEDIUM POTATOES, PEELED AND CUT
   INTO BITE-SIZE CHUNKS
1 CUP CANNED DICED TOMATOES
¹/2 CINNAMON STICK
1 BAY LEAF
2 CUPS HOT WATER
SALT
2¹/2 TABLESPOONS CHOPPED FRESH PARSLEY

Sausage and potato goulash

This is a great, quick, tasty, meal-in-one that will serve quite a few people or leave you with enough leftovers for the next day. Adults can serve theirs with a twist of pepper. This can be completely prepared in advance and just warmed up to serve. It's important to use good-quality sausages —Italian sausages are also good.

Slice the sausages into rounds about ¹/2 inch thick. Heat the oil and butter in a large heavy-bottomed pan (cast iron is good) and sauté the onion for a couple of minutes over medium heat. Stir in the paprika, cook for 30 seconds or so, and then add the sausages. Continue cooking, stirring fairly often, until the sausages turn golden in places. Add the potatoes, tomatoes, cinnamon, bay leaf, and 2 cups of hot water. Season with salt and bring to a boil.

   Lower the heat, cover, and simmer for about 20 minutes until the potatoes are softened and the goulash is thick and stewy. Stir with a wooden spoon from time to time and loosen the bits at the bottom to make sure they don't stick. If the potatoes are not quite done after that time, take the pan off the heat and leave it with the lid on for the potatoes to continue steaming. Mix the parsley through and serve hot, or even at room temperature.

Serves 8

1/2 CUP FIRMLY PACKED LIGHT BROWN SUGAR
1 1/2 CUPS FRESHLY SQUEEZED ORANGE JUICE
3/4 CUP CANNED TOMATO SAUCE
1 1/2 TABLESPOONS SOY SAUCE
1 1/2 TABLESPOONS WORCESTERSHIRE SAUCE
6 CHICKEN DRUMSTICKS
6 CHICKEN WINGS

Chicken drumsticks and wings with orange-tomato glaze

This is my friend Alan's recipe. He is somebody I trust completely with food and wine, and he says this recipe is also beautiful with pork, especially the parts that benefit from a long cooking time.

Preheat the oven to 325°F. Put the sugar, orange juice, tomato sauce, soy sauce, and Worcestershire sauce in a pan, and bring to a boil, stirring to dissolve the sugar. Simmer for 5 minutes.

Spread the chicken drumsticks and wings in a roasting pan just large enough to fit them in a single layer and pour the sauce over the top. Bake for 2 to 2 1/2 hours, basting and turning the pieces over every now and then, until the chicken is crispy and sticky and the sauce is a thick sticky glaze. Serve warm, or even at room temperature.

Serve 6

I loved the orange quarters at half-time in school netball matches. We would rip at them. We never minded having bits of orange stuck in our teeth for the rest of the game. And I liked them at home in the cooler afternoons, scattered with a smidgen of salt.

½ SMALL WINTER SQUASH
SALT
5 TO 8 TABLESPOONS OLIVE OIL
1 CUP ALL-PURPOSE FLOUR, FOR DUSTING
1 (8-OUNCE) CAN TOMATO SAUCE
1 TO 2 TEASPOONS DRIED OREGANO
1 CUP GRATED MOZZARELLA CHEESE

Winter squash pizza

This is my friend Caterina's recipe and is something she often makes for her kids. It's not really a pizza, but they call it that. It is very important to make the winter squash slices as thin and long as possible, and you can keep the seeds, rinse them, and bake them in the oven to serve as a snack with a sprinkling of salt. Next time you make this, you could even try adding a few dollops of leftover cooked ground beef between the layers of winter squash.

Peel the winter squash, cut out the seeds, and cut the flesh into very thin, long slices about ¹/₁₆ inch thick. Put the slices in a colander, sprinkle with salt and leave for about 1 hour. Rinse them very well and pat them dry. Preheat the oven to 350°F.

Drizzle 2½ tablespoons of olive oil into a round 10 to 12-inch baking pan and spread it to coat the bottom of the pan. Put the flour on a plate and pat both sides of the squash slices in it. Make a slightly overlapping layer of slices in the baking pan. Trickle the tiniest bit of olive oil over this layer, then repeat the layering and oiling until you have used up all the squash (you should have four or five layers).

Mix a little salt into the tomato sauce and dot here and there over the top of the squash. Put into the oven and bake for about 50 minutes, until the bottom is sizzling and the top is turning quite golden. Scatter the oregano over the top, crushing it between your fingers. Sprinkle with the mozzarella and return to the oven for 5 or 10 minutes, until the cheese melts and browns slightly. Cool a little before serving in wedges like pizza.

Serves 6

1 1/2 ORANGES
1 1/2 LEMONS
4 TABLESPOONS OLIVE OIL
2 TABLESPOONS BUTTER
ABOUT 1 1/2 POUNDS VEAL LEG, OR ROUND ROAST,
    TIED WITH STRING TO KEEP ITS SHAPE
2 CLOVES GARLIC, UNPEELED
2 SHALLOTS, PEELED AND HALVED LENGTHWISE
SALT AND FRESHLY GROUND BLACK PEPPER
4 CARROTS, PEELED AND CUT INTO THIRDS
2 ROSEMARY SPRIGS
4 THYME SPRIGS
1/2 CUP WHITE WINE

Roast veal with oranges and lemons

I made this with Luca and Luisa—my brother and sister-in-law, who are fantastic cooks—and it left me incredibly happy. There is not too much orange and lemon, just a hint, but I love the citrus wedges and a roasted thyme sprig served on the plate with the veal so that you know exactly what has gone into the cooking. (If you want, you can add more orange and lemon wedges toward the end of the cooking time, although they could make the sauce a little more tart.) The meat should be deep golden on the outside and cooked but just slightly rosy inside. You will need a small roasting pan (mine is about 7 by 10 inches) that fits the meat and vegetables quite compactly and can transfer to the stovetop.

Preheat the oven to 400°F. Cut the whole orange and lemon into quarters lengthwise (or into 6 wedges, if they are large) and put to one side. Keep the halves for later.

Put the oil and butter in a flameproof roasting pan and put over medium heat until the butter melts. Add the veal, garlic, shallots, and carrots, turn the heat to high, and brown the meat, salting and peppering the done sides and turning the vegetables over when you turn the meat.

Add the rosemary and thyme, and put the pan in the oven. Roast for about 20 minutes, or until the surface of the veal looks bubbling and golden, then turn it over. Squeeze in the juice from the orange and lemon halves, and add the wine. Roast for 10 minutes, then add the orange and lemon wedges. Reduce the temperature to 350°F and roast for another 10 minutes. Turn the wedges, taking care not to pierce them and ruin their shape, then roast for a final 20 minutes. Remove from the oven and let the dish sit for about 15 minutes.

Remove the string before carving the meat into fine slices. Serve with the pan juices, some carrots, and an orange and lemon wedge for each person.

Serves 4 to 5

1 1/4 POUNDS TURKEY BREAST IN ONE
   SLICE, LESS THAN 1/2 INCH THICK
9 DRIED APRICOTS
9 THIN SLICES UNSMOKED PANCETTA
1 EGG
SALT AND FRESHLY GROUND BLACK
   PEPPER
2 1/2 TABLESPOONS ALL-PURPOSE FLOUR
2 1/2 TABLESPOONS FINE POLENTA
5 TABLESPOONS OLIVE OIL
ABOUT 15 LARGE SHALLOTS, PEELED
   AND QUARTERED LENGTHWISE
4 TABLESPOONS WHITE WINE
4 TABLESPOONS WATER

Turkey breast with dried apricots and pancetta

This is my sister-in-law Luisa's. Her kids loved this kind of thing when they were young. You can also make it with two chicken breasts, making two smaller bundles.

Heat the oven to 350°F, and lay the turkey breast flat on a board. Roll up each apricot in a slice of pancetta and sit them in a line along one long side of the turkey breast. Roll up the turkey and secure the seam closed with a few metal skewers or toothpicks.

Break the egg into a large flat dish and whip with salt and pepper. Soak the turkey roll in the egg for 5 minutes or so, turning it over so that it is well coated. Hold it up so that the excess egg drips off and then pat the flour all over it. Dip it again in the egg, covering it well, then pat with the polenta, making sure that it is covered everywhere.

Heat half the oil in a nonstick frying pan and fry the turkey roll over medium heat to seal the crumbs. Turn over very gently, but only when the polenta crust is lightly golden and has set, or it will stick to the pan and come away.

Put the shallots in a roasting pan and drizzle with the wine and the remaining oil. Toss the shallots to coat them well and then put the turkey on top. Put in the oven for 40 to 50 minutes, turning the turkey when the top is golden and stirring the shallots. Once the wine has almost evaporated, add about 4 tablespoons of water and finish cooking. Serve in slices with some shallots on the side and the pan juices spooned over the top.

Serves 4 to 5

2 FENNEL BULBS, TRIMMED
2¼ POUNDS PORK LOIN CROWN ROAST
2 LONG ROSEMARY SPRIGS
SALT AND FRESHLY GROUND BLACK
    PEPPER
4 MEDIUM POTATOES, PEELED AND
    CUT INTO LONG WEDGES
5 SHALLOTS, PEELED
2 OR 3 CLOVES GARLIC, UNPEELED
2 FRESH BAY LEAVES
⅔ CUP OLIVE OIL
½ CUP WHITE WINE
½ CUP WATER
3 OR 4 SAGE SPRIGS
2½ TABLESPOONS RUNNY HONEY
1 TEASPOON MUSTARD POWDER

Roast rack of pork with fennel and honey

This is really quite simple even though it may seem fussy. Ask your butcher to prepare the meat for you by cutting it away from the bone and leaving it attached just at the bottom. Then, to serve, all you have to do is detach the last bottom bit and slice it up. Roasting it with the bones just gives extra flavor to the dish and it looks good. But if you prefer, you can cook it from the beginning deboned—a simple loin of pork. You can easily get a bigger piece than this, depending on how many you will be feeding. If you prefer, use unsweetened clear apple juice in place of the wine. And you can brush the pork with some mandarin orange jam and mustard instead of the honey, if you happen to have some. Or leave out the last step of brushing with honey mustard and serve a plain unsweetened roast instead.

Preheat the oven to 400°F. Cut the fennel bulbs lengthwise into 4 or 6 wedges that are still attached at the bottom. Bring a large saucepan of salted water to a boil and simmer the fennel for about 7 to 8 minutes to soften it a little, then drain.

Put the pork in a roasting pan and tuck the rosemary sprigs between the bone and the meat. Secure it closed with a skewer, or tie it with string so that it stays in place while cooking. Season all over with salt and pepper. Scatter the potatoes, shallots, garlic, bay leaves, and fennel around the meat. Sprinkle a little salt over the potatoes, drizzle the olive oil over the meat and potatoes, and pour the wine and 1/2 cup of water around. Put one sage sprig on top of the meat like a crown and tuck the rest under the vegetables.

Put the pan in the oven and roast for about 1 1/2 hours, turning the potatoes, shallots, and fennel over and basting them a few times. The meat won't need basting or turning over. By the end of the cooking time, the potatoes should be juicy and crisp on the outside and the meat nicely golden and cooked through, but still soft inside. If something is ready before everything else, remove it from the pan and put it in an ovenproof dish. This can be put in the oven to heat through for a few minutes before serving.

Meanwhile, mix together the honey and mustard until smooth, pressing down with a spoon to squash out any lumps.

Preheat the broiler to high. Remove the roasting pan from the oven and move the vegetables to the ovenproof dish to keep warm in the oven. Brush the honey mustard over the meat and put it under the broiler for about 5 minutes, until it crisps up and becomes nicely golden. Cut the meat completely off the bone and serve on a platter, carved in slices as thin or thick as you like. Arrange the vegetables on the platter around the meat and drizzle some of the melted honey juices over the potatoes before serving.

Serves 5 to 6

ABOUT 5 CUPS FINELY SLICED CABBAGE
1 TEASPOON SALT
2 SMALLISH LEAFY CELERY STALKS, FINELY SLICED
2 WHOLE ORANGES (BLOOD ORANGES, WHEN
   IN SEASON)

DRESSING:
4 TABLESPOONS OLIVE OIL
1 ½ TABLESPOONS LEMON JUICE
2 TEASPOONS BALSAMIC VINEGAR
SALT AND FRESHLY GROUND BLACK PEPPER
½ TEASPOON DRIED OREGANO, CRUSHED
   THROUGH YOUR FINGERS

GROUND CHILE, TO SERVE

Cabbage salad with oranges and lemons

A soft cabbage like savoy is best here, as the dressing will happily cling to it. You can easily add other ingredients—sometimes I sprinkle in some crushed dried mint or freshly chopped parsley, ground coriander seeds, or caraway seeds (although not for my children, who say they look like "gogos"—a word we used in South Africa for something small and insecty). Finely sliced fennel and coarsely grated carrots are also good, and you could use some beautiful purple cabbage for extra color. It is also lovely with a peeled, cored, and chopped apple tossed through. Walnuts are great, too. I normally use blood oranges, but when they are out of season, orange oranges are fine—just make sure that they are bright, sweet, and at their very best.

Put the cabbage in a large bowl, sprinkle with 1 teaspoon of salt and cover with cold water. Leave to soak for an hour or so. This will help draw away any acid from the cabbage. Drain, rinse, and put it in your serving bowl with the celery. Cut the skin and all the pith from the oranges. Slice the oranges into fine wheels (picking out any seeds) and add to the cabbage.

For the dressing, lightly whisk the oil, lemon juice, balsamic vinegar, and oregano together. Season with salt and pepper, and pour over the cabbage. Mix through well. Let it settle, then mix through a few more times so that the cabbage is completely coated. Toss through a sprinkling of ground chile just before serving, or pass it around separately for those who want it.

Serve in winter (when cabbage is at its best) with roast pork or chicken, or in summer with grilled meats.

Serves 6

4 TABLESPOONS OLIVE OIL
1 1/2 POUNDS BEEF ROUND, OR STEWING
   BEEF, CUT INTO 1 1/2-INCH CUBES
SALT
1 RED ONION, FINELY CHOPPED
2 TABLESPOONS BUTTER
2 CLOVES GARLIC, CHOPPED
4 THYME SPRIGS
1/2 CUP LIGHT RED WINE
1/2 CUP CANNED TOMATO SAUCE
3 CUPS HOT WATER
3 CARROTS, PEELED AND CUT DIAGONALLY
   INTO 1 1/2-INCH CHUNKS

Beef stew with carrots

This will be really soft and should have a nice amount of sauce after it has been cooking for a couple of hours. It is wonderful served with the sage and rosemary mashed potatoes (page 94). You decide if you want to leave a bit of fat on the meat or not—sometimes I do and sometimes I don't.

Heat the oil in a large flameproof casserole. Add the beef and brown it over high heat until it is deep golden on all sides, salting the done parts as you go. Add the onion and fry until it is lightly browned and looking a bit sticky. Add the butter, garlic, and thyme, and cook until you can smell the garlic. Add the wine, cook until it has evaporated, and then add the tomato sauce.

Add 3 cups of hot water and bring to a boil. Cover, turn the heat to minimum, and simmer for 1 1/2 to 2 hours, giving it a stir now and then. The meat should be soft and there should be a good amount of liquid.

Add the carrots and sprinkle them with a little salt. Cook uncovered for another 20 to 30 minutes, until the carrots are cooked all the way through but not collapsing, the meat is meltingly soft, and the sauce fairly thickened. Remove from the heat, leave with the lid on for 10 minutes or so and then serve with mashed potatoes.

Serves 4

5 MEDIUM POTATOES, PEELED AND
    CUT INTO CHUNKS
4 TABLESPOONS OLIVE OIL
1 LARGE CLOVE GARLIC, PEELED AND
    SQUASHED A BIT
2 SAGE SPRIGS
1 ROSEMARY SPRIG
4½ TABLESPOONS BUTTER
½ CUP MILK
4 TABLESPOONS HEAVY WHIPPING
    CREAM
SALT (OPTIONAL)

Sage and rosemary mashed potatoes

You can make these plain without the herb-flavored oil, if you like. This is easy, and once you get past the idea that there might be more dishes to wash, it's quick to make. There really is nothing to compare with a dollop of creamy mashed potatoes on your plate, especially with a stewy saucy dish like the beef stew with carrots (page 92).

Bring a saucepan of salted water to a boil. Add the potatoes and cook them for about 20 minutes, until you can pierce right through them and they look frayed at the edges. Drain well.

Heat the oil in a nonstick frying pan. Add the garlic, sage, and rosemary, and cook over medium heat for just long enough to lightly flavor the oil. Add the potato chunks and sauté for a few minutes so that they are well coated in oil and absorb the flavors.

Heat the butter, milk, and cream in a small saucepan just until the butter has melted. Pass just the potatoes through a food mill into a bowl, or mash with a potato masher. Add the hot milk mixture and fluff it through with a wooden spoon, trying not to overmix but keeping it light and fluffy. Add a little extra milk and cream if it seems too stiff, and add salt if needed. Serve immediately.

Serves 4

8 MEDIUM CARROTS, PEELED AND COARSELY CHOPPED
1 BAY LEAF
2 THYME SPRIGS
1 SMALL LEAFY CELERY STALK, HALVED
2 PARSLEY STALKS
A FEW WHOLE PEPPERCORNS
$4\frac{1}{2}$ TABLESPOONS BUTTER, DICED
SALT AND FRESHLY GROUND BLACK PEPPER
GROUND CINNAMON, TO SERVE

Carrot purée

The color of this is so very appealing. Serve in a small heap with roast pork, veal, or chicken. Use sweet, bright orange carrots.

Put the carrots in a pan of boiling salted water with the bay leaf, thyme, celery, parsley, and peppercorns. Simmer for about 20 minutes until the carrots are soft. Transfer just the carrots to a food processor, keeping about $\frac{1}{2}$ cup of the cooking liquid. Purée until completely smooth, adding teaspoonfuls of the cooking liquid if you need to. Add the butter and process just enough for it to melt. Taste for salt and pepper, and serve warm, sprinkled with cinnamon.

Serves 6

----

8 MEDIUM CARROTS, PEELED AND CUT INTO $\frac{1}{2}$-INCH ROUNDS
2 TABLESPOONS BUTTER
1 TO 2 TABLESPOONS CHOPPED FRESH PARSLEY
$\frac{1}{2}$ CUP HEAVY WHIPPING CREAM

Creamy carrots

This is a very simple carrot sauté that renders them soft and sweet and easy to eat. Make sure your carrots are bright orange and sweet to start with—the kind that you would like to eat raw. Sometimes we like these with grated parmesan sprinkled over the top and sometimes just plain.

Simmer the carrots in salted water for 10 to 15 minutes until they are quite soft and almost fraying on the outside, but still just a bit firm inside. Drain and put them in a large nonstick frying pan with the butter and the parsley. Sauté over medium heat until the butter starts to sizzle and turn a little golden, then pour in the cream. Let the cream bubble up and reduce a little, then serve hot.

Serves 4

3½ TABLESPOONS BUTTER
2¼ POUNDS UNPEELED BUTTERNUT SQUASH
¼ TO ⅓ CUP LIGHT BROWN SUGAR
SALT
4 TABLESPOONS WATER
2 BAY LEAVES

Baked butternut with butter and sugar

This is lovely and sweet and goes very well with roast pork or chicken, and also game if you happen to be serving that. I use organic butternut, which is a beautiful creamy orange outside and bright orange inside. Make sure you start off with a lovely butternut, but if you suspect yours is not very ripe and tasty, you could add a little more sugar. You might like to add another vegetable here, too, like turnips or other root vegetables. You can also add some ground cinnamon before baking. I use a 12-inch round baking dish, but you can work out how many you need to serve and what size dish will be right, as these are very easy amounts to adjust.

Preheat the oven to 350°F and generously butter the bottom of a large round ovenproof dish with some of the butter. Peel the butternut by first cutting it in half, then scooping out the seeds with a spoon (save the seeds to toast in the oven for a snack, or to plant). Cut the squash into long slices that are about an inch thick. Using a small sharp knife, carefully cut away the skin, keeping the shape of the squash slices and taking care that you don't cut yourself, as the skin is hard. You should have about 1½ pounds of butternut.

Scatter some of the sugar over the bottom of the dish and then lay the butternut slices flat, in a single layer. Scatter the rest of the sugar over the top, dot with the rest of the butter, and sprinkle with a little salt. Pour 4 tablespoons of water around the side and add the bay leaves. Put into the oven for about 1 hour, or until the butternut is soft and golden, even dark in places, and there is some thick golden juice bubbling away at the bottom. Spoon the pan juices over the squash a couple of times during the cooking—if it looks a little too dry, add a dribble more water. Serve warm. If you aren't serving it immediately, then reheat gently so that the butter melts again.

Serves 6

1 1/4 POUNDS WINTER SQUASH (ABOUT
   3 CUPS, ONCE PEELED, DESEEDED, AND
   CHOPPED)
1/2 CUP ALL-PURPOSE FLOUR
A LARGE PINCH OF BAKING SODA
2 EGGS, LIGHTLY BEATEN
1/2 TEASPOON SALT
FRESHLY GROUND BLACK PEPPER
5 TABLESPOONS SUPERFINE SUGAR
1 TEASPOON GROUND CINNAMON
BUTTER, FOR FRYING

Winter squash fritters

I use beautiful organic winter squash for this—they are small with reddish-orange skin outside and very bright autumny orange inside. This dish is best warm but also quite nice and stodgy when at room temperature (because we don't always get round to frying things and serving them immediately). If you have clarified butter, use that for frying because it doesn't burn so quickly. Otherwise, just use ordinary butter and throw in a few extra blobs from time to time to cool it down.

Cut the winter squash into chunks and boil in a large pan of water for 15 minutes or so until very soft. Drain well and then leave on a plate for a few minutes for the excess water to evaporate. Put it into a bowl and mash very well. You should get about a cupful of mash.

Add the flour, baking soda, eggs, 1/2 teaspoon of salt, and a couple of grindings of pepper, and mix it all together well. Mix the sugar and cinnamon together on a large flat plate.

Heat enough butter in a nonstick frying pan to just cover the bottom. When it sizzles, turn the heat to medium and dollop in a few large tablespoonfuls of the squash mixture, letting them settle into fritters. Don't touch them until they have set, with some holes appearing on their tops, and their bottoms are golden brown. Swiftly flip them over with a metal spatula and cook until the new bottoms turn golden. Lift them out onto a plate lined with paper towels to soak up the oil, and then pat them richly on both sides in the cinnamon sugar. If the butter looks dark and as if it's starting to burn, wipe out the pan with a paper towel and add fresh butter. Carry on frying the rest, adding fresh butter as needed.

Makes about 18 fritters

4 EGGS, SEPARATED
1 TEASPOON VANILLA EXTRACT
1 CUP SUPERFINE SUGAR
1/4 CUP FIRMLY PACKED LIGHT BROWN SUGAR
3/4 CUP OLIVE OIL
3 1/3 CUPS ALL-PURPOSE FLOUR
1 HEAPING TEASPOON BAKING POWDER
FINELY GRATED RIND OF 1 ORANGE
1 CUP FRESHLY SQUEEZED ORANGE
   JUICE (JUICE OF ABOUT 4 ORANGES)
1/2 CUP PINE NUTS

Orange juice and olive oil cake with pine nuts

I like making this in two small pans—they look good together and you can take one to a friend. I just love what's in it and I love it when my kids eat things like this. You could dress it up for a snack with a creamy yogurt on the side or just serve it for what it is: an honest simple sponge.

Preheat the oven to 350°F. Brush two 8 1/2-inch springform pans with olive oil and dust with flour. Whip the egg whites in a large bowl until they are firm and snowy white (keep them in the fridge in hot weather, and don't leave them too long or they could collapse). Whip the yolks with the vanilla until they bulk up and become foamy. Whisk in the superfine and brown sugars, then add the olive oil bit by bit, mixing well after each addition. Add the flour, baking powder, orange rind, and juice, and beat well until you have a smooth batter. Gently fold in the egg whites.

   Scrape out half the batter into each pan and sprinkle each cake with pine nuts. Bake for a,bout 35 minutes, or until the tops are golden and crusty and a skewer poked into the middle comes out clean. Leave to cool before serving. This will keep well in a sealed container for 4 or 5 days.

Makes two 8 1/2-inch cakes

2 WHOLE ORANGES OR BLOOD ORANGES
SUGAR (OPTIONAL)
1/2 CUP SWEETENED CONDENSED MILK
FINELY GRATED RIND AND JUICE OF
  1 SMALL ORANGE
1 1/4 CUPS GREEK-STYLE PLAIN YOGURT

Greek yogurt with condensed milk and oranges

The basis of this recipe was given to me—thank you, Ioanna. I added the oranges, but you might like to add another fruit. I sometimes use blood oranges, sometimes ordinary. Whatever sort you use, make sure they are sweet as sweet. You could actually serve this with any other fruit you like, keeping the orange juice and rind for mixing into the yogurt, and then spooning this over any other cut fruit—bananas, mangoes, plums would be beautiful . . .

Use a small sharp knife to cut away the skin of the oranges, leaving no pith. Slice the oranges into substantial wheels, maybe 1/4 inch thick, and then halve those. Put the cut slices in a bowl to collect their juice. If you don't think they're very sweet, sprinkle a tablespoon or so of sugar over them.

Put the condensed milk, half of the orange rind, and 5 tablespoons of the orange juice in a pouring cup (you can drink the rest of the orange juice). Slowly mix this into the yogurt, bit by bit. Cover and put in the fridge for a couple of hours until it has set to a very soft and creamy pudding. Serve a few orange slices with a dollop of the yogurt, some juice dribbled over the top, and a tiny hill of leftover rind, just for extra color.

Serves 4

These are the rabbits that my sister, Ludi, and I tucked tightly into our pockets. We never left home without our rabbits.

PASTRY:
1 1/3 CUPS WHOLE WHEAT FLOUR
1/3 CUP FIRMLY PACKED LIGHT BROWN SUGAR
7 TABLESPOONS CHILLED BUTTER, CUT INTO CUBES
1 EGG, PLUS 1 EGG YOLK
A FEW DROPS OF VANILLA EXTRACT

ABOUT 3 APPLES
3 TABLESPOONS BUTTER
2 TABLESPOONS LIGHT BROWN SUGAR
1 TABLESPOON WATER
1 TEASPOON GROUND CINNAMON
ABOUT 10 FRESH APRICOTS, HALVED
   (OR QUARTERED, IF LARGE), PITS REMOVED
ABOUT 3 TABLESPOONS SUPERFINE SUGAR

Whole wheat apricot and apple pie

You can use absolutely any fruit you like here—fresh figs are good. I use apple purée for the crust and then put apricot halves on top, but you can stick to all apples, strawberries, or nectarines, and plums are beautiful. You can serve this with one part Greek-style yogurt and one part lightly sweetened whipped cream with a couple of drops of vanilla extract stirred through. This is dripping with health, I feel—I love to have things like this in my kitchen when the kids ask for a snack.

To make the pastry, put the flour, sugar, and butter in a bowl. Work it all together with your fingers until you have a sandy mixture. Add the egg, extra egg yolk, and vanilla, and carry on mixing until you have a smooth ball. Wrap it up in plastic wrap, flatten and put it in the fridge for about 30 minutes.

   Meanwhile, peel and core the apples, and cut them into chunks. Put half the butter in a nonstick pan and add the apple chunks, the brown sugar, and a tablespoon of water. Put the lid on and cook over medium heat for about 15 to 20 minutes, until the apples collapse and turn slightly golden on the bottom. Stir in the cinnamon and squash the apples into a purée with a wooden spoon. Remove from the heat.

   Preheat the oven to 400°F. Roll out the pastry on a sheet of parchment paper to a circle of about 12 to 13 inches, dusting with a little all-purpose flour if necessary. Using the parchment paper, flip the pastry over into an ungreased 9 1/2-inch springform pan. Let it settle in before peeling off the paper and pressing the pastry onto the bottom and sides of the pan. Don't worry if the pastry tears, just patch it and press the gaps together.

   Spread the apple over the bottom and put the apricots on top. Scatter with superfine sugar, more or less, depending on the sweetness of your fruit. Dot with the rest of the butter, then fold the pastry edge in and over to cover the edge of the filling. Bake for about 40 minutes, or until the top of the fruit is golden brown in places, and the pastry crisp. Serve plain or with yogurt and whipped cream.

Serves 6 to 8

8 MANDARIN ORANGES (ABOUT 2³/4 POUNDS)
2²/3 CUPS SUPERFINE SUGAR
2 CUPS WATER

Mandarin orange jam

It is a bit of a job peeling the mandarin oranges, but you can't leave the skins on to make this beautiful jam. It is quite a quantity to get through, but if you have three or four friends over, this will move really quickly while everyone catches up on news. Working alone, you may well end up in a trance from the monotonous concentration. Use brightly colored, sweet, seedless mandarin oranges if possible. You can add a piece of cinnamon or some cardamom for a different touch, but I love this jam just simply on the breakfast table next to chocolate loaf, white loaf, and strawberry jam. It makes me feel as if I'm strolling through a citrus grove. This is also great for using as a crust on pork. Roast a pork loin, spread it with mustard, this jam, and some bread crumbs and bake for another half an hour, until the crust is crisp.

First of all, sterilize your jars for when you have a panful of hot jam ready to bottle. It is always best to use several small jars, rather than one or two big ones. Wash the jars and lids in hot soapy water, or in the dishwasher, and rinse well in hot water. Then put the jars (and the lids) on a baking sheet and leave in a 250°F oven for at least 20 minutes, or until you are ready to use them. (Don't use a dish towel to dry them—they should dry thoroughly in the oven.)

Rinse the mandarin oranges in warm water and then peel them. Keep the peel from half of them, taking off the black eye where the stem connected to the fruit.

Divide all the mandarins into segments, then remove the skin from each segment. A small pair of scissors or a sharp paring knife will be useful in cutting the pith line, then gently pulling this up will help loosen the skin. Sometimes they come away easily, sometimes not. Try to keep some segments whole if possible, but it is not a problem if they break up (many of them will). Put the segments in a colander set over another bowl to catch the juice.

Roughly tear up the peel you have saved and put it in a large heavy-bottomed pan with the sugar, the collected mandarin orange juice, and 2 cups of water. Bring to a boil, then lower the heat, and simmer uncovered for 20 minutes or so, or until the peel starts to look glazed. Purée until it is as smooth as you can get it.

Add the mandarin segments, keeping a small handful back, and any further juice that has accumulated. Bring back to a boil and simmer for another 30 minutes or so, taking care that the jam doesn't color and caramelize. Stir often with a wooden spoon to make sure that nothing sticks to the bottom. Test that the jam is ready by dropping a heaping teaspoonful onto a plate. When you slightly tilt the plate, the jam should not run off, but cling and slowly glide down. If the jam isn't ready, put it back on the heat for a while.

Add the handful of mandarin segments about 5 minutes before the jam is ready, to add a splash of brighter color and some texture. Spoon into the warm sterilized jars and close the lids tightly. Turn the jars upside down, cover with a dish towel, and leave to completely cool (this creates a vacuum that can be seen on the lid). Turn upright and store in a cool dark place. The jam will keep for 10 to 12 months before it is opened. After opening, you need to keep it in the fridge.

Makes 2 1/3 cups

1/2 CUP SUGAR
A FEW DROPS OF VANILLA EXTRACT
1 1/2 CUPS WATER
ABOUT 15 RIPE APRICOTS, HALVED,
    PITS REMOVED

Apricot sauce

I serve this over Greek-style yogurt and it would be ideal on pancakes or ice cream. I also like it chilled as a summer drink, topped up with ice-cold sparkling water (two-thirds sauce, one-third water) in tall glasses. I don't like my sauces overly sweet, but you can add more sugar if your apricots seem a little sour, and if you prefer the sauce a little thicker, then simmer for a few moments more with the lid off. This makes quite a bit, so when you have an abundance of apricots, make this and freeze some for an emergency future sauce.

Put the sugar and vanilla in a large saucepan with 1 1/2 cups of water. Bring to a boil, stirring until the sugar dissolves. Simmer for a few minutes and then add the apricots. Cover the pan and simmer over low heat for about 10 minutes, until the apricots start to lose their shape. Purée until totally smooth and then chill, depending on how you're serving it. Serve over vanilla ice cream or with pancakes or waffles.

Makes about 3 cups

ORANGE

2 LARGE RIPE MANGOES
1/2 CUP SUPERFINE SUGAR
FINELY GRATED RIND OF 1 LIME
JUICE OF 2 LIMES

Mango sorbet

This is pure frozen mango—wonderful, thick, plain and simple, yet a splash of color. It looks fantastic served with a scoop of pomegranate or strawberry sorbet. Seek out the best-quality fruit—your sorbet will only ever be as good as the mangoes you start off with. You can also serve this unfrozen as a mango purée to pour over ice cream or yogurt.

Peel the mangoes and cut as much flesh as possible from the pit. Cut the flesh into small chunks and put it in a bowl with the sugar, lime rind, and lime juice. Stir, cover, and leave overnight in the fridge to draw out the juice. Purée until smooth and, if necessary, pass through a sieve to extract the very pulpy and stringy bits. Taste for sweetness and add extra superfine sugar, a teaspoon at a time, if you think it needs it (this will depend on the variety and ripeness of your mangoes). Top up the purée with water to give 2 cups.

Pour the purée into a bowl or container that has a lid. Put the lid on and put it in the freezer. After an hour, give the mixture an energetic whisk with a hand whisk or an electric beater. Put it back in the freezer and then whisk again after another couple of hours. When the sorbet is nearly firm, give one last whisk and put it back in the freezer to set.

Alternatively, pour into your ice cream machine and churn, following the manufacturer's instructions.

Serves 4 to 6

We always saved our mango pits. We tore off every scrap with our teeth and then washed and scrubbed them carefully, running our nails first in one direction and then the other until they were clean of all mango. After they were towel-dried, we kept our mango pets and brushed their lovely hair with our old toothbrushes. They still needed a bath and looking after now and then.

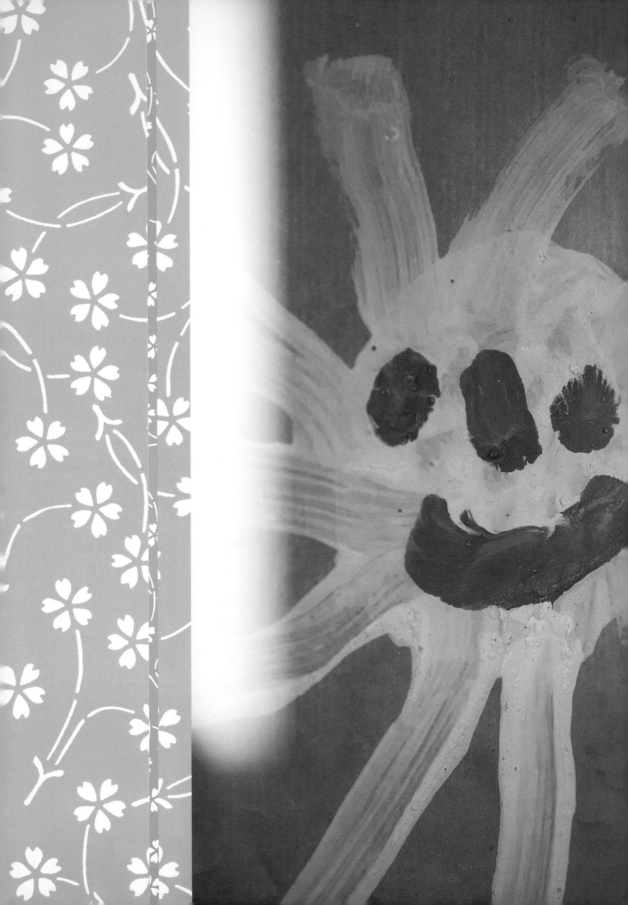

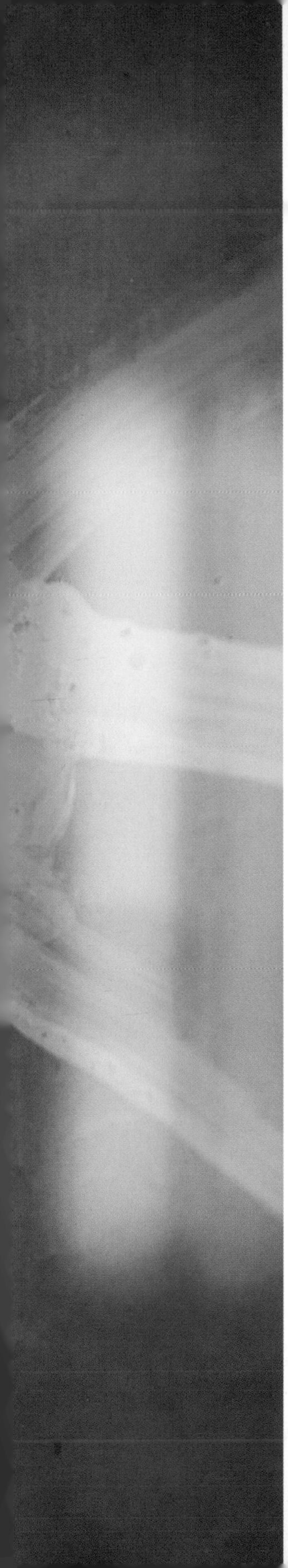

yellow

Lemonade
Fizzy orange
Risotto with fried egg
Spaghettini with egg and toasted parsley
  bread crumbs
Grilled fish skewers
Barbecued mixed grill with corn
Chicken sautéed with cheese and milk
Ham and cheese omelette
Eggs with bread and butter
Sautéed potatoes with egg
Fun dough
Egg custard
Fried custard squares
Lemon sandwiches with raspberries and cream
Lemon curd ice cream
Lemon meringue ice cream cake

- Memory -

There is children's laughter escaping out
through the iron gates and past the oleander
and daffodils, sprinkling onto the just-cut
lawns that line the road and fluttering up
to me through my open window, falling
over my shoulders like fairy glitter. And that
atmosphere of sleeping head to tail in trains
and on vacation, and knocking on walls to
see if others are awake.

1/3 CUP SUPERFINE SUGAR
ONE LONG STRIP OF LEMON RIND, PITH REMOVED
4 TABLESPOONS WATER
JUICE OF 2 1/2 LEMONS (ABOUT 1/2 CUP)
2 CUPS ICE-COLD SPARKLING WATER

Lemonade

This is a lovely basic to which you can add more or less sugar or lemons and double, halve, or triple quantities as you like. If you and your children prefer, you can use still, not fizzy, water. On a hot summer day, this always has been, and always will be, amazing. I like to put the sparkling water in the freezer so that it is really cold, make up the syrup (and leave it to cool), and then pour in the ice-cold water just before serving so that the bubbles don't disappear. I think you could probably make a lovely limeade in this way, too, and soon I might try it with pink grapefruits for a brunch.

Put the sugar, lemon rind, and 4 tablespoons of tap water in a small pan. Bring to a boil, stirring so that the sugar dissolves completely, then boil for a few minutes so that the lemon rind flavors the syrup. Add the lemon juice (I like to leave in some fleshy bits that might get through, but no seeds) and let that bubble up for a minute or two. Pour into a large pitcher and cover with a cloth or lid as you'll probably be making this in summer and there might be flies. Leave to cool completely. When you're ready to serve, pour in the sparkling water, and mix well. Ladle out into glasses and add ice if you like.

Makes 2 1/2 cups

We are all born to play a role, from our early days . . . remember the lemonade maker, the one who set up the stall on the side of the road, the passerby?

4 TABLESPOONS SUPERFINE SUGAR
ONE LONG STRIP OF ORANGE RIND, PITH REMOVED
4 TABLESPOONS WATER
JUICE OF 4 ORANGES (ABOUT 1 1/3 CUPS)
2 CUPS ICE-COLD SPARKLING WATER

Fizzy orange

If lemons aren't readily available, or lemonade is slightly tart for your children, you can make up a pitcher of fizzy orange, which, I find, always goes down well. If you like, you can strain the drink at the end. I prefer it with some bits in, personally—and so does one of my daughters, but the other will drink it only if I strain it. For adults, who might want a bit of extra pizzazz, you could make a pitcher with added spices such as a vanilla bean or a small stick of cinnamon.

Put the sugar, orange rind, and 4 tablespoons of tap water into a small pan. Bring to a boil, stirring so that the sugar dissolves completely, then boil for a few minutes so that the orange rind flavors the syrup. Add the orange juice (I like to leave in some fleshy bits that might get through, but no seeds) and let that bubble for about 5 minutes, or until it looks slightly denser. Pour into a pitcher and cover with a cloth or lid to keep the flies out. Leave to cool completely.

When you're ready to serve, pour in the sparkling water, and mix well. Ladle out into glasses and add ice if you like.

Makes 3 1/3 cups

YELLOW

3 TABLESPOONS BUTTER
4 TABLESPOONS OLIVE OIL
2 SHALLOTS, CHOPPED
1²/₃ CUPS RISOTTO RICE
½ CUP WHITE WINE
4 CUPS HOT VEGETABLE BROTH
FRESHLY GRATED NUTMEG
SALT
½ CUP GRATED PARMESAN OR GRANA
    CHEESE
ABOUT 8 FRESH SAGE LEAVES
4 EGGS, AT ROOM TEMPERATURE
GRATED PARMESAN CHEESE, TO SERVE
FRESHLY GROUND BLACK PEPPER,
    TO SERVE

Risotto with fried egg

These are all the things my family loves—white risotto, egg, Parmesan—on one plate. The egg yolk must be soft when you serve it so that it can drip into the rice, and we like the white to be golden and frayed around the edge.

Heat half the butter and 2 tablespoons of oil in a heavy-bottomed pan suitable for making risotto. Sauté the shallots over low heat until light gold and then stir in the rice with a wooden spoon. Stir for a few minutes to completely coat the rice and let it cook just a bit. Add the wine, and when that has evaporated, add all of the broth. Add a few good grinds of nutmeg and taste for salt (your broth will probably be seasoned enough). Simmer uncovered over high heat for about 15 minutes, or until the rice has absorbed much of the liquid. If it seems as if it needs a bit more liquid, add some hot water. Remove from the heat and stir in the remaining butter and the Parmesan. Taste for salt, adjusting if necessary. Leave with the lid on so that the steam continues to cook the rice.

Heat the remaining oil in a large nonstick frying pan and briefly fry the sage leaves until crisp. Remove with tongs. Gently break the eggs into the pan and sprinkle a little salt on the yolks. Cook until the edges of the white are a bit golden. Cover the pan with a lid and fry until the yolks are just slightly opaque on the surface but still soft inside (they are best when the undersides are golden and a bit crisp).

Scoop the rice onto serving plates and top each serving with an egg and a couple of sage leaves, being careful not to break the yolk just yet. Serve with a sprinkling of Parmesan and a few grinds of black pepper for those who want it.

Serves 4

4 EGGS, AT ROOM TEMPERATURE
5 TABLESPOONS OLIVE OIL
SALT
2/3 (16-OUNCE) PACKAGE SPAGHETTINI
2 SLICES SOFT WHITE BREAD, BROKEN UP INTO
    COARSE CRUMBS
2 ANCHOVY FILLETS, FINELY CHOPPED
1 CLOVE GARLIC, FINELY CHOPPED
1 HEAPING TABLESPOON CHOPPED FRESH
    PARSLEY
FINELY GRATED ZEST OF 1/2 LEMON
OLIVE OIL, TO SERVE
GRATED PARMESAN CHEESE, TO SERVE
FRESHLY GROUND BLACK PEPPER, TO SERVE

Spaghettini with egg and toasted parsley bread crumbs

This is nice and simple. The anchovies and garlic can be left out, and you could also add baby capers or maybe some chopped olives. This could nicely precede a simple sautéed chicken breast or fish fillet.

Bring a large pan of salted water to a boil. Add the eggs and boil for 4 minutes. Lift out the eggs with a slotted spoon, run under cold water, and peel off the shells. Put the eggs in a large serving bowl and mash up into small bits with a fork. Add a couple of tablespoons of olive oil and a little salt.

Add the spaghettini to the boiling water and cook, following the package instructions. Meanwhile, heat $2^1/2$ tablespoons of oil in a nonstick frying pan, add the bread crumbs, anchovies, and garlic, and sauté over medium heat until the bread crumbs are golden and crisp. Remove from the heat and stir in the parsley and lemon zest.

Drain the spaghettini, keeping some of the cooking water. Add the pasta to the egg with a few spoonfuls of the cooking water. Toss through very well and serve immediately. Drizzle each serving with some olive oil and scatter parsley bread crumbs over the top. Pass around the Parmesan and some black pepper for those who like it.

Serves 4

ABOUT 1 POUND SWORDFISH, 3/4 INCH THICK
ABOUT 1 POUND FRESH TUNA, 3/4 INCH THICK
1 POUND RAW SHRIMP
1 1/4 POUNDS SMALL SQUID
3 HEAPING TABLESPOONS CHOPPED FRESH PARSLEY
1 LARGE CLOVE GARLIC, FINELY CHOPPED
ABOUT 1/2 CUP DRY BREAD CRUMBS
SALT
OLIVE OIL, FOR THE GRILL

DRESSING:
1/2 CUP OLIVE OIL
2 CLOVES GARLIC, PEELED AND SQUASHED A BIT
JUICE OF 1 LARGE JUICY LEMON
SALT AND FRESHLY GROUND BLACK PEPPER

Grilled fish skewers

Your fish has got to be super-fresh with that almost-sweet smell. Tuna should be lovely and bright red; swordfish white. You can choose another type of fish here, as long as you can cut it easily into squares and thread it onto skewers. These are passed through a bread crumb, parsley, and garlic mix and then grilled so they turn golden dark and crispy in places. It is important that they are still soft and moist inside but cooked through. You could add some chopped herbs or even finely chopped red chile to the dressing.

Cut the swordfish and tuna into 3/4-inch blocks. Peel and devein the shrimp, leaving the tails on. Clean the squid and cut the bodies into thick rings (you won't need the wings or tentacles here, so save them for something else).

Using short metal skewers, or bamboo ones that have been soaked in cold water for an hour, thread a block of swordfish, a block of tuna, a squid ring, then a shrimp (spiking this through in two places), then another block of swordfish, and finally tuna. You should have enough to make about 12 skewers, and you might need to juggle the order around a bit at the end depending on how much of each fish you have left.

Heat the grill to high. Mix the parsley, garlic, bread crumbs, and a little salt together on a large plate. Pat the skewers on all sides in this mixture so that they're lightly coated.

For the dressing, mix together the oil, garlic, and lemon juice, and add some salt and black pepper.

Brush the grill rack with a little oil and grill the skewers until they are charred deep golden in some parts, but not for so long that they dry out. Reduce the heat or move the rack farther from the coals if the crust starts to burn before the fish cooks through. Serve hot, with some dressing drizzled over, and a sprinkling of salt.

Makes about 12 skewers

1/4 POUND PLUS 1 TABLESPOON BUTTER, SOFTENED
2 TABLESPOONS FINELY CHOPPED FRESH HERBS (THYME, BASIL, PARSLEY, MINT)
6 POTATOES, SCRUBBED BUT NOT PEELED
SALT
6 SMALL RED ONIONS, PEELED
JUICE OF 1 1/2 LEMONS
5 TABLESPOONS OLIVE OIL
1 TEASPOON DRIED OREGANO, CRUSHED BETWEEN YOUR FINGERS
FRESHLY GROUND BLACK PEPPER
3/4 POUND VEAL FILLET, IN ONE PIECE
ABOUT 14 YOUNG LAMB RIB CHOPS, FRENCHED
6 EARS CORN, HUSKS REMOVED, HALVED IF LARGE
1 1/3 CUPS SOUR CREAM OR GREEK-STYLE PLAIN YOGURT
BUTTER, TO SERVE

Barbecued mixed grill with corn

I am crazy about mixed grills—they are something my mother always made for us and remind me of restaurants in Greece where you can order lamb chops by the pound and they come out barbecue-grilled with oregano and a squeeze of lemon. Here I make them with a whole fillet of veal, and potatoes and onions roasted amongst the coals. We love a dollop of sour cream or Greek-style yogurt and an extra drizzle of olive oil over our potatoes. You might like a tomato salad and bread to finish off this display.

Beat the butter and herbs together. Put on a sheet of aluminum foil in a fat little sausage shape, roll up tightly, and put in the fridge to firm up.

Preheat the barbecue or chargrill. Rinse the potatoes and prick the skins here and there. While they are still wet, lay each potato on a square of foil. Sprinkle quite generously all over with salt, then wrap up the foil parcels tightly. Do the same with the onions. Put the parcels directly into the coals, if that's the style of your barbecue, or over the flame on a rack. Cook for 10 minutes, turning a couple of times with tongs, before you add the meat.

Meanwhile, mix the lemon juice with the oil and add the oregano. Add a few grinds of black pepper and 1/2 teaspoon or so of salt. Put the whole veal fillet onto the barbecue rack and cook until the underside is deep golden. Turn, brushing the cooked side with the lemon dressing. Add the rib chops and corn to the grill and, when the undersides are golden, turn them over and brush the chops with the dressing. Keep turning the potatoes and onions, too. Turn the meat and corn again, brushing the meat with dressing. When the meat is golden and a bit crispy in places, put it on a serving platter and drizzle the remaining dressing over the top. The whole fillet should ideally be cooked through but still pink inside. Leave them to rest for a minute or so and then cut the fillet into fairly thick slices.

Check that the potatoes and onions are soft, then unwrap and add to the platter. Cut a deep slash in the potatoes, pinch their bottoms to fluff them up, and then mash the tops a bit with a fork. Top with sour cream or yogurt. Slice the herb butter and serve alongside some plain butter for people to have with their corn.

Serves 6

2 SMALL CHICKEN BREASTS
ABOUT 4 TABLESPOONS ALL-PURPOSE FLOUR,
    FOR DUSTING
2½ TABLESPOONS OLIVE OIL
SALT
4 LARGE THIN SLICES FONTINA CHEESE
½ CUP MILK

Chicken sautéed with cheese and milk

I find there is something really encouraging about serving this to my kids.
It is warm and homely and the kind of thing I like to call them downstairs
to after their bath . . . to have it sitting on that ready table, a small vase of
flowers, some pan-fried potatoes with rosemary and sage (page 245), and
maybe even a small pan of sautéed broccoli.

Slice each chicken breast horizontally to give two thin cutlets. Cover them with a
sheet of plastic wrap and pound with a meat mallet until they are of an even
thickness and a bit thinner. Dust in flour.
    Heat the oil in a large frying pan. Add the four chicken cutlets and cook over
medium heat until the underneaths are nicely browned. Turn over and season the
cooked sides with salt. Cook until golden underneath and then turn them again
and season. Put a slice of cheese over each cutlet so that it covers the chicken
completely. Add the milk to the pan, put the lid on, and cook until the cheese has
melted and there is a bubbly, thickened sauce. Check that the chicken is soft and
cooked through, but be careful not to overcook it. Remove from the heat and leave
the lid on the pan until the very last second before serving so that the cheese
carries on melting. Serve hot.

Serves 4

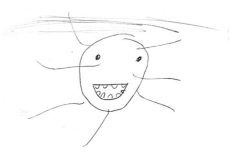

1 EGG
SALT
1 TEASPOON BUTTER
1 THIN SLICE HAM, CHOPPED
1 TABLESPOON GRATED PARMESAN CHEESE

Ham and cheese omelette

We like this with a handful of pan-fried potatoes and sautéed zucchini. The quantities can be doubled and made in a larger pan.

Whip the egg with a touch of salt. Melt the butter in a 6-inch nonstick frying pan over medium heat until it is fizzling. Pour in the egg and swirl it around the pan to cover the bottom evenly. Lower the heat a little and fry the egg, making some holes when it starts to set to allow the uncooked egg to run through. Shake the pan to dislodge the omelette, then scatter the ham and cheese over the top. Roll it up gently, slide it out onto a plate and serve immediately.

Serves 1

---

1 VERY FRESH LARGE EGG, AT ROOM TEMPERATURE
1 TO 2 TEASPOONS SOFT BUTTER
1 SLICE FRESH SOFT WHITE OR BROWN BREAD
SALT

Eggs with bread and butter

This is what my mom gave us so often—it is one of my earliest food memories. I have only to smell it and it takes me sailing back in time and fills me with wonderful memories. It is amazing how an egg and slice of bread can do that.

Put the egg in a pan of cold water and bring to a boil. Cook for $2\frac{1}{2}$ minutes from when the water comes to a boil (the white should have just set and the yolk will still be soft and runny). Lift out with a slotted spoon. Meanwhile, butter the bread, break it into small bits, and put in a little bowl. Hold the egg over the bowl, give it a sharp crack through the middle with a knife, and scoop out the egg with a teaspoon. Add a little salt and mash together well with a fork. Serve immediately.

Serves 1

3 MEDIUM POTATOES, PEELED AND CUT INTO
    CHUNKS
2½ TABLESPOONS OLIVE OIL
1½ TABLESPOONS BUTTER
2 CLOVES GARLIC, PEELED BUT LEFT WHOLE
3 SAGE SPRIGS
SALT
2 EGGS

Sautéed potatoes with egg

If you want just potatoes on their own, you can double this amount and add an extra spoonful of oil, but if you'll be adding the eggs to the pan, you'll need this smallish amount of potatoes with a fairly large nonstick frying pan. The one I use is about 12 inches. I love making just this amount and taking the pan straight to the table to my two waiting children. You could also easily serve a chicken cutlet on the side, or maybe another vegetable like sautéed broccoli or creamed spinach.

Boil the potato chunks in boiling salted water until they are cooked through but not breaking up.

Put the olive oil, butter, garlic, and sage in a large nonstick frying pan and heat until the butter melts. Add the potatoes with a slotted spoon straight from their pan, letting all the water drip off first. Sauté over fairly high heat at first, then once they start to look golden, lower the heat slightly, and leave them on the stovetop to get crusty, tossing them carefully from time to time. Take care not to mush them up, although just a bit is fine if it gives extra crusty bits. If the garlic looks like it may burn, sit it on top of the potatoes. Try to get the sage to the bottom of the pan so it crisps up nicely. Taste to see if there is enough salt.

When the potatoes are golden all over and crisp in parts, push them to the side to make two big spaces for the eggs; like a pair of sunglasses in the pan. Break an egg into each space, sprinkle with a little salt, and put the lid on. Cook over medium-low heat until the whites are just set. Serve at once, trying not to break the egg yolks because it's nice to mix them with the potatoes on your plate.

Serves 2

1 CUP ALL-PURPOSE FLOUR
1 CUP FINE SALT
A FEW DROPS OF FOOD COLORING (OPTIONAL)
5 TABLESPOONS WATER

Fun dough

Sometimes, when you have a lot of cooking to get through and you don't
need small helping hands, this can be fun. So, this is not to eat—but just
an easy pastry dough for children to work with while you get on with
things. If they want, you can bake the shapes or leave them to dry out
over the heaters in colder months. Make sure you put a good plastic
covering on the table so that they can roll out the dough without giving
you a cleaning-up nightmare. This keeps for a day in a plastic bag in
the fridge.

Put the flour and salt in a bowl and mix it through with your hands. If you're
using food color, add it now, and work in about 5 tablespoons of water bit by bit.
You may need a bit more or a bit less, so add it slowly until you get a soft dough.
Knead it well for a minute or two until smooth. Let the children make shapes,
either their own or using cookie cutters. If they want to bake them, put them on
a baking sheet, and bake at 200°F for about 30 to 40 minutes, depending on the
thickness, to dry them out.

---

1 1/4 CUPS MILK
1 1/4 CUPS HEAVY WHIPPING CREAM
1 1/2 TEASPOONS VANILLA EXTRACT
6 EGG YOLKS
1/4 CUP SUPERFINE SUGAR
1 1/2 TABLESPOONS CORNSTARCH

Egg custard

I like custard this way—a little thick—eaten on its own straight from the
fridge, or at room temperature with a fruit crisp or baked fruit. This is a
good way to use up the egg yolks after you've made pavlovas and is best
eaten on the day you make it. Use top-quality vanilla extract.

Put the milk and cream in a heavy-bottomed saucepan and heat gently to just
below boiling point. Remove from the heat and stir in the vanilla extract.

Beat the egg yolks, sugar, and cornstarch in a heatproof bowl for a few minutes, until the sugar has dissolved and the mixture is pale and thick. Gradually add the warm milk, mixing constantly. When everything is mixed together, pour it back into the pan over low heat. Cook, stirring or whisking almost continuously, for about 4 minutes, until the custard has thickened. Don't let it get too hot or it will scramble, so take the pan off the heat once or twice if necessary. Pour into a serving bowl and either serve straightaway or cover the surface with plastic wrap (this stops a skin forming) and put it in the fridge to chill.

Makes 3 cups

---

3 CUPS MILK
1 LONG STRIP OF LEMON RIND
1 TEASPOON VANILLA EXTRACT
3 EGGS
$\frac{1}{4}$ CUP SUGAR
1 $\frac{1}{4}$ CUPS ALL-PURPOSE FLOUR,
  SIFTED, PLUS EXTRA, TO COAT
ABOUT 5 $\frac{1}{2}$ TABLESPOONS BUTTER
SUPERFINE SUGAR, TO SERVE

Fried custard squares

This is the sort of thing that would have appealed to my sweet tooth in childhood. It's what some Italians remember from theirs.

Put the milk in a heavy-bottomed pan and add the lemon rind and vanilla. Bring just to a boil. Meanwhile, whip 2 eggs in a bowl until they are creamy, then whisk in the sugar. Add the flour and whisk to a smooth cream. Just as the milk comes to a rolling boil, whisk a ladleful into the eggs. Whisking constantly, add another ladleful or two of milk. Spoon it all back into the milk pan and put over the lowest heat, whisking all the time. It will thicken quickly, so you may have to remove the pan for a minute and whisk vigorously until it's smooth. Put back on the heat for a few minutes to cook the flour, whisking until it's completely smooth and very thick.

Lightly grease a 6 $\frac{1}{2}$ by 11-inch baking pan. Spoon the custard into the pan, smoothing the surface with a spatula. Let it cool and set completely, then turn out and cut into 2-inch squares. Break the last egg into a small flat bowl and scatter some flour on a plate. Melt 2 to 3 tablespoons of butter in a nonstick frying pan over medium–low heat. Working in batches, dip squares of custard first in the egg and then in the flour to coat lightly. Fry in the butter until golden on both sides, turning them gently. Add blobs of butter along the way to prevent burning. Lift the squares out onto paper towels to drain and then serve warm, sprinkled with some superfine sugar.

Makes 15

½ POUND PLUS 2 TABLESPOONS BUTTER, SOFTENED
1¼ CUPS SUPERFINE SUGAR
3 EGGS
2½ CUPS ALL-PURPOSE FLOUR
1½ TEASPOONS BAKING POWDER
FINELY GRATED ZEST AND JUICE OF 1 LEMON
¾ CUP HEAVY WHIPPING CREAM
1 TEASPOON VANILLA EXTRACT

FILLING:
½ CUP HEAVY WHIPPING CREAM
2 TEASPOONS CONFECTIONERS' SUGAR
½ CUP GREEK-STYLE PLAIN YOGURT
1 CUP FRESH RASPBERRIES, HALVED

CONFECTIONERS' SUGAR, FOR DUSTING

Lemon sandwiches with raspberries and cream

This basic lemon cake is very good on its own, fresh from the oven. But for something special, or to use the leftover cake, you can make these little sandwiches and serve them with coffee, or at an afternoon party. I use fresh raspberries and cream in these ones, but you could use raspberry or strawberry jam and cream. The sandwiches are easier to cut when the cake is a day old.

Preheat the oven to 325°F and butter and flour a 12 by 4-inch loaf pan.
    Cream together the butter and sugar until light and fluffy. Beat in the eggs one by one. Sift in the flour and baking powder, then add the lemon zest, lemon juice, cream, and vanilla. Whisk well to get a smooth batter.
    Spoon into the loaf pan and bake for about 1 hour 10 minutes, or until a skewer poked into the center comes out clean. If the top looks like it's getting too brown before the cooking time is up, cover it with aluminum foil. Remove and leave to cool completely in the pan.
    For the filling, whip the cream and confectioners' sugar together until the cream holds peaks, then fold the yogurt through. Cut the cake like a loaf of bread into slices about about ¼ inch thick. Spread half the slices with cream, and then top with the raspberries and the rest of the cake slices to make sandwiches. Dust with confectioners' sugar to serve.

Makes about 20 sandwiches

4 EGG YOLKS
3/4 CUP SUPERFINE SUGAR
3 TABLESPOONS BUTTER, CUT INTO BITS
FINELY GRATED ZEST OF 1 LEMON
JUICE OF 2 LEMONS
1 CUP MILK
1 1/2 CUPS HEAVY WHIPPING CREAM

Lemon curd ice cream

This is for the lemon meringue ice cream cake, opposite (because it gives you something perfect to make with your egg whites), but you can also just make this on its own and serve it with a bowl of cherries or raspberries. If you won't be making the meringue layers, then freeze your egg whites until you need them to make pavlova.

Bring a pan half-full of water to a boil and then lower the heat to the absolute minimum. Put the egg yolks and sugar in a wide glass or stainless steel bowl and whisk until they are thick and creamy. Sit the bowl atop the pan of water, add the butter and let it melt. Whisk until it starts to get thicker and creamier, then add the lemon zest and juice and carry on whisking until it thickens. It doesn't have to be cooked out like a proper lemon curd, but just until it has thickened and the egg is cooked through from the warmth of the simmering water.

Meanwhile, warm up the milk a little. Whisk it into the lemony eggs and then remove the bowl from the heat. Whisk from time to time until it's cool before you whisk in the cream. Put the bowl in the fridge until it's completely cool and then, if your bowl doesn't have a lid, pour the mixture into one that does.

Cover the bowl and put in the freezer. After an hour, give the mixture an energetic whisk with a hand whisk or an electric mixer. Put it back in the freezer and whisk again after another couple of hours. When the ice cream is nearly firm, give one last whisk and put it back in the freezer to set.

Alternatively, pour the mixture into your ice cream machine and churn, following the manufacturer's instructions.

Makes 7 cups

7 CUPS LEMON CURD ICE CREAM (OPPOSITE)

MERINGUE:
4 EGG WHITES
1 CUP SUPERFINE SUGAR
1½ TABLESPOONS DESICCATED COCONUT
A FEW DROPS OF VANILLA EXTRACT
1 TEASPOON WHITE WINE VINEGAR

Lemon meringue ice cream cake

I like to throw some petals over the top of this, or some whole cherries or raspberries. It is really very lovely on a summer or spring day. When you come to putting the cake together, take out your ice cream beforehand so that it is manageable and you don't break up the meringue when you're trying to spread it. However, too soft and it may drip down the sides— you'll have to decide, according to the season.

Preheat the oven to 250°F. Get two sheets of parchment paper and, on each one, draw around the bottom of a 9½-inch springform pan. Put each sheet of paper on a baking sheet (with the drawn side down so that it doesn't mark the meringue).

For the meringue, put the egg whites into a comfortable wide bowl and whisk until they are firm and glossy. Add a third of the sugar and carry on whisking until they are even stiffer, then add another third of the sugar. Whisk again until the meringue is almost climbing up the beaters. Add the last of the sugar and the coconut, vanilla, and vinegar, whisking them in quickly and well.

Divide the meringue into two and spread half over each circle, flicking your wrists and using a spatula to smooth it out. Make a very slight indentation in the top of each.

Put both in the oven for 45 minutes, then swap them around and bake for another 45 minutes, or until they are firm and pale beige. Turn off the oven and leave them inside for 10 minutes with the door slightly ajar before removing them to cool completely. If you will not be putting the cake together immediately, wrap up the meringues in plastic wrap.

To assemble, take the ice cream out of the freezer 5 or 10 minutes in advance so that it softens a little and you can spread it more easily. Put a layer of meringue onto a lovely and freezer-friendly serving plate. Spoon the ice cream on top and spread it gently to cover the meringue, leaving just the edges showing. Top with the next layer of meringue. Cover with plastic wrap and put back into the freezer until you are ready to serve it.

Let the cake soften for 5 or 10 minutes before cutting it, using a clean cut instead of sawing so that you don't destroy the meringue. It might crack a bit, but that's fine, as long as it stays intact.

Serves 10 to 12

pink

Beet gnocchi
Baked ham and cheese savory custard
Penne with shrimp, cream, and tomato
Shrimp and spinach brown rice risotto
Poached fruit in vanilla syrup
Greek yogurt with honey, cinnamon,
  pecans, and pomegranate
Pomegranate sorbet
Pear and berry crisp
Fruit butters
Tiny cupcakes with pink icing

- memory -

We had huge sacks of marbles. The most
important people had the most important and
biggest sacks; others just carried theirs in an
old sock or jam jar. At the end of break,
everyone would scurry along to stuff their bags
into their lockers. The thought of them is what
kept us going through the fraying edges of
school. It looped it all together. This and those
writing papers. I would lie in bed at night
concentrating hard on the zillions of floral
papers that other girls had and that we would
swap at school. I would fall asleep watching
papers in my mind. I dreamed of two in
particular that I loved.
We all had our loops of elastic ready as we
hopscotched our way two-by-two into the
schoolyard, past other pairs playing cat's cradle
with bright yarn. The same partner that you
sat with, and hung out with. It was not okay to
not be a couple. We made cups and saucers
with the yarn and never ever got bored of
swapping bits and pieces. But my mother's
collection still impressed me most of all.
Writing paper and stickers kept my heart
beating—I dreamed of having them. Oh, the
careful trading that went on.

GNOCCHI:
3 MEDIUM POTATOES, SCRUBBED BUT NOT
   PEELED
1 SMALL BEET, STEAMED AND PEELED
1 2/3 CUPS ALL-PURPOSE FLOUR
1/2 CUP GRATED PARMESAN CHEESE
1 EGG, LIGHTLY BEATEN
SALT

TO SERVE:
12 LARGE BASIL LEAVES
1/4 CUP PINE NUTS, LIGHTLY TOASTED
2 1/2 TABLESPOONS GRATED PARMESAN CHEESE
8 TABLESPOONS OLIVE OIL
SALT AND FRESHLY GROUND BLACK PEPPER
4 GOOD BLOBS OF BUTTER
GRATED PARMESAN CHEESE, TO SERVE

Beet gnocchi

The beet here is mainly for its uplifting color. These gnocchi are also very good with just a blob of butter on each serving and a handful of grated Parmesan scattered over. The color pales a little when the gnocchi are boiled, but then seems to win its strength back almost immediately.

Bring a large pan of salted water to a boil, add the potatoes, and boil for about 25 minutes until they are soft. Drain and, when they are cool enough to handle, peel them, and pass them through a food mill into a bowl, or mash thoroughly.

Purée the beet in a food processor or blender until it is absolutely totally smooth (you will need just over 1/2 cup of purée). Fold the purée into the potatoes, then add the flour, Parmesan, egg, and salt to taste. Mix first with a wooden spoon and then by hand until you have a completely smooth soft dough. The gnocchi need to be shaped and cooked straightaway to avoid your having to add more flour, which would make them hard.

Chop up the basil leaves quite coarsely and chop most of the pine nuts, leaving a few whole. Put them in a bowl, add the Parmesan and olive oil, and mix through. You could add a dash of salt and a grind of pepper if you like. Bring a large saucepan of salted water to a boil and have a flattish dish ready with the blobs of butter in the bottom.

Divide the dough into four and roll out each portion into a long salami about 5/8 inch in diameter. Try to avoid adding flour to your work surface, but you may need to lightly flour your hands. Cut each salami into short lengths (say, 1/2 inch) and don't worry if they are all different shapes and don't look completely perfect. Cook them in two batches—drop them into the boiling water and give a gentle stir. They are ready as soon as they bob up to the surface (this will take only about half a minute), then quickly lift them out with a slotted spoon, put them in the dish, and toss them in the butter. Drizzle the basil dressing all over and sprinkle with Parmesan. Serve immediately.

Serves 4

3 EGGS
1 CUP MILK
1 CUP HEAVY WHIPPING CREAM
FRESHLY GRATED NUTMEG
SALT
ABOUT 5½ TABLESPOONS BUTTER, SOFTENED
1 LOAF (ABOUT 14 SLICES) WHITE BREAD, SLICED
   ½ INCH THICK, CRUSTS REMOVED
8 OUNCES FINELY SLICED HAM
1⅔ CUPS COARSELY GRATED FONTINA, EDAM,
   SWEET PECORINO, OR SIMILAR CHEESE
⅔ CUP GRATED PARMESAN CHEESE

Baked ham and cheese savory custard

This is a quick, tasty meal—a variation on ham and cheese sandwiches. For a richer dish, swap some of the milk for more cream. Use a home-made white loaf (page 263) or a bought one. It is easy to add other ingredients between the layers if there's something you particularly like.

Preheat the oven to 350°F and lightly butter a 12 by 8 by 2-inch ovenproof dish.

Whip the eggs in a bowl, then whisk in the milk and cream. Season with a good grinding of nutmeg and a touch of salt.

Butter the bread slices on one side only. Lay half of them, buttered side up, in the dish in a slightly overlapping layer. If you need to, cut the slices so that they snugly cover the bottom of the dish. Pour over half the eggy milk and leave for 5 minutes for the bread to soak some of it up. Layer half the ham over the bread and then sprinkle with half the fontina and Parmesan cheeses. Repeat the bread and butter layer, then cover with the remaining eggy milk and the rest of the ham. Press down gently on the ham so that some of the eggy milk leaks through, then finish off with the rest of the cheese.

Bake in the oven for 25 to 30 minutes, until the top is golden and crusty here and there. Turn off the oven, open the door and leave the custard inside to cool for a while before cutting into serving squares. Serve warm.

Serves 6

3 TABLESPOONS BUTTER
1/2 (14-OUNCE) CAN TOMATOES WITH JUICE, PUREED
SALT AND FRESHLY GROUND BLACK PEPPER
2/3 (16-OUNCE) PACKAGE PENNE
2 TEASPOONS OLIVE OIL
1 1/4 POUNDS RAW SHRIMP, PEELED AND DEVEINED
2 CLOVES GARLIC, PEELED AND SQUASHED A BIT
2 1/2 TABLESPOONS CALVADOS
3 TABLESPOONS HEAVY WHIPPING CREAM
1 1/2 TABLESPOONS CHOPPED FRESH PARSLEY

Penne with shrimp, cream, and tomato

This is simple and not too rich. I use Calvados just because I like the way it turned out once when I didn't have brandy. The shrimp here are not too many—so you can pick them out at the end and serve more to some, less to others. And there is just a little cream, to sweeten things up even more . . .

Melt half of the butter in a smallish pan and, when it is sizzling, add the tomatoes. Season with salt and a dash of pepper and then cook over medium heat for about 10 minutes, until it is thick.

Cook the pasta in a large pan of boiling salted water, following the package instructions. Meanwhile, heat a large nonstick frying pan over high heat. Add the oil and the rest of the butter and, when it is sizzling, add the shrimp and garlic. Over the highest heat possible, cook the shrimp until they are quite bright and the undersides are golden and crusty in places. It is important that the heat is high and that you have a nonstick pan so that the shrimp fry quickly rather than boil in their own liquid. Turn them with tongs and, when they are cooked, scatter salt over them. Add the Calvados and cook until it evaporates.

Drain the pasta, keeping a cupful of the cooking water. Add the tomato sauce to the shrimp, along with the cream and parsley. Heat until just bubbling. Add the pasta and toss well. If it seems like you need it, add a little of the cooking water to help the sauce coat the pasta. Serve immediately with a grinding of pepper.

Serves 3

8 RAW SHRIMP
5 TABLESPOONS OLIVE OIL
2 CLOVES GARLIC, FINELY CHOPPED
1 CUP CANNED TOMATO SAUCE
5 CUPS HOT WATER
4 PARSLEY STALKS, PLUS 1 1/2 TABLESPOONS
    CHOPPED FRESH PARSLEY
2 SLICES LEMON
SALT AND FRESHLY GROUND BLACK PEPPER
1 1/2 TABLESPOONS BUTTER
2 SHALLOTS, FINELY CHOPPED
1 1/2 CUPS BROWN RICE
2 CUPS FIRMLY PACKED SPINACH LEAVES,
    CHOPPED
2 TABLESPOONS BUTTER, EXTRA

Shrimp and spinach brown rice risotto

This is a very adaptable recipe with ingredients that can be easily swapped for others if you prefer. You can also make it with white rice: Just add your broth as instructed and follow the same method, but the cooking time will be much shorter (about 20 minutes).

Peel and devein the shrimp (keeping the shells), leaving the tails on four of them, if you like. Butterfly these four and chop up the rest. Put the butterflied shrimp in one side of a bowl, the chopped shrimp in the other side, then cover the bowl and keep it in the fridge.

Put the shrimp shells and half the oil into a pan and cook on high for about a minute, stirring a few times, until the shells turn pink. Add the garlic and, when you can smell it, add the tomato sauce. Sauté for a few more minutes. Add 5 cups of hot water, the parsley stalks and lemon slices. Season with salt and pepper and bring to a boil. Simmer for about 20 minutes, then strain into a clean pan and keep warm over very low heat.

Heat the butter and the remaining oil in a heavy-bottomed pan suitable for making risotto. Add the shallots and sauté for a few minutes over medium heat until lightly golden and softened, then add the rice. Stir and turn it for a few minutes so that it is well coated. Add a ladleful of the broth and stir with a wooden spoon until the liquid has been absorbed. Reduce the heat to low, add another ladleful of broth, and stir until it has been absorbed. Carry on like this for about 40 minutes, then add the chopped shrimp, chopped parsley, and spinach. Continue cooking in the same way for another 10 minutes or so, until the rice is tender but still a little bit firm in the center. If you run out of broth before this time, just carry on with hot water. Add the extra butter, sit the whole shrimp atop the rice, and cook for a few minutes more until the shrimp are pink. Sprinkle a little salt over the shrimp, put a cloth over the rice, remove from the heat, and leave to stand for 10 minutes before serving.

Serves 3 to 4

2 SMALL RIPE BUT FIRM PEARS
3 BRIGHT-RED RIPE BUT FIRM PLUMS
2 JUICY BUT FIRM PEACHES OR NECTARINES
A HANDFUL OF SEEDLESS GREEN AND BLACK GRAPES
4 CUPS COLD WATER
1 CUP SUPERFINE SUGAR
1 STRIP LEMON OR LIME RIND, PITH REMOVED
JUICE OF HALF A LEMON OR LIME
HALF A VANILLA BEAN, SPLIT LENGTHWISE

Poached fruit in vanilla syrup

This is just fruit served in a bath of syrup. Use any fruit you like, but I feel color is important here, so a couple of berries or cherries can be splashed in at the last moment if you don't have very red plums. Choose fruit with a beautiful shape. I love serving something like this with a scoop of snow-white yogurt or buttermilk ice cream. This is lovely for breakfast or dessert, or just as a snack, and you could also serve it with a fruit sorbet (mango or pomegranate, pages 110 and 162). Ladle any leftover syrup into cups for children to drink. You could also add different spices to your poaching syrup—a small cinnamon stick, cloves, a bay leaf, for instance.

Peel the pears, keeping their smooth shape. Halve lengthwise and cut out the cores. Halve the unpeeled plums lengthwise and remove their pits by gently twisting the halves. If the pits are stubborn, edge them out with a spoon or the point of a potato peeler. Cut each half in half again lengthwise, if they are large. Do the same with the peaches or nectarines, and halve the grapes, too.

Put 4 cups of cold water in a large saucepan and add the sugar, lemon or lime rind, and the juice. Scrape the seeds from the vanilla bean into the pan and then throw in the bean as well. Bring to a boil and then simmer for about 5 minutes. Lower the heat and add the fruit you think will take the longest—probably the pears. Poach them gently for about 5 minutes, turning them with a slotted spoon so that they are totally immersed in syrup and don't darken in parts. Add the plums and peaches, and carry on simmering for another 5 minutes or so, just until they surrender their firmness and have absorbed the syrup (not too long, or they will become soggy). Next add the grapes, which will need only a couple of minutes. In the meantime, if some of the fruit looks ready, remove it very carefully with the slotted spoon, and put in a wide bowl, taking care not to mark the fruits with cuts or dents. If you have overdone it at any stage, pop the bowl into the freezer for a few minutes to cool down the fruit and stop it cooking further.

Cool the fruits at room temperature in a fly-free zone. If the skins of the peaches are wrinkled, slip them off. Otherwise leave them on, and leave the plum skins on, too. When the syrup has cooled, pour it over the fruit. Serve very slightly warm or at room temperature, and it is even good cold from the fridge in summer. This will keep well in the fridge, covered, for up to 5 days.

Serves 5 to 6

APPLES FOR SAM

SEEDS FROM ¼ POMEGRANATE
ABOUT ¼ CUP SHELLED PECANS, BROKEN INTO
   BIG CHUNKS
1 ⅓ CUPS GREEK-STYLE PLAIN YOGURT
4 TEASPOONS THICK, CLEAR HONEY
GROUND CINNAMON

Greek yogurt with honey, cinnamon, pecans, and pomegranate

I would make my kids swallow pomegranate seeds whole if I could. Just for their sheer beauty and vitamins. This is a quick "healthy" snack that you can literally produce in one minute if you have all the ingredients. The Greek-style yogurt is important—its thick and creamy nature allows the honey, nuts, and cinnamon to sit on it like a crown. The pomegranates dress it up well, and the seeds from the rest of the pomegranate can be served up later to nibble on with a glass of prosecco, or saved for filling little tartlets.

Pick all the seeds out of the pomegranate, making sure there is no white pith still attached. In a small dry frying pan, lightly toast the pecans just enough to bring out their flavor and crisp them up (take care not to overdo them or they'll be bitter and taste burnt). Leave them to cool.
   Spoon the yogurt into bowls, scatter a child's fistful of nuts over the top, drizzle with honey and finish with a small scattering of pomegranate seeds and cinnamon. Best served immediately.

Serves 2

4 RIPE POMEGRANATES
JUICE OF 1 LEMON
1/4 CUP SUPERFINE SUGAR

Pomegranate sorbet

My children are incredibly enthusiastic about this. I think it is probably the color that delights them most: I make this when I have lovely rosy pomegranates. The color of your sorbet will vary in intensity, depending on the color of your pomegranate seeds. Sometimes I serve this on its own and sometimes with a scoop of vanilla ice cream. It looks beautifully colorful with a ball of bright mango sorbet next to it in the bowl, too (page 110).

Juice the pomegranates very thoroughly, using a levered juice extractor or a citrus juicer, and then strain. You should have about 1 3/4 cups of juice. Put the lemon juice in a small saucepan with the sugar and 3 to 4 tablespoons of the pomegranate juice. Heat, stirring, over medium-low heat until the sugar has dissolved. Remove from the heat, leave to cool a little, and then stir in the rest of the pomegranate juice.

Pour the mixture into a bowl or container that has a lid. Put the lid on, and put it in the freezer. After an hour, give the mixture an energetic whisk with a hand whisk or an electric mixer. Put it back in the freezer and then whisk again after another couple of hours. When the sorbet is nearly firm, give one last whisk, and put it back in the freezer to set.

Alternatively, pour into your ice cream machine and churn, following the manufacturer's instructions.

Serves 4

3 LARGE PEARS
1 CUP OF MIXED BERRIES
1/3 CUP SUPERFINE SUGAR
1 2/3 CUPS ALL-PURPOSE FLOUR
1/4 CUP FIRMLY PACKED LIGHT BROWN SUGAR
1/4 POUND PLUS 3 TABLESPOONS BUTTER,
   SOFTENED
1 TEASPOON VANILLA EXTRACT

Pear and berry crisp

You can use any ripe sweet fruit you like for this, really—peaches, apples, apricots, nectarines, pineapples. . . . This is best served warm, when it has cooled down a bit, with some warm custard or just a blob of thick or clotted cream on the side, and a dusting of confectioners' sugar. Sometimes I like the crisp topping to be soft soft, and then I use 1/2 cup of confectioners' sugar instead of the brown sugar and superfine sugar. If you feel your fruit might not be sweet enough, sprinkle a dash more sugar over it before the crisp topping goes on. You can mix some chopped shelled walnuts (about 1/4 cup) through the topping for a nutty crunch.

Preheat your oven to 375°F. Generously butter a 14 by 8 1/2 by 2 1/2-inch ovenproof dish. Peel, core, and slice the pears, and put them in the dish. Mix in the berries and scatter half the superfine sugar over the fruit.

Mix together the flour, brown sugar, and the other half of the superfine sugar in a bowl. Add the butter and vanilla and rub them in with your fingertips, working until the mixture isn't smooth but looks like damp clustery sand. Your fingers might be tired.

Scatter the topping over the fruit to cover it completely in a good thick layer. Bake for about 45 minutes, or until the top is nicely golden and some berry juice has oozed up a bit over the crust and darkened it here and there.

Let it cool down a touch and then serve warm with whipped cream, a bowl of custard, or vanilla ice cream.

Serves 8

¼ POUND PLUS ½ TABLESPOON UNSALTED BUTTER,
  SOFTENED
5 TABLESPOONS FRUIT PUREE (BELOW)

PERSIMMON PUREE:
1 LARGE VERY RIPE PERSIMMON
1 TEASPOON LEMON JUICE
ABOUT 1 TEASPOON CONFECTIONERS' SUGAR

PLUM PUREE:
2 SMALL DARK-FLESHED PLUMS
ABOUT 1 TABLESPOON SUPERFINE SUGAR

RASPBERRY PUREE:
1 CUP FRESH RASPBERRIES (FROZEN
  RASPBERRIES WON'T WORK)
1 ½ TABLESPOONS CONFECTIONERS' SUGAR
2 TEASPOONS LEMON JUICE

BLUEBERRY BUTTER:
¼ POUND PLUS ½ TABLESPOON UNSALTED BUTTER,
  SOFTENED
1 ½ TABLESPOONS CONFECTIONERS' SUGAR
¾ CUP BLUEBERRIES

Fruit
butters

These are wonderful for a special breakfast where everyone can choose what they want. Serve them with toast, rolls, or brioche. I think mandarin orange, cranberry, and strawberry butters would all be good, too. It's important to use unsalted butter here.

With a wooden spoon, beat the butter in a bowl until it is smooth. Add the purée a little at a time and, when it is all mixed through, beat the butter well until very smooth. Cover and keep in the fridge. It is spreadable even straight from the fridge.

Any fruit purée can be used, but here are some to try.

PERSIMMON: Pull the persimmon into pieces and put it in a food processor or blender, skin and all. Add the lemon juice and confectioners' sugar and purée until very smooth. Taste for sweetness and add more confectioners' sugar if it's needed.

PLUM: Halve the plums, throwing away the pits, and cut them into quarters. Put them in a frying pan, scatter with the sugar, and stir them over medium-low heat for about 5 minutes, until they start to soften and caramelize slightly. Put into a food processor or blender and whiz until smooth. Taste for sweetness and add more sugar if it's needed.

RASPBERRY: Put the raspberries, confectioners' sugar, and lemon juice in a food processor or blender and whiz until smooth.

And this one doesn't even require you to make a purée first.

BLUEBERRY: With a wooden spoon, beat the butter and confectioners' sugar together in a bowl until smooth. Add the blueberries and mix just until the butter turns slightly pinkish and the blueberries are still mostly whole.

1/4 POUND PLUS 2 TABLESPOONS (2 1/4 STICKS) BUTTER, SOFTENED
1 CUP SUPERFINE SUGAR
3 EGGS
1 TEASPOON VANILLA EXTRACT
2 1/3 CUPS ALL-PURPOSE FLOUR
1 1/2 TEASPOONS BAKING POWDER
3/4 CUP MILK OR HALF-AND-HALF

ICING:
2 CUPS CONFECTIONERS' SUGAR
RED FOOD COLORING
4 TABLESPOONS COLD WATER

Tiny cupcakes with pink icing

This makes about 60 small cakes in paper liners. They are always successful at a party—perhaps for their exuberant color once they are iced. I use tiny (1 1/2 by 3/4-inch) paper liners. Make up half the quantity of icing at a time if you want to make two colors, a quarter quantity if you want four colors, rather than making the whole quantity and dividing it up to color and then having the icing harden as you work. Plain iced are good, but you could add extra decorations on top—jelly beans, colored sprinkles, M&M's, or other candies. When I am in an all-natural mood, I use beet juice to color the icing.

Preheat your oven to 350°F. In a large bowl, thoroughly beat together the butter and sugar. Add the eggs one at a time, beating well after each one goes in. Add the vanilla and then sift in the flour and baking powder. Beat well, adding the milk or half-and-half a little at a time. You should have a thick and creamy batter.

Spoon heaping teaspoons of batter into small paper cupcake liners. Don't put in too much batter or the cakes will puff up too much, and these look lovely when the icing is flush with the top of the liners.

Put the filled paper liners on baking sheets and bake in batches for 15 minutes or so, until they are golden on top. Cool completely before icing.

For the icing, put the confectioners' sugar in a bowl, add a few drops of food coloring, and gradually stir in 4 tablespoons of cold water until you have a smooth but thick icing that is stiff enough to cling to the cakes. Add more coloring if you think you'd like it brighter. Working a few at a time, drop about a teaspoon of icing on top of each cake, and spread it gently with the back of the spoon so that it covers the top. If the icing gets too thick as you are working, add a few more drops of water. Sprinkle on any decorations before the icing dries.

Once the icing has dried, the cakes can be stored in a container for 5 to 6 days.

Makes about 60

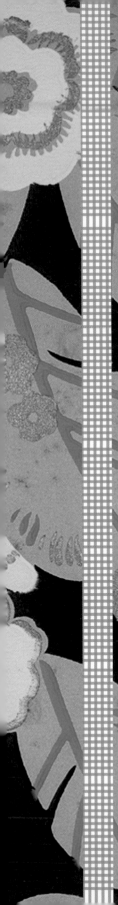

Green

Broccoli soup
Green vegetable soup with egg and lemon
Pasta with squid and peas
Spinach and ricotta cannelloni
Meat cannelloni
Pork, veal, and rice dumplings with dill,
    egg, and lemon sauce
Angel hair pasta with zucchini,
    mint, and feta
Chicken cutlets with parsley and capers
Lamb and green bean casserole
Sole bundles with spinach
Zucchini omelette
Paillard
Pea and potato mash
Watercress omelette
Creamy spinach with feta
Sautéed broccoli with tomato
Squashed zucchini
Gratinéed broccoli
Gratinéed celery with tomato and Parmesan
Green bean soufflé loaf
Peppermint crisp pie

- memory -

Our friends had a big jungle swing, right in the middle of their vegetable patch. I kept wondering if I would ever see a monkey as I swung up and down and dreamed of being in the circus with the other acrobatic and stylish swinging ladies. There were ducks following their mamma around everywhere while our mammas were inside rolling out pans of pizza for our lunch. We would roll down the steep and grassy hill and stare up, squinting, at the bright sun through the kaleidoscope of our minds to see dinosaur- and butterfly-shaped clouds. After a thick slice of pizza, we might fiddle about making mud pies, or sit in a circle and play princesses for a while. The longest-haired girl would always be the princess. We had time to follow the trail of snails all the way to where it finished and then examine the snails before we moved them to brighter green lawns, to better homes. We'd look for secret places filled with more and more secrets. At night then, our mammas would pile us all into the same bath, and there would be quite a bit of splashing about and water marks on the wall afterward. We loved the soft pale fluffy towels that they would bundle us into, and we would sit drying, smelling of soap, and flicking through books.

6 CUPS CHOPPED BROCCOLI
7 CUPS COLD WATER
SALT
2 MEDIUM POTATOES, PEELED AND CUT INTO
 BIG CHUNKS
1 RED ONION, PEELED AND QUARTERED
3/4 CUP HEAVY WHIPPING CREAM
FRESHLY GROUND BLACK PEPPER
 (OPTIONAL)

Broccoli soup

This is such a simple soup, consisting of a few ingredients, and is a perfect example of how good some straightforward things can be. You could really make it with your eyes closed. Adults should add a generous grinding of black pepper to this—which is what I believe makes the soup—and sometimes my kids ask for a tiny twist of pepper over theirs. I like to serve this as a first course for them, followed by a plate of cheese, and their favorite buttered bread. Make sure your broccoli is deep chlorophyl-green in its florets and hasn't been sitting for days in your fridge getting paler and paler. My children like to see a deep green soup with creamy swirls in it and are upset if I forget and stir in all the cream. So do it like this—just make sure you take the cream out of the fridge well beforehand so you don't ice up the soup with your swirl.

Save a handful of the florets and put the rest in a large saucepan with the potatoes and onion. Add 7 cups of cold water, season with one or two teaspoons of salt, and bring to a boil. Skim the surface if necessary. Lower the heat slightly, and simmer uncovered for about 45 minutes. Add the other handful of florets 10 minutes before the end of this time. You should be able to squash the broccoli easily on the side of the pan with a wooden spoon.

Purée all this in a blender until it is completely smooth (and hope that you didn't get a woody broccoli to start with). It should be thick, but if you find it too thick then you can add some hot water. If it is too thin then carry on cooking it uncovered for a while to reduce the liquid. Add salt until you can really taste the depth of the broccoli. Swirl in half the cream and heat through. Serve immediately, with another swirl of cream through each portion and a good grinding of pepper for those who like it.

Serves 6

3 TABLESPOONS OLIVE OIL
3 OR 4 SCALLIONS (GREEN AND WHITE PARTS),
    CHOPPED
A COUPLE OF LEAFY CELERY STALKS, CHOPPED
3 OR 4 SMALL ZUCCHINI, CUT INTO BLOCKS
2 MEDIUM POTATOES, PEELED AND CUT
    INTO BLOCKS
2/3 CUP FRESH SHELLED PEAS
1 1/2 CUPS SHREDDED LETTUCE (ROMAINE OR
    BUTTER)
1 1/2 CUPS CHOPPED WATERCRESS TIPS
6 CUPS WATER
SALT
2 1/3 CUPS SHREDDED BABY SPINACH LEAVES
2 EGGS
JUICE OF 1 LARGE JUICY LEMON
GRATED PARMESAN CHEESE, TO SERVE
FRESHLY GROUND BLACK PEPPER, TO SERVE

Green vegetable soup with egg and lemon

You can add any vegetables you like to this, preferably those that are in season. I like to use butter or romaine lettuce.

Heat the oil in a fairly large stockpot. Gently sauté the scallions and celery until they have softened but not colored, then add the zucchini, potatoes, peas, and half of the lettuce and watercress.

Add 6 cups of water, salt well, and bring to a boil. Put the lid on, lower the heat, and simmer for 30 minutes, or until the potatoes are soft. Add the remaining lettuce and watercress and the baby spinach and cook for 1 or 2 minutes more. Meanwhile, whip the eggs in a bowl and then whisk in the lemon juice and a pinch of salt. Take a ladleful of the hot broth from the soup and whisk it into the eggs to acclimatize them. Then add a couple more ladlefuls, whisking them in well.

Take the soup off the heat and tip all the egg mixture back into the pan, mixing all the time. Keep mixing, and put the pan back over the lowest possible heat for just a minute so the eggs cook through but don't scramble. Taste for salt, and serve warm with a generous scattering of Parmesan, more lemon juice to taste, and a good grinding of black pepper, if you like it.

Serves 6 to 8

APPLES FOR SAM

4 TABLESPOONS OLIVE OIL
1 RED ONION, FINELY CHOPPED
1 1/4 POUNDS SMALL SQUID, CLEANED
    AND SLICED INTO RINGS
2 CLOVES GARLIC, FINELY CHOPPED
1/2 CUP WHITE WINE
1/2 (14-OUNCE) CAN DICED TOMATOES
1 CUP WATER
SALT AND FRESHLY GROUND BLACK
    PEPPER
1 CUP FRESH SHELLED PEAS
2 1/2 TABLESPOONS CHOPPED FRESH
    PARSLEY
3/4 (16-OUNCE) PACKAGE PASTA

Pasta with squid and peas

This sauce could be served with some bread, boiled rice, or potatoes. Here it is mixed through pasta, which I think works well for kids. You can make the sauce well in advance and just warm it up to serve at the last moment. If you prefer, ask your fishmonger to clean and slice the squid for you (you'll end up with about 12 ounces once it's cleaned).

Heat the oil in a frying pan and sauté the onion over medium heat until golden but not oversoft. Add the squid, turn up the heat, and stir with a wooden spoon until most of the liquid has evaporated. Stir in the garlic, cook for another minute, and then add the wine. Cook until most of the wine has evaporated, and then add the tomato. Let that bubble up, squashing bits down with your wooden spoon, and then add 1 cup of water and season with salt and pepper. Let it come back to a boil, lower the heat, and simmer, covered, for about 45 minutes or until the squid is very soft. Check it from time to time and add a few more drops of water if it is looking too dry.

    Add the peas and parsley and cook for another 10 minutes or so, until the peas are soft. Remove from the heat. There should be a good amount of sauce to serve with the pasta, so add water if necessary.

    Leave the lid on and let it sit off the heat while you cook the pasta.

    Cook the pasta in a large saucepan of boiling salted water, following the package instructions. Drain well, keeping a few tablespoons of the cooking water.

    Put the warm squid and pea sauce in a serving bowl, add the pasta, and toss together. If you think it needs it, add a bit of the cooking water to give a good coating. Serve immediately.

Serves 4

CREPES:
3 EGGS
1½ CUPS ALL-PURPOSE FLOUR
SALT
3½ TABLESPOONS BUTTER, MELTED, PLUS EXTRA
   BUTTER FOR FRYING
1 CUP MILK

TOMATO SAUCE:
1 CLOVE GARLIC, PEELED AND SQUASHED A BIT
3 TABLESPOONS OLIVE OIL
SALT
1 (14-OUNCE) CAN DICED TOMATOES
ABOUT 4 BASIL LEAVES
½ CUP WATER

FILLING:
6 CUPS FIRMLY PACKED SPINACH LEAVES,
   COARSELY CHOPPED
2 CUPS FRESH RICOTTA
1 EGG, LIGHTLY BEATEN
¾ CUP GRATED PARMESAN CHEESE
FRESHLY GRATED NUTMEG
SALT AND FRESHLY GROUND BLACK PEPPER

BÉCHAMEL SAUCE:
4½ TABLESPOONS BUTTER
⅓ CUP ALL-PURPOSE FLOUR
2¼ CUPS MILK, WARMED
SALT AND FRESHLY GROUND BLACK PEPPER
FRESHLY GRATED NUTMEG

½ CUP GRATED PARMESAN CHEESE

Spinach and ricotta cannelloni

I learned to make these with my brother and sister-in-law, Luca and
Luisa. They really are amazing proper Italian cooks, who put this
together effortlessly, as though they were just ironing a shirt.
Sometimes they use fresh egg pasta squares instead of the crepes,
boiling them first to soften, and laying them out on clean dish
towels to dry. Although this might seem a bit fiddly, it's worth it in
the end because you can just take this one lovely dish to the table.
If you want to break up the workload a bit, fry the crepes and make
the tomato sauce and spinach mix in advance, keeping them covered
until you are ready to use them. Then, at the last moment, you can
heat up your oven, make the béchamel, fill and roll the crepes, dot the
béchamel and tomatoes over the top, and bake. Your oven dish needs
to be about 8 by 12 inches so that you can fit 12 rolled crepes in two
rows. If the rolled crepes won't quite fit your dish, you can trim off their
ends—it is a little fiddly, but they do look very smart that way.

For the crepes, whisk the eggs in a bowl, and then whisk in the flour and a couple of pinches of salt. Add the butter, still whisking, and then slowly incorporate the milk to make a smooth batter. Leave it to stand for 20 minutes or so.

Heat a little butter in a 6-inch nonstick frying pan. Add half a ladleful of batter and quickly swirl the pan around so that the batter covers it as evenly as possible. Cook until the underneath is golden, then flip the crepe over with a spatula and cook the other side. Move to a plate with the spatula and cook the rest of the batter. You will need 12 crepes and you should have enough mixture to allow for a couple of disasters.

For the tomato sauce, heat the garlic with the oil in a saucepan and, when you begin to smell the garlic, add the tomatoes. Season with salt, bring to a boil, then lower the heat and simmer for about 15 minutes, until the tomatoes have melted. Add the basil and 1/2 cup of water toward the end of this time. Purée to a smooth sauce.

For the filling, rinse the spinach under cold water, shake off the excess, and then put in a saucepan with just the water clinging to the leaves. Cook over medium-low heat, turning with a wooden spoon, until the leaves have wilted. Cool a little, and then squeeze out as much water as you can and chop the spinach. Put the spinach in a bowl with the ricotta, egg, Parmesan, nutmeg, and salt and pepper to taste. Mix well.

To make the béchamel, melt the butter in a small saucepan over low heat. Whisk in the flour and cook for a few minutes, stirring constantly, then begin adding the warm milk. It will be immediately absorbed, so work quickly, whisking with one hand while adding ladlefuls of milk with the other. When the sauce seems to be smooth and not too stiff, add salt, pepper, and a grating of nutmeg, and continue cooking, even after it comes to a boil, for 5 minutes or so, mixing all the time. It should be a very thick and smooth sauce.

Meanwhile, preheat the oven to 350°F, and grease an 8 by 12-inch baking dish.

To put together, dollop some béchamel in the bottom of the dish, and rock it from side to side so that the béchamel thinly covers the bottom. Spoon a couple of tablespoons of filling along one side of a crepe and then roll it up tightly. Repeat with all the crepes and lay them on the béchamel like soldiers in two rows of six. Pour the rest of the béchamel over the top, then dot generously with the tomato sauce. Sprinkle with the Parmesan and bake for about 40 minutes, until golden and bubbling nicely. Let it cool a little before serving, then check carefully where each crepe begins and ends and lift them out with a spatula.

Serves 6

APPLES FOR SAM

CREPES:
3 EGGS
1½ CUPS ALL-PURPOSE FLOUR
SALT
3½ TABLESPOONS BUTTER, MELTED,
   PLUS EXTRA BUTTER FOR FRYING
1 CUP MILK

MEAT SAUCE:
4 TABLESPOONS OLIVE OIL
1 ONION, CHOPPED
1 CLOVE GARLIC, FINELY CHOPPED
1 POUND GROUND BEEF
1 BAY LEAF
½ CINNAMON STICK
1 TABLESPOON WORCESTERSHIRE SAUCE
½ TEASPOON DRIED MINT
1 TEASPOON SWEET PAPRIKA
¾ CUP WHITE WINE
1½ CUPS WATER
SALT
1 (14-OUNCE) CAN DICED TOMATOES
1 HANDFUL FRESH PARSLEY, CHOPPED

TOMATO SAUCE:
1 CLOVE GARLIC, PEELED AND SQUASHED
   A BIT
2½ TABLESPOONS OLIVE OIL
1 (14-OUNCE) CAN DICED TOMATOES
SALT
ABOUT 4 BASIL LEAVES
½ CUP WATER

BÉCHAMEL SAUCE:
4½ TABLESPOONS BUTTER
⅓ CUP ALL-PURPOSE FLOUR
2¼ CUPS MILK, WARMED
SALT AND FRESHLY GROUND BLACK
   PEPPER
FRESHLY GRATED NUTMEG

½ CUP GRATED PARMESAN CHEESE

Meat cannelloni

This is a bit of a job—but great. You can do it all in one go, or cook the meat sauce the day before and make the crepes in the morning with the tomato sauce. Then all you have do is make up a béchamel, assemble it all together, and bake. If not, I find it quite satisfying to put the whole thing together in a morning. Your baking dish needs to be about 12 by 8 inches and about 2½ inches deep so that two lines of filled crepes will fit together. Otherwise, it starts to get quite fiddly if you have to trim the crepes to fit your dish (although they do look very smart that way).

For the crepes, whisk the eggs in a bowl, and then whisk in the flour and a couple of pinches of salt. Add the butter, still whisking, and then slowly incorporate the milk to make a smooth batter. Leave it to stand for 20 minutes or so.

Heat a little butter in a 6-inch nonstick frying pan. Add half a ladleful of batter and quickly swirl the pan around so the batter covers it as evenly as possible. Cook until the underneath is golden, then flip the crepe over with a spatula, and cook the other side. Move to a plate with the spatula and cook the rest of the batter. You will need 12 crepes and you should have enough mixture to allow for a couple of disasters.

For the meat sauce, heat the olive oil in a large pan and sauté the onions over medium heat until quite golden. Stir in the garlic, then add the ground beef, bay leaf, cinnamon stick, Worcestershire sauce, mint, and paprika. Sauté over high heat for about 8 minutes until the meat starts to brown, stirring often to prevent sticking, and to brown all the meat. Add the wine and cook for a few minutes until it has evaporated. Add the tomatoes, cook for a few minutes, and then add 1 1/2 cups of water. Season with salt. Bring to a boil, lower the heat, and simmer uncovered for about 45 minutes. Add the parsley for the last 10 minutes of the cooking time.

For the tomato sauce, heat the garlic with the oil in a saucepan, and when you begin to smell the garlic, add the tomatoes. Season with salt, bring to a boil, then lower the heat and simmer for about 15 minutes, until the tomatoes have melted. Add the basil and 1/2 cup of water towards the end of this time. Purée to a smooth sauce.

To make the béchamel, melt the butter in a small saucepan over low heat. Whisk in the flour and cook for a few minutes, stirring constantly, then begin adding the warm milk. It will be immediately absorbed, so work quickly, whisking with one hand while adding ladlefuls of milk with the other. When the sauce seems to be smooth and not too stiff, add salt, pepper, and a grating of nutmeg, and continue cooking, even after it comes to a boil, for 5 minutes or so, mixing all the time. It should be a very thick and smooth sauce.

Meanwhile, preheat the oven to 350°F and grease an 8 by 12-inch baking dish.

To put it all together, spread 3 to 4 tablespoons of tomato sauce over the bottom of the dish. Spoon 4 tablespoons of meat filling along one side of a crepe and then roll it up tightly. Repeat with all the crepes and lay them in two rows of six over the tomato sauce in the dish. Dollop the béchamel over the top, here, there, and everywhere, and then spoon tomato sauce on top and in between so that you can still see patches of béchamel. Scatter the Parmesan over the top and bake for about 40 minutes, until it is bubbling nicely, and is golden here and there. Let it cool a little before serving.

Serves 6

DUMPLINGS:
2¼ POUNDS GROUND PORK AND VEAL
½ TEASPOON OREGANO
4 TABLESPOONS CHOPPED FRESH DILL
4 TABLESPOONS CHOPPED FRESH PARSLEY
1 EGG
¾ CUP LONG-GRAIN RICE
1 LARGE RED ONION, GRATED
⅔ CUP MILK
SALT
4 TO 5 TABLESPOONS OLIVE OIL
2 CLOVES GARLIC, PEELED BUT LEFT WHOLE
5 CUPS HOT WATER

SAUCE:
1 EGG
JUICE OF 2 LEMONS
SALT
3 TABLESPOONS CHOPPED FRESH DILL

Pork, veal, and rice dumplings with dill, egg, and lemon sauce

These are wonderfully soft meat and rice dumplings that most Greek children eat on a regular basis. If you think that your children might not appreciate the green flecks of dill in the sauce then you can leave it out—they probably won't notice it in the dumplings, and it does give a special and definite flavor.

For the dumplings, put the ground meat, oregano, dill, parsley, egg, rice, and onion in a mixing bowl with the milk and season well with salt. Knead with your hands so it is all very well mixed. Shape the dumplings by breaking off chunks about the size of a large walnut and quickly patting them into balls or ovals.

Heat the oil and garlic in a nonstick frying pan and fry the dumplings in batches over medium-high heat, turning them carefully when they are lightly golden on the underside, and lifting the dumplings into a large flameproof casserole when they are golden all over.

When all the dumplings are in the casserole, gently pour in 5 cups of hot water. Add a little extra salt and bring to a gentle boil. Lower the heat to a bare simmer, cover with a lid, and cook for an hour. There should be a fair amount of liquid still at the end. Remove from the heat.

For the sauce, whip the egg in a bowl, and then whisk in the lemon juice and a pinch of salt. Add a ladleful of the hot liquid from the pan (which you will have to tip to the side to get to). Quickly whisk the hot liquid into the egg mixture to acclimatize the eggs, then add another couple of ladlefuls along with the dill, mixing well.

With the pan off the heat, pour all the egg and lemon sauce back in, quickly swirling the pan around to shift everything so that the eggs don't scramble. Cover the pan and let it sit for a few minutes—there should be enough heat left in the pan to just cook the eggs through. Taste that there is enough salt before serving, perhaps with a grinding of black pepper. Best served warm, but also good at room temperature.

Serves 5 to 6

---

4 TABLESPOONS OLIVE OIL
2 SMALL ZUCCHINI, FINELY SLICED
2 CLOVES GARLIC, PEELED AND SQUASHED A BIT
SALT
1/2 TEASPOON DRIED MINT
3/4 CUP SMALL CUBES FETA CHEESE
1 1/2 TABLESPOONS LEMON JUICE
2/3 (16-OUNCE) PACKAGE ANGEL HAIR PASTA
OLIVE OIL, TO SERVE
GRATED PARMESAN CHEESE, TO SERVE

Angel hair pasta with zucchini, mint, and feta

This is light, elegant, and very quick. You can get the preparation done and sauté the zucchini while the pasta is cooking and then just mix it all together.

Heat the olive oil in a large nonstick frying pan and add the zucchini and garlic. Sauté over quite high heat until the zucchini are cooked through and golden in places. If the garlic starts to burn, sit it on top of the zucchini. Season very lightly with salt and remove from the heat. Toss in the mint, crushing it between your fingers, and add the feta and lemon juice to the pan.

Meanwhile, cook the pasta in boiling salted water, following the package instructions. Drain the pasta, not too thoroughly, and save a little cooking water. Toss the pasta directly into the zucchini pan, if it fits. If not, return it to its own pan and add the zucchini sauce. Add 2 to 3 tablespoons of olive oil and toss quickly and thoroughly to mix it all through (add a little cooking water if it seems at all dry). Serve immediately, with Parmesan and an extra drizzle of olive oil, if you like.

Serves 3

3 CHICKEN CUTLETS
ABOUT 4 TABLESPOONS ALL-PURPOSE FLOUR
4 TABLESPOONS OLIVE OIL
1 CLOVE GARLIC, PEELED AND SQUASHED A BIT
SALT AND FRESHLY GROUND BLACK PEPPER
JUICE OF HALF A LEMON
1 ½ TABLESPOONS CAPERS IN VINEGAR, DRAINED
   AND CHOPPED
3 TABLESPOONS CHOPPED FRESH PARSLEY
3 TABLESPOONS HOT WATER

Chicken cutlets with parsley and capers

This is another very simple way to prepare a chicken breast. You can buy cutlets from your butcher, or simply slice a chicken breast horizontally into three or four thin flat slices. You could even pound them out a bit thinner with a meat mallet, if you like. This is nice with mashed or boiled potatoes, or fries and a simple vegetable like sautéed cauliflower.

Lightly pat both sides of the chicken in flour. Heat the oil with the garlic in a large frying pan over medium-high heat and add the chicken. Fry until lightly golden on the underside, then turn over, and season the done sides with salt and pepper. When the new undersides are golden, turn them again, season, and squeeze in the lemon juice. Add the capers, half the parsley, and 2 to 3 tablespoons of hot water. Let it bubble up, then put a lid on the pan, and cook for an extra minute or two to make sure that the chicken is cooked through but still soft and moist and there is some liquid in the pan. Turn off the heat and leave the pan with the lid on for a few minutes. Mix in the remaining parsley and serve immediately.

Serves 3

Walking barefoot through fields, knowing to zigzag if you see a snake. The medicine chest is full—I have covered mosquito bites and bee stings.

GREEN

3 TABLESPOONS OLIVE OIL
1 1/4 POUNDS DEBONED, TRIMMED LEG
   OR SHOULDER OF LAMB, CUT INTO
   1 1/2-INCH CHUNKS
1 RED ONION, FINELY CHOPPED
1 1/2 TABLESPOONS BUTTER
2 CLOVES GARLIC, CHOPPED
3/4 (14-OUNCE) CAN DICED TOMATOES
SALT
1 SMALL PIECE CINNAMON STICK
3 CUPS WATER
3/4 POUND GREEN BEANS, TRIMMED
   (LEAVE THE TAILS ON)
1 1/2 CUPS SMALL CUBES FETA CHEESE

Lamb and green bean casserole

I like to make this in advance and then leave it in the oven to cool down completely. This seems to make the meat even softer, and then I just warm it up a bit on the stovetop to serve. This is a great one-pan meal that needs just the time to prepare and chop up the ingredients, and not much more attention from then on. You can use chunks of lamb or beef here, and throw in a couple of potatoes, cut up into chunks, with the beans, if you like. The green beans alone are also delicious cooked like this; still served with crumblings of feta that melt a little into the tomato sauce.

Preheat the oven to 350°F. Heat the oil in a heavy-bottomed casserole over high heat. When it is very hot, add the meat, and brown on all sides. Add the onion and cook, stirring, for a few minutes to soften it. When the onion starts to brown, add the butter and garlic. When you can smell the garlic, add the tomatoes. Season with salt and add the cinnamon. Add 2 cups of water and bring to a boil. Put on the lid and put the casserole in the oven.

   Cook for 45 minutes or so until the meat is soft, and then add the beans, a little more salt, and another 1 cup of water if it needs it. Mix through well, cover, and put the casserole back into the oven for another hour. Remove the lid and cook for another 15 minutes, until it turns a little golden on the top. Turn off the oven, put the lid back on, and leave the casserole in there for about an hour so that the meat is soft and melting. You can warm it up on the stovetop to serve.

   Sprinkle the feta over the hot servings so that it melts slightly, and serve with chunks of bread.

Serves 3

5 TABLESPOONS OLIVE OIL
2 CLOVES GARLIC, PEELED AND SQUASHED A BIT
1/2 (14-OUNCE) CAN DICED TOMATOES
2 BASIL LEAVES, TORN
SALT
3 CUPS FIRMLY PACKED SPINACH LEAVES, CHOPPED
1/3 CUP GRATED PARMESAN CHEESE
8 SOLE FILLETS, WITHOUT SKIN
ALL-PURPOSE FLOUR, FOR DUSTING
LEMON WEDGES, TO SERVE

Sole bundles with spinach

This is nice with mashed potatoes or french fries, or just on its own with some bread. If you can't get sole, use fillets from another white-fleshed fish, such as cod or flounder. They need to be long fillets—fine-flaked, narrow, and about 1/4 inch thick so that they can be rolled easily.

Heat 4 tablespoons of the oil and a garlic clove in a nonstick deep frying pan that will hold all the sole bundles later on. Add the tomato and basil, season lightly with salt, and simmer over low heat for about 10 minutes, or until everything has melted together into a sauce.

Heat the remainder of the oil with the other garlic clove in a saucepan and add the spinach. Sauté for a few minutes to wilt the leaves. Remove from the heat, season with salt, and stir in the Parmesan. Remove the garlic clove.

Lay the fish fillets on a flat surface, former-skin-side down. Put about a teaspoon of the spinach mixture onto the tapered end of each fillet and roll up the fish compactly around the spinach. Secure with toothpicks. Roll the fish bundles in flour to coat lightly. Arrange them in a single layer over the tomato sauce in the pan and sprinkle with a little extra salt.

Put the lid on the pan and simmer for 5 minutes or so, until the undersides of the fish bundles become lightly golden. Very gently turn them over, sprinkle with salt, and put the lid back on. Simmer for another 5 minutes, or until the inside of the fish is cooked. If the sauce seems at all dry, add a few drops of hot water, and heat through. Serve with lemon wedges.

Serves 4

ABOUT 1½ TABLESPOONS OLIVE OIL
1 CLOVE GARLIC, PEELED AND SQUASHED A BIT
1 TO 2 SMALL GREEN ZUCCHINI, FINELY SLICED
SALT
3 OR 4 BASIL LEAVES, TORN UP
4 EGGS
6 TABLESPOONS GRATED PARMESAN CHEESE
A LITTLE LEMON JUICE

Zucchini omelette

The amount of zucchini here is enough to make four individual omelettes.
Just reduce the zucchini and eggs accordingly if you only want one or two.

Heat 2 teaspoons of oil in a nonstick pan. Add the garlic and zucchini and sauté
over medium-high heat until lightly golden, shuffling them with a wooden spoon
so that they cook evenly. Season with salt and mix in the basil. Remove from the
heat and remove the garlic.

    Whisk one egg in a bowl. Heat 1 teaspoon of oil in a 6-inch nonstick frying pan
over medium-low heat. Add the egg, swirling it evenly around the pan. Scatter
about a quarter of the zucchini over the omelette and about 1½ tablespoons
of Parmesan. Cook until the omelette is set and the underside is lightly golden.
Slip out onto a warm plate while you make the rest, adding more oil to the pan as
needed. Serve with a few drops of lemon juice and a grinding of pepper, if you like.

Serves 4

---

3 TABLESPOONS OLIVE OIL
1 CLOVE GARLIC, PEELED AND
SQUASHED A BIT
1 SMALL ROSEMARY SPRIG
2 LARGE SLICES OF VEAL, CUT ABOUT
⅛ INCH THICK
SALT
2 LEMON WEDGES, TO SERVE

Paillard

This is a wonderful piece of meat to give children—very tender and soft.
Ask your butcher for long pieces of veal, about ⅛ inch thick. It is essential
that the meat is just seared on the pan and doesn't simmer and harden. It
needs just a couple of minutes cooking in total, and your grill pan must be
incredibly hot before you put the meat on it. You need to think ahead a
little and put your herbs and oil in a bowl a while before you cook. This is
very nice with pea and potato mash (opposite) or with pan-fried potatoes.

Put the olive oil, garlic, and rosemary sprig in a small bowl and leave for about 45 minutes to flavor the oil.

If it's necessary, pound the veal slices (first covered with a sheet of plastic wrap) with a meat mallet to make them an even thickness.

Put your grill pan over a high flame and let it stay there until it is very hot. Put the veal slices on the pan, one at a time if they won't both fit. They should sear immediately. As soon as the undersides come away easily with a pair of tongs and there are obvious grill marks, turn them over and do the other side. Both sides should take less than 30 seconds.

Remove to a plate, drizzle some of the oil over each one, and add a small scattering of salt. Serve immediately, with a lemon wedge on the side.

Serves 2

---

2 TO 3 MEDIUM POTATOES, PEELED AND CUT INTO LARGE CHUNKS
4 TABLESPOONS OLIVE OIL
1 SHALLOT, PEELED BUT LEFT WHOLE
2 CLOVES GARLIC, PEELED BUT LEFT WHOLE
1 1/3 CUPS SHELLED PEAS, FRESH OR FROZEN
SALT
1/2 CUP HOT WATER
1/2 CUP MILK
ABOUT 2 TABLESPOONS BUTTER

Pea and potato mash

Sometimes I like this with variegated ripples of color and sometimes I mix it in to make it all green. This is also delicious made with chickpeas (page 346). It is good next to any broiled meat or fish, and is best served immediately. If that's not feasible, you can heat it up over a double boiler, or directly in the pan with a little milk so that it doesn't stick.

Boil the potatoes in salted water until they are soft enough to mash.

Meanwhile, heat the olive oil, shallot, and garlic in a saucepan over medium heat. Once you can smell the garlic, add the peas (straight from the freezer, if you're using frozen), and season with salt. Sauté for about 15 minutes, until they are soft and cooked through, but still bright green. When the liquid has evaporated, add 1/2 cup or so of hot water, and carry on cooking until most of it has evaporated. Remove the shallot and garlic, and purée the peas so that they are rather smooth. Drain the potatoes and put them through a food mill back into the pan, or use a potato masher to make a light mash.

Meanwhile, heat the milk and butter in a small saucepan over low heat until the butter melts. Pour into the potatoes and mix through. Add the peas and either mix them in completely or just fold them through to get a rippled effect. Serve hot.

Serves 5

1 1/2 TABLESPOONS OLIVE OIL
1 CLOVE GARLIC, PEELED AND SQUASHED A BIT
5 CUPS WATERCRESS LEAVES WITH JUST THE
 TIPS OF THE STALKS
4 EGGS
SALT AND FRESHLY GROUND BLACK PEPPER
1/3 CUP GRATED PARMESAN CHEESE
4 MINT LEAVES, TORN
1 1/2 TABLESPOONS BUTTER
A COUPLE OF LEMON WEDGES, TO SERVE

Watercress omelette

You can use any soft green leafy vegetable here: spinach is good, or even lettuce.

Heat the oil and garlic in a large saucepan and add the watercress. Cook over medium-high heat for about half a minute, turning the watercress over with a wooden spoon until it has just wilted. Remove the garlic clove.

Whip the eggs with a little salt and pepper in a bowl. Add the watercress, Parmesan, and mint and mix together.

Melt the butter in a large nonstick frying pan. Pour in the eggs and swirl them around. Cook for a few minutes over medium heat, swirling the pan around again to spread out any uncooked egg. Using a straight-edged wooden spatula, make a few holes on the bottom of the omelette, and shake the pan so that the uncooked egg leaks through and sets. Loosen the sides and bottom to make sure the omelette doesn't stick. The top will still be slightly soft and the bottom lightly golden. Remove from the heat and cut into wedges with the spatula. Serve hot from the pan, with a few drops of lemon juice squeezed over the top.

Serves 2 to 3

APPLES FOR SAM

4 CUPS WATER
SALT
10 CUPS FIRMLY PACKED SPINACH LEAVES,
    ROUGHLY CHOPPED
4 TABLESPOONS OLIVE OIL
2 CLOVES GARLIC, PEELED BUT LEFT WHOLE
1 CUP CRUMBLED FETA CHEESE
1/3 CUP GRATED PARMESAN CHEESE

Creamy spinach with feta

I remember eating this as a child, and I still like it this way now. Don't throw the spinach cooking water away—save it to make white risotto in spinach broth (page 267).

Put about 4 cups of water in a large pan, add a little salt, and bring to a boil. Add the spinach, return to a boil, and simmer for just about a minute, until the spinach has wilted. Drain, reserving the water.

Put the olive oil and garlic cloves in a large frying pan over medium heat. When you can smell the garlic, add the spinach, turning it over with a wooden spoon to collect the oil. Add the feta and 1/2 cup of the spinach water. Mix the feta through, mashing it in with the spoon so it dissolves. Still at medium heat, sauté for a couple of minutes until everything has blended together and there is only a bit of liquid left in the pan. Remove from the heat, stir in the Parmesan, and taste for salt. Serve immediately, with some black pepper for adults only.

Serves 5

4½ CUPS BROCCOLI FLORETS
5 TABLESPOONS OLIVE OIL
½ CUP CANNED DICED TOMATOES
SALT
2 CLOVES GARLIC, PEELED AND SQUASHED A BIT
CHILE OIL, TO SERVE

Sautéed broccoli with tomato

This is a similar idea to the sautéed cauliflower (page 241), but with tomato, and to me it transforms something like plain boiled broccoli into an actual dish—comfortably dressed to show up at any type of meal. The leftover cooking water can be kept and used to cook rice or pasta.

Drop the broccoli into boiling salted water for a couple of minutes. Drain well, keeping about 4 tablespoons of the cooking water. Heat 1½ tablespoons of the oil in a small saucepan and add the tomato and a dash of salt. Simmer over low heat for about 10 minutes, until it melts into a smoothish sauce. Heat the rest of the oil in a large nonstick frying pan over medium heat and add the garlic. When you can smell the garlic, add the broccoli. Sauté for a few minutes until it is a little crusty and then add the saved broccoli water. Dot the tomato here and there, put a lid on, and cook for a few minutes so that everything mingles together. Serve warm or at room temperature, definitely with a drizzle of chile oil for the adults.

Serves 4

We blew away our fallen eyelashes and the ladybugs that landed on us, together with our wishes, to the nearest star.

1 CLOVE GARLIC, PEELED AND SQUASHED A BIT
4 TABLESPOONS OLIVE OIL
8 ZUCCHINI
4 BASIL LEAVES, TORN
SEA SALT FLAKES, TO SERVE
OLIVE OIL, TO SERVE

Squashed zucchini

This is hardly a recipe, but Giovanni's mother does them like this, and so did his grandmother. Although as a young boy he didn't enjoy them, he grew into these. The zucchini tastes more concentrated somehow—more like a pattypan squash this way. I love this sort of thing that has been passed down through a family.

Put the garlic and oil in small bowl. Bring a large pan of salted water to a boil, add the zucchini, and boil them for 20 minutes or so until they are nice and soft. Remove them with a slotted spoon and line them up on a plate. Put another plate on top and press down a little to squash the water out of the zucchini. Pour off the water and do the same thing again so all the liquid is removed. Drizzle the garlic oil over the top, scatter with the basil leaves, and sprinkle with salt flakes. Serve warm, whole or in thick slices, drizzled with more olive oil if you like it.

Serves 8

BÉCHAMEL SAUCE:
3½ TABLESPOONS BUTTER
¼ CUP ALL-PURPOSE FLOUR
1½ CUPS MILK, WARMED
SALT AND FRESHLY GROUND BLACK
    PEPPER
A LITTLE FRESHLY GRATED NUTMEG

4½ CUPS BROCCOLI FLORETS
½ CUP GRATED PARMESAN CHEESE

Gratinéed broccoli

As well as boiled broccoli dressed with olive oil and lemon, my children also like this gratinéed classic. Remove the harder broccoli stems and use only the florets. Don't throw out the hard stems; they can be added to a vegetable soup or boiled and then sautéed with garlic and olive oil.

Preheat the oven to 350°F and grease a 4-cup shallow ovenproof dish that is suitable to take directly to the table. To make the béchamel, melt the butter in a small saucepan over low heat. Whisk in the flour and cook for a few minutes, stirring constantly, then begin adding the warm milk. It will be immediately absorbed, so work quickly, whisking with one hand while adding ladlefuls of milk with the other. When the sauce seems to be smooth and not too stiff, add salt, pepper, and a grating of nutmeg, and continue cooking, even after it comes to a boil, for 5 minutes or so, mixing all the time. It should be a very thick and smooth sauce.

Meanwhile, bring a saucepan of salted water to a boil, and cook the broccoli for a few minutes until it has softened a little but is still bright green. Lift out with a slotted spoon, letting the water drain off, and put it in the baking dish. (Save the broccoli water for cooking rice or pasta, or adding to a roast instead of water.)

Stir the Parmesan into the béchamel sauce and pour over the broccoli, leaving some florets still showing. Bake for about 30 minutes and then serve hot.

Serves 4

ABOUT 4 INNER CELERY STALKS, TRIMMED
3 TABLESPOONS OLIVE OIL
1 CLOVE GARLIC, PEELED AND SQUASHED A BIT
3/4 CUP CANNED TOMATO SAUCE
4 TABLESPOONS WATER
SALT AND FRESHLY GROUND BLACK PEPPER
3 BASIL LEAVES, TORN
ABOUT 5 TABLESPOONS ALL-PURPOSE FLOUR
5 TABLESPOONS GRATED PARMESAN CHEESE

Gratinéed celery with tomato and Parmesan

This is Aunt Julietta's recipe. I love having these types of things at her home—she always serves them alongside a beautiful roast. This also works very well with cauliflower broken up into smaller bits, zucchini, or the thicker stems of Swiss chard, and is especially good with winter squash slices. It is very good fried first and then arranged on the tomato, but that's a bit more of a job.

With a sharp knife, trim the strings from the celery stalks and cut into short lengths (about 1 1/2 inches). Bring a pan of salted water to a boil and cook the celery for about 20 minutes, until it is soft but not collapsing. Preheat the oven to 400°F and lightly grease a 7-inch square shallow ovenproof dish.

Heat the olive oil and garlic in a small pan over medium heat. When you can smell the garlic, add the tomato sauce and 4 tablespoons of water. Season with salt and pepper, and add the basil. Simmer over low heat for about 10 minutes for the flavors to mingle and the sauce to thicken a little. Remove the garlic clove and throw it away.

Drain the celery. Spread the flour on a plate and pat the celery pieces lightly into it to coat both sides. Spread about a third of the tomato sauce over the bottom of the dish. Arrange the celery on top, in a single layer or slightly overlapping. Dollop the rest of the tomato sauce on top. Bake for 20 minutes, or until the top is golden in places. Sprinkle with the Parmesan and bake for another 10 minutes or so until it is golden and crusty. Leave to cool for a few minutes before serving.

Serves 5

2¼ POUNDS GREEN BEANS, TRIMMED
SALT
ABOUT ½ CUP DRY BREAD CRUMBS

BÉCHAMEL SAUCE:
3½ TABLESPOONS BUTTER
⅔ CUP ALL-PURPOSE FLOUR
1⅔ CUPS MILK, WARMED
SALT AND FRESHLY GROUND BLACK
    PEPPER
FRESHLY GRATED NUTMEG

4 EGGS
¾ CUP GRATED PARMESAN CHEESE
½ TABLESPOON CHOPPED DILL

Green bean
soufflé loaf

I like the idea of wrapping this up and taking it along on an autumn picnic, perhaps with a pile of schnitzels and the pear butter cake (page 248). Cooked beans are puréed and folded into a dense béchamel in a loaf pan, baked, and served in thick slices . . . a little like a cross between a soufflé and a loaf. You can use another herb in place of dill, if you'd prefer. This makes two loaves, but you could easily halve the quantity, and you can use any shape pan you prefer.

Steam the beans over a pan of boiling water for about 20 minutes until tender. Put them in a blender or processor and pulse so that most are smooth, but there are some small bits, too. Pour into a bowl, season well with salt, and leave to cool a bit.

Preheat the oven to 350°F. Grease two 8 by 4-inch loaf pans and sprinkle the bottoms and sides with bread crumbs. Shake out the excess.

To make the béchamel, melt the butter in a small saucepan over low heat. Whisk in the flour and cook for a few minutes, stirring constantly, then begin adding the warm milk. It will be immediately absorbed, so work quickly, whisking with one hand while adding ladlefuls of milk with the other. When the sauce seems to be smooth and not too stiff, add salt, pepper, and a grating of nutmeg, and continue cooking, even after it comes to a boil, for 5 minutes or so, mixing all the time. It should be a very thick and smooth sauce.

Whisk the eggs, Parmesan, and dill together, then fold through the puréed beans. Whisk in the béchamel and add some salt, nutmeg, or pepper if needed. Ladle into the pans and sprinkle the tops with a teaspoon or so of bread crumbs. Put side by side in the oven and bake for about 45 minutes, or until they are set and the tops are nicely golden and crusty. Cool for a while before slicing to serve.

Serves 10

ABOUT 3/4 (14 1/2-OUNCE) PACKAGE
    GRAHAM CRACKERS
7 TABLESPOONS BUTTER, MELTED
1 1/2 CANS CARAMELIZED
    SWEETENED CONDENSED MILK
1 2/3 CUPS HEAVY WHIPPING
    CREAM
4 OUNCES PEPPERMINT CRISP
    BARS, OR PEPPERMINT
    CHOCOLATE, CRUMBLED OR
    COARSELY GRATED

Peppermint crisp pie

This outrageous pie has a base of crushed crackers, a layer of caramel, a
layer of whipped cream, and then a scattering of crisp peppermint candy
covered in milk chocolate. It is incredibly rich and should probably be
served in small spoonfuls, depending, of course, on your personal tastes.
It makes me think of boarding school midnight feasts in books from the
1950s. If you can't get peppermint crisp bars, grated peppermint-flavored
chocolate is a good substitute, although your pie will not have the bits of
crunchy green candy. In South Africa, we made this with "tennis" cookies,
but graham crackers work just as well. It is possible to buy condensed
milk already boiled into caramel. If you can't get it, you will have to
simmer the condensed milk in a double boiler for about 1 1/2 hours until
it turns nutty golden brown and is caramelized.

Crush the crackers and put them in a bowl with the butter. Mix together well and
then press firmly onto the bottom and a little way up the sides of a 10 1/2-inch pie
dish. Put in the fridge to set.
    Beat the caramel in a bowl with a wooden spoon until smooth. Carefully spread
over the cracker crust, trying not to lift any of the cracker crumbs.
    Whip the cream until it holds its shape well, but take care not to overwhip it.
Spoon it over the caramel to cover the whole surface, and then scatter the
peppermint chocolate over the top. Keep in the fridge before serving in slices if
you can manage it, or dollops if you can't. This is also good the next day.

Serves 10 to 12

gold

Olive oil focaccia
Whole wheat focaccia
Half-moon rolls
Cheese pies
Steak pie
Fried mozzarella sandwiches
Macaroni cheese
Fried squid
Pan-fried sole with lemon garlic butter
Beef and potato croquettes
Scallopini with ham and cheese
Fried buttermilk-marinated chicken
Chicken cutlets with lemon and butter
Boiled potatoes with parsley
Sautéed chicken with bay leaves and juniper berries
Roast chicken and potatoes with thyme, lemon, and garlic
Fish cakes
Very thin fries
Mayonnaise
Sautéed cauliflower
Fried potato halves with oregano
Pan-fried potatoes with rosemary and sage
White loaf with honey, butter, and pecans
Toffee sauce
Pear butter cake
Semolina puddings with caramel
Pancakes
Waffles
Sweet crepes

- memory -

I could hardly wait to spring out of bed in the mornings, onto my bicycle down the drive. We played circus over Dixie's kennel and brushed Sumpi till she shone. Later were water-drinking competitions and just about anything else that came into our lush minds. Sometimes it was just such a drag to come in for a meal . . . we far preferred to take our plates to the shelter that the tree had made into a cave for us— or under the weeping willow. We didn't really mind if it was real Parmesan—it was the shapes and the flavors that could carry us away and link arms with our fairies. I watch that same energy in my children, their days just tinged with trust and newness and full of spontaneous wonder, miracle, and flowing along with whatever is happening. Sitting on hilltops and dreaming of being kings in other places.

1³/₄ CUPS WARM (COMFORTABLE TO YOUR
   FINGERS) WATER
1 (³/₄-OUNCE) CAKE FRESH YEAST, CRUMBLED, OR
   1 (¹/₄-OUNCE) PACKAGE ACTIVE DRY YEAST
1 TEASPOON HONEY
2¹/₂ TABLESPOONS OLIVE OIL
5 CUPS ALL-PURPOSE FLOUR
2¹/₂ TEASPOONS SALT
¹/₂ CUP HOT WATER

Olive oil focaccia

This is nice left to rise up high so that it is soft and can be split for filling sandwiches. A couple of squares of this filled with thinly sliced ham or salami, bresaola, chopped egg, herbs, tomato, and ricotta or mozzarella, or roasted tomato and pesto makes a good lunch or emergency snack. The bread can also be frozen in bags in small portions and pulled out to thaw quickly. This is lovely also with some fresh herbs such as rosemary strewn across the top before baking. If you use rosemary, strip the leaves off a couple of stalks and chop them up very finely (as I think the long needles might not be appreciated by the kids). The amount of water and flour you need may vary slightly, but the dough should be sticky and difficult to knead.

Put the water, yeast, honey, half the olive oil, and 3 fistfuls of the flour in a bowl. Mix with an electric beater until smooth. Cover and leave for 20 to 30 minutes, until it all froths up and looks foamy on the top. Mix in the rest of the flour and 1¹/₂ teaspoons of salt. Now, using a dough hook, mix for 4 to 5 minutes so that it is well incorporated. If you don't have a dough hook, then mix it with your hands in the bowl, just slapping it from one side to the other, as it will be too soft to knead. Cover the bowl with a couple of cloths and leave it in a warm and draft-free place for about 1¹/₂ hours, or until it has puffed up well.

Lightly grease an 11 by 15 by 1¹/₂-inch baking pan. Punch down the dough to flatten it. Spread the dough out gently into the pan, right out to the edges. If it won't stretch easily, leave it to relax for another 5 minutes and then gently stretch it out, starting from the center. Make sure the dough doesn't break anywhere and that it is spread more or less evenly. Put in a warm, draft-free place. So the dough doesn't stick to the cloth, arrange four glasses around the pan and drape a couple of dish towels or a towel over them like a tent to completely cover the pan. Leave for about 45 minutes, until the dough puffs up.

Meanwhile, preheat the oven to 450°F. In a small bowl, mix the remaining oil with ¹/₂ cup of hot water and 1 teaspoon of salt and stir until the salt dissolves. Make some dimples on the top of the bread with your fingertips and then brush well with the saltwater mixture.

Put in the oven and bake for around 20 to 30 minutes, until the bread is golden, a bit crusty here and there, and sounds hollow when tapped. Remove from the oven and cool a little before cutting into pieces. This is best warm but can also be served at room temperature or reheated.

Cuts up into 10 to 12 pieces

1 1/2 CUPS WARM (COMFORTABLE TO YOUR
    FINGERS) WATER
1 (3/4-OUNCE) CAKE FRESH YEAST, CRUMBLED,
    OR 1 (1/4-OUNCE) PACKAGE ACTIVE DRY YEAST
1 1/2 TABLESPOONS SUPERFINE SUGAR
2 CUPS WHITE BREAD FLOUR
2 1/3 CUPS WHOLE WHEAT FLOUR
5 TABLESPOONS OLIVE OIL
2 TEASPOONS SALT
1/2 CUP HOT WATER

Whole wheat focaccia

Here is a whole wheat version of the focaccia on page 211. You can use any proportion of whole wheat flour to white, or you could use another type, too, such as spelt flour instead of the whole wheat. You could also incorporate this into the pizza rossa on page 53, swapping some of the white flour for whole wheat and carrying on with the tomato topping.

Put the water, yeast, and sugar in a large bowl with 2 fistfuls of the white flour. Mix with an electric beater until smooth. Cover and leave for about 30 minutes, until it all froths up and looks foamy on the top. Add the rest of the all-purpose flour, the whole wheat flour, half the oil, and 1 teaspoon of salt. Mix well with your hands: it will be very soft, but try to work it without adding more flour. If it's too soft to knead, just slap it around in the bowl for 4 to 5 minutes until it starts to feel elastic. Cover the bowl with a couple of cloths and leave it in a warm and draft-free place for about 1 1/2 hours, or until it has puffed up well.

Lightly grease an 11 by 15 by 1 1/2-inch baking pan. Punch down the dough to flatten it. Spread the dough out gently into the pan, right out to the edges. If it won't stretch easily, leave it to relax for another 5 minutes and then gently stretch it out, starting from the center. Make sure the dough doesn't break anywhere and that it is spread more or less evenly. Put in a warm, draft-free place. So the dough doesn't stick to the cloth, arrange four glasses around the pan and drape a couple of dish towels or a towel over them like a tent to completely cover the pan. Leave for about 45 minutes to 1 hour, until the dough puffs up.

Meanwhile, preheat the oven to 450°F. In a small bowl, mix the remaining oil with 1/2 cup of hot water and 1 teaspoon of salt, and stir until the salt dissolves. Make some dimples on the top of the bread with your fingertips and then brush well with the saltwater mixture.

Put in the oven and bake for around 20 to 30 minutes, until the bread is golden, a bit crusty here and there, and sounds hollow when tapped. Remove from the oven and cool a little before cutting into pieces. This is best warm but can also be served at room temperature or reheated.

Cuts up into 10 to 12 pieces

1/2 CUP WARM (COMFORTABLE TO YOUR
    FINGERS) MILK
1/3 CUP WARM (COMFORTABLE TO YOUR
    FINGERS) WATER
1 (1/2-OUNCE) CAKE FRESH YEAST, CRUMBLED, OR
    1 (1/4-OUNCE) PACKAGE ACTIVE DRY YEAST
1 TEASPOON HONEY
3 1/4 CUPS CAKE FLOUR
1/2 TEASPOON SALT
3 TABLESPOONS BUTTER, MELTED

TO GLAZE:
1 EGG, LIGHTLY BEATEN WITH A LITTLE MILK
POPPY SEEDS
SESAME SEEDS

Half-moon rolls

My kids love these for breakfast with butter and jam. You can freeze them easily and take out a couple as you need them. For people who have never made their own bread and think it sounds daunting, these are so much easier to make than you would think. You can even freeze the dough once it's been shaped . . . that way it has its second rising as it thaws.

Put the milk, water, yeast, and honey in a small bowl, and stir until the honey melts. Leave it for about 10 minutes, or until it begins to froth a bit. Put the flour and 1/2 teaspoon of salt into a larger bowl. Add the yeast mixture and melted butter, and mix through well. Knead for 10 minutes or so until you have a soft elastic ball. Only add extra flour if the dough is so sticky that it is unkneadable. Cover the bowl with a cloth and leave it to rise in a warm, draft-free place for 1 1/2 to 2 hours, or until it has puffed up well. Punch down the dough to flatten it, and divide it approximately in half.

    On a lightly floured work surface, roll or stretch each piece of dough into a circle like a pizza crust, about 14 inches in diameter and 1/8 inch thick. If the dough is hard to stretch, leave it for 5 minutes to relax before rolling it out. Cut each circle into eight wedges like you would cut a pizza. Working with one wedge at a time, stretch out the two outside corners a little, then roll up the dough tightly from the outside and finishing at the point of the triangle. With this point to the top, curve the roll slightly into a crescent shape.

    Line two baking sheets with parchment paper and arrange 8 rolls on each. Cover with a cloth and leave to rise in the warm place for 30 to 45 minutes. Brush with the egg and scatter seeds over the top.

    Preheat the oven to 350°F. Bake one sheet at a time for about 15 minutes, or until the rolls are lightly golden and the bottoms sound hollow when tapped. Serve warm or at room temperature with your favorite filling.

Makes 16

PASTRY:
2½ CUPS ALL-PURPOSE FLOUR
¼ POUND PLUS 6 TABLESPOONS (1¾ STICKS)
   BUTTER, CUT INTO BLOCKS
½ TEASPOON SALT
1 SMALL EGG, LIGHTLY BEATEN
3½ TABLESPOONS MILK
2 TEASPOONS WHITE VINEGAR

FILLING:
¾ CUP CRUMBLED FETA
½ CUP SMOOTH RICOTTA
2 TEASPOONS FINELY GRATED PARMESAN CHEESE
½ TEASPOON CRUSHED DRIED MINT
2 SMALL EGGS
½ TEASPOON SWEET PAPRIKA
ABOUT 1 TEASPOON MILK

Cheese pies

One of these works well as a snack, and two or three could be a meal, perhaps served alongside a vegetable soup. You could even add some sautéed chopped leeks or spinach to the cheese filling. Sometimes I sprinkle the pies with sesame seeds after I have brushed them with the egg wash and then I dab at the tops a little more with the egg (I always feel that a few extra vitamins is a good idea wherever possible).

For the pastry, put the flour and butter in a bowl and add ½ teaspoon of salt. Rub the butter into the flour with your fingertips until it is crumbly, like sand. Add the egg and milk, and continue working it until it comes together in a loose dough. Then add the vinegar and mix it in well so that the dough forms a loose ball. Flatten it slightly, cover with plastic wrap, and refrigerate for an hour or so.
   Preheat the oven to 350°F and line two baking sheets with parchment paper (unless you have a very large oven and can fit everything on one big sheet).
   For the filling, mash the feta with a fork until smooth. Work in the ricotta, Parmesan, and the mint. Add 1 egg and the paprika, and mix well.
   Whip the remaining egg and milk together in a small bowl for a glaze. Roll out the pastry on a lightly floured surface to about ⅛ inch thick. Cut 4-inch rounds with a cookie cutter or a glass, cutting them as close to each other as you can. Reroll the scraps if you need to. Brush around the edges of the pastry circles with the glaze. Dollop a fairly heaping teaspoon of filling in the center of each one, spreading it out very slightly into an oval (you want enough filling to make your pies tasty—but not so much that it bursts out during cooking).
   Flip the pastry over your thumb and forefinger to make half-moons. Stretch out the ends to lengthen and thin them a bit. Press the edges together firmly to seal, then roll them over to make a lip so that no filling can escape.
   Put the pies on the sheets and brush the tops with glaze. Bake one sheet at a time for 20 minutes, or until the pies have golden tops and bottoms and look ready to eat. Leave to cool for a while—they are best eaten just warm, not piping hot.

Makes about 20 small pies

PASTRY:
2½ CUPS ALL-PURPOSE FLOUR
¼ POUND PLUS 6 TABLESPOONS (1¾ STICKS)
    BUTTER, CUT INTO BLOCKS
½ TEASPOON SALT
1 EGG, LIGHTLY BEATEN
3½ TABLESPOONS MILK
2 TEASPOONS WHITE WINE VINEGAR

FILLING:
5 TABLESPOONS OLIVE OIL
1 RED ONION, CHOPPED
3 SHALLOTS, CHOPPED
2 CLOVES GARLIC, FINELY CHOPPED
ABOUT 2 POUNDS SIRLOIN OR RUMP STEAK
    IN THICK SLICES, TRIMMED AND CUT INTO
    1¼-INCH CHUNKS
5 TABLESPOONS ALL-PURPOSE FLOUR
1½ TABLESPOONS BUTTER
1½ TABLESPOONS COGNAC
3 TABLESPOONS WORCESTERSHIRE SAUCE
3 CUPS HOT WATER
SALT AND FRESHLY GROUND BLACK PEPPER
ABOUT 7 ALLSPICE BERRIES
1 EGG YOLK
1 TEASPOON MILK

Steak pie

This is also lovely made into individual pies, and you could even add a few lentils, carrots, potatoes, or other vegetables to the filling. I serve this with some boiled broccoli, potatoes in their skins, and zucchini—all dressed with good olive oil and a small squeeze of lemon to make an honest square meal. It's also stunning with mashed potatoes and peas.

For the pastry, put the flour and butter in a large bowl with ½ teaspoon of salt. Work the butter into the flour with your fingertips until it is crumbly and looks like sand. Add the egg and milk, and continue working it until it comes together in a loose dough. Add the vinegar and mix it in well, until the dough forms a loose ball. Flatten it slightly, cover with plastic wrap, and refrigerate for an hour or so.

For the filling, heat half the oil in a large heavy-bottomed pan and sauté the onion and shallots over medium-low heat until they are nicely golden and sticky, stirring often so they don't stick. Add the garlic and cook until you can smell it.

In the meantime, heat the remaining oil in a nonstick frying pan. Toss the meat pieces in the flour and fry in the oil, in two or three batches, until browned. Add each batch to the onions as it is done.

When all the meat is in the pan, add the butter and cook until it melts, then add the Cognac. When that has evaporated, add the Worcestershire sauce. Cook for a minute or two and then add 2 cups of hot water. Bring to a boil, season with salt and pepper, and add the allspice berries. Remember how many you have added so that you can take them all out later. Simmer uncovered for 30 minutes, stirring now and then.

Add 1 cup of hot water, put on the lid, and simmer very slowly for another hour, stirring very often so nothing gets stuck on the bottom of the pan, until you have soft meat and a thick gravy. Add a little more water if it seems necessary, or cook for longer with the lid off if there is too much liquid. Leave to cool slightly, and remove all the allspice berries.

Preheat your oven to 350°F. Divide the dough into two, one part slightly larger than the other. Roll out the bigger portion on a lightly floured surface to a thickness of about 1/8 inch. Lower it into a 9 1/2-inch pie dish or springform cake pan, patting it flat against the side of the pan. Spoon in the filling and then trim the dough so that you have a 1-inch edge. Roll out the second piece of dough to about 1/8 inch thick, then cut out a neat circle to match the diameter of the pan. Fit this over the meat and then fold the edge of the lower piece of dough over it, pressing the edge gently to seal it.

Mix the egg with the milk and brush generously over the top. If you have any leftover pastry, you can make shapes or letters to decorate the top and brush those, too, with the egg wash. Bake for about 45 minutes, until the pastry is crisp and deep golden. Take out of the oven and leave to cool slightly before serving.

Serves 4

I am ironing a shirt, keeping an eye on the cake and the chicken and an ear outside, as the kids are on their bikes. I am praying it will rain so I won't have to water the flowers today and it will cool everyone down a bit.

It is almost time for us to leave for tennis lessons. I notice Yasmine has a hole in her stocking. I call them in 5 minutes early—so that we will only be 5 minutes late—and I hope my gas is above half. I love it when it is; such freedom. Why didn't I fill it up yesterday when I had those spare two hours?

2 EGGS
SALT
4 TO 5 TABLESPOONS ALL-PURPOSE FLOUR
ABOUT 5 TABLESPOONS DRY BREAD CRUMBS
2 THIN HAM SLICES, ABOUT THE SAME SIZE AS
　　THE BREAD
ABOUT 3 OUNCES THINLY SLICED MOZZARELLA
　　CHEESE
4 SLICES WHITE BREAD, CRUSTS REMOVED
OLIVE OIL, FOR FRYING

Fried mozzarella sandwiches

This can be a meal in itself. I like to serve it with a tomato salad dressed with olive oil, a drop of balsamic, and a couple of torn basil leaves. You can just double up the bread and mozzarella, making as much as you need. Use good white bread and cut it about about 5/8 inch thick. Make these with or without the ham—they are good either way.

Whip the eggs with a little salt in a flattish bowl. Sprinkle the flour over one plate and the breadcrumbs over another.

Make two ham and mozzarella sandwiches, using two slices of bread for each, and using up all the ham and cheese (if you have any mozzarella left over, you can nibble at it while you work). Cut each sandwich in half.

Heat enough oil to come about 1/2 inch up the side of your frying pan. Holding each sandwich together firmly, dip them first in the flour on all sides, then in the egg, and then in the bread crumbs so that they are well coated. Fry them over medium heat until they are golden on both sides. Lift them out onto a plate lined with paper towels to soak up the excess oil. Serve immediately.

Serves 2 to 4, depending on whether it's a meal or a snack

MINI

1 1/2 TABLESPOONS FINE DRY BREAD CRUMBS

BÉCHAMEL SAUCE:
5 TABLESPOONS BUTTER
1/3 CUP ALL-PURPOSE FLOUR
2 1/4 CUPS MILK, WARMED
SALT AND FRESHLY GROUND BLACK PEPPER
FRESHLY GRATED NUTMEG

2/3 (16-OUNCE) PACKAGE SHORT PASTA, SUCH AS PENNE
1 OUNCE THICKLY SLICED HAM, CUT INTO CHUNKS OR STRIPS
1/2 CUP GRATED PARMESAN CHEESE

Macaroni cheese

I have to say that pasta in bianco in some form or another is definitely my children's first choice favorite for dinner. When I make them plain pasta with Parmesan and olive oil or butter, they smile and behave well. So this is another version of macaroni cheese with Parmesan—but you might want to use another cheese, if you prefer. This version also has some chopped up ham added to it, and some sautéed peas might be good, too, depending on what you think your family will like. If not, just totally white is also good. You can just put this onto the table and not worry about anything. We also make a plain cheese version often. Here I use short penne, because you can get them into your mouth easily, but you can use any: ordinary penne, rigatoni, macaroni, etc. . . . I make it in this fairly small dish as it's not fantastic the next day.

Preheat the oven to 325°F. Grease a 10 by 6-inch shallow ovenproof dish and scatter the bread crumbs over it. To make the béchamel, melt 3 1/2 tablespoons of the butter in a small saucepan over low heat. Whisk in the flour and cook for a few minutes, stirring constantly, then begin adding the warm milk. It will be immediately absorbed, so work quickly, whisking with one hand while adding ladlefuls of milk with the other. When the sauce seems to be smooth and not too stiff, add salt, pepper, and a grating of nutmeg, and continue cooking, even after it comes to a boil, for 5 minutes or so, mixing all the time. It should be a very thick and smooth sauce.

Meanwhile, cook the pasta in a large pan of boiling salted water for a little less time than it says on the package so that it is still a bit firm. Drain well and then tip into a bowl. Add the rest of the butter and half of the béchamel, and mix until the butter melts. Scrape half the pasta into the ovenproof dish and level it out. Scatter the ham over the top, then a couple of tablespoons of the Parmesan. Top with the rest of the pasta, then spread the remaining béchamel over this. Scatter the rest of the Parmesan over the top. Bake for 20 to 30 minutes, until the top is getting a little bit crusty, then put it under a hot broiler until it is golden and crisp in places. Serve hot, scooped out in rough squares.

Serves 6

1 1/4 POUNDS SQUID, ABOUT 4 INCHES LONG
ABOUT 2 CUPS MILK
3/4 CUP ALL-PURPOSE FLOUR
SALT AND FRESHLY GROUND BLACK PEPPER
LIGHT OLIVE OIL OR SUNFLOWER OIL, FOR FRYING
LEMON WEDGES, TO SERVE

Fried squid

I love eating fried food out in a restaurant, but sometimes I make it at home, too. My children like these quite plain—and if you find making fries at the same time is just too much of a job with all that frying, then serve some broken up bits of tender crunchy lettuce hearts with feta and a light drizzling of dressing. The important thing here really is the quality of the squid, which must be tender to start with (although soaking them in the milk first helps make them beautifully tender). You could also add a few shelled shrimp here with the squid. I use a deep wok-type pan for this—you have to take care as the squid are quite unpredictable and often spit and splutter just as they are ready.

Clean out the squid and peel off their skin and wings. Halve the tentacles, if they are large, and cut the bodies into 1-inch rings. Rinse them well, put them in a bowl, and pour in enough milk to cover them. Cover the bowl and leave it in the fridge for at least a couple of hours or overnight.

Drain the squid well and pat them dry. Sprinkle the flour over a plate and season with salt and pepper. Pour enough oil into a wok or pan to comfortably fry the squid and put it over medium heat. Pat the squid in the flour so that they are well but lightly covered.

When the oil is hot, fry the squid in batches, turning them as the undersides become golden and crispy. Take care with the hot oil and jumping squid—you might need to stand back and reach out with long tongs to turn and lift them out when they are ready. Put them on a plate lined with a couple of layers of paper towels to soak up the oil, then transfer them to a clean plate and serve straight-away with lemon wedges and salt.

Serves 4

SAUCE:
3 TABLESPOONS BUTTER
2 CLOVES GARLIC, PEELED AND SQUASHED A BIT
1/4 TEASPOON SWEET PAPRIKA
SALT
JUICE OF 1 LEMON

ABOUT 5 TABLESPOONS ALL-PURPOSE FLOUR
2 WHOLE SOLE, ABOUT 7 OR 8 OUNCES EACH,
    SKINNED AND GUTTED
2 TABLESPOONS BUTTER
SALT
1 1/2 TABLESPOONS CHOPPED FRESH PARSLEY

Pan-fried sole with lemon garlic butter

This sauce is also very good over a broiled chicken breast or steak. You can make as much or as little of it as you need, but I try to have at least two generous tablespoons per serving. Your fishmonger should be able to skin the fish when he guts them (and you can use different fish, if you prefer). It's best to decide beforehand how you are going to serve the sole—you can cook them ready-filleted or cook them whole and serve with sauce spooned over and let everyone fillet their own on their plate. They come away from the bone easily, but it's still always worth double-checking for tiny missed bones. They do look impressive served whole—so often I serve them like that, then move the fish to a clean empty plate, quickly fillet it and return the fillets to the plate of sauce. You will need to work quickly, so have everything ready before you start.

For the sauce, put the butter and garlic in a small pan and cook over medium heat until sizzling. Add the paprika, season well with salt, and sizzle a bit more so that the flavors mingle. When it starts looking a bit golden brown, add the lemon juice and cook for a minute longer. Keep warm.

Sprinkle the flour over a plate and lightly pat both sides of the fish in it. Heat the butter in a large nonstick frying pan and add the fish. Cook over medium-high heat until their undersides are nicely golden. Sprinkle with salt and then gently flip them over. Salt the cooked side and fry until the new underside is golden. Cover the pan with a lid now and cook for a few minutes to make sure the fish are cooked through. If you think there is not enough butter or it is browning too much, then add another blob of butter to the pan. Remove the fish to plates.

Add about 2 1/2 tablespoons of your sauce to the frying pan and heat through to collect the pan flavors. Spoon over the fish and sprinkle with parsley. Serve immediately, with the remaining warm sauce spooned over.

Serves 2

ABOUT 4 POTATOES, SCRUBBED
3/4 POUND GOOD-QUALITY GROUND BEEF
1/2 CUP GRATED PARMESAN CHEESE
1 EGG
1 TEASPOON SALT
ABOUT 1 CUP DRY BREAD CRUMBS
ABOUT 5 TABLESPOONS OLIVE OIL

Beef and potato croquettes

These are very popular and seem to just disappear when there are kids around. You could also add some freshly chopped parsley to the mix.

Put a pan of salted water on to boil. Add the unpeeled potatoes and boil, covered, for about 20 minutes, or until they are soft and completely cooked through. Preheat the oven to 350°F.

Drain the potatoes and, when they are cool enough, peel them. Mash them well in a wide bowl. Add the beef, parmesan, egg, and salt, and mix thoroughly with your hands.

Roll into balls about the size of small walnuts and then flatten them a bit into little ovals. Put the bread crumbs on a plate and pat the croquettes in them to coat both sides. Drizzle about 2 1/2 tablespoons of oil over the bottom of a large baking pan, spreading it around with the back of a spoon. Pack the croquettes like tight soldiers on the pan and drizzle lightly with another couple of tablespoons of oil.

Put the pan in the oven and bake the croquettes for about 30 minutes, or until the undersides are nicely golden and a bit crisp. Turn them over gently and bake for another 10 minutes, or longer if necessary, until the new undersides become nicely golden (even a little crisp here and there—but not dried out).

Serve warm or at room temperature with a small scattering of salt, if you think they need it.

Makes about 40 small croquettes

BECHAMEL SAUCE:
1 1/2 TABLESPOONS BUTTER
1 1/2 TABLESPOONS ALL-PURPOSE FLOUR
1/2 CUP MILK, WARMED
SALT AND FRESHLY GROUND BLACK PEPPER
FRESHLY GRATED NUTMEG

4 LARGE THIN SLICES BEEF, ABOUT 2 OUNCES
   EACH AND 1/16 INCH THICK
4 THIN SMALL SLICES FONTINA OR SIMILAR CHEESE
4 THIN SMALL SLICES HAM
ABOUT 5 TABLESPOONS ALL-PURPOSE FLOUR
FRESHLY GROUND BLACK PEPPER
1 EGG
SALT
ABOUT 2/3 CUP DRY BREAD CRUMBS
1 1/2 TABLESPOONS BUTTER
2 1/2 TABLESPOONS OLIVE OIL

Scallopini with ham and cheese

This is a definite favorite for most of the kids I hang around with. I serve it with the potato and chickpea mash (page 346), and it's greatly appreciated. The important thing is to have quite large flat slices of meat as you need to fold them over double.

To make the béchamel, melt the butter in a small saucepan over low heat. Whisk in the flour and cook for a few minutes, stirring constantly, then begin adding the warm milk. It will be immediately absorbed, so work quickly, whisking with one hand while adding ladlefuls of milk with the other. When the sauce seems to be smooth and not too stiff, add salt, pepper, and a grating of nutmeg. Continue cooking, even after it comes to a boil, for 5 minutes or so, mixing all the time. It should be a very thick and smooth sauce. Remove from the heat to cool a little.

Lay a slice of beef flat on a board. Lay a slice of cheese over one half of it and put a slice of ham on top of that. Add a dollop of béchamel and spread it gently to almost cover the ham, but leaving a border all around the edge. Fold the other half of the meat over the béchamel, pressing it down well to seal the edges.

Put the flour on a large plate and season with a twist or two of pepper, if you like. Break the egg into a flat bowl and whisk with a little salt, and put the bread crumbs on a large plate. Pat the meat parcels gently in the flour, coating both sides, and then dip in the egg, turning them to coat well. Now pat them in the bread crumbs so that they are well covered.

Heat the butter and oil in a nonstick frying pan over medium-high heat until sizzling. Add the parcels and fry until they start to become firm and are deep golden on the underside. Adjust the heat so they don't burn. Turn over carefully, taking care not to pierce them, and cook the other side. Don't worry if some of the filling starts to ooze out. Lift out onto a plate lined with paper towels to soak up the excess oil. Serve warm with a small sprinkling of salt, if necessary.

Serves 4

1 CHICKEN, CUT INTO 10 PIECES, WITH SKIN
2 CLOVES GARLIC, PEELED BUT LEFT WHOLE
2 ROSEMARY STALKS
2 TEASPOONS SALT
1 1/3 CUPS BUTTERMILK
ABOUT 1 CUP ALL-PURPOSE FLOUR
2 TEASPOONS SWEET PAPRIKA
FRESHLY GROUND BLACK PEPPER
  (OPTIONAL)
LIGHT OLIVE OIL, FOR FRYING
LEMON WEDGES, TO SERVE

Fried buttermilk-marinated chicken

My friend Anabelle told me about this—that the buttermilk makes the chicken really soft and this is the way a lot of proper fried chicken is cooked in the Deep South. You will need to marinate the chicken for 12 to 24 hours (the longer, the better). This dish has a very honest and simple flavor at the end so you might like to add some extras—adults might appreciate some chile and extra herbs mixed into the paprika flour. You can also do this with skinless chicken breasts—just flatten them out a bit, fry them in the same way and serve them in hamburger buns with lettuce and mayonnaise. Or you could cut the breast into strips, then you might like to make a dip with a bit of mustard, honey, some lemon, and salt if your family like to dip into sauces. I like to serve this with the potato and yogurt salad (page 271) and also the cabbage salad with oranges and lemons (page 89).

Put the chicken pieces in a large bowl. Add the garlic and rosemary, sprinkle with a teaspoon of fine salt and pour in the buttermilk. Turn the chicken over to coat well—it needs to be covered by the buttermilk. Cover with plastic wrap and put into the fridge for at least 12 hours, even for over 24 hours. Turn the chicken once or twice to distribute the flavors.

Pour into a colander to drain (you don't need to keep the buttermilk marinade). Put the flour on a plate and add the paprika and about 1 teaspoon of fine salt. Add pepper, if you like, and mix everything together.

Pour at least 2 inches of oil into a large frying pan over medium heat. Heat until the oil is hot. Pat the chicken in the flour to coat it on all sides, making sure that it is completely covered. Add the chicken to the hot oil and fry until it is crispy and golden. If the chicken seems to be browning too quickly, turn down the heat a little. It is important that the chicken is cooked right through to the bone—use tongs to turn the pieces over a couple of times until you are satisfied that they are deep golden and cooked through. Lift out onto a plate lined with paper towels to absorb the excess oil. Serve immediately, with a sprinkling of salt and some lemon wedges to squeeze over the top.

Serves 4

ABOUT 5 TABLESPOONS ALL-PURPOSE FLOUR
4 CHICKEN CUTLETS
1 1/2 TABLESPOONS OLIVE OIL
3 1/2 TABLESPOONS BUTTER
SALT
1 CLOVE GARLIC, PEELED AND SQUASHED A BIT
8 SAGE LEAVES
JUICE OF HALF A LEMON

Chicken cutlets with lemon and butter

Buy chicken cutlets from your butcher, or buy one chicken breast and thinly slice it horizontally into three or four cutlets. It is important not to overcook the chicken—you want to end up with a thin chicken breast with a little sauce to cover it. You will need to have all your ingredients organized before you start, and then this simple dish is ready to serve in a matter of minutes. You can serve them straight from the pan (once the cutlets have cooled a little). You might also like to throw some finely chopped fresh herbs into the pan at the last moment—parsley, basil, thyme, or mint—which will add a totally different flavor.

Put the flour on a plate and dust the chicken on both sides. Heat the oil with roughly a third of the butter in a large nonstick saucepan over medium-high heat. Add the chicken when the pan is sizzling and cook until the underside is lightly golden. Turn over and salt this side. Add the garlic, sage leaves, and another third of butter to the pan (this helps to prevent the rest of the butter burning). Cook until the underside of the chicken is golden, turn again, and sprinkle lightly with salt. If at any time the garlic or sage look like they are overbrowning, sit them on top of the chicken. Add the last of the butter and, when it all sizzles up, add the lemon juice. Let it bubble up for a minute and then serve immediately with a good spoonful of sauce over each serving and maybe some bread to wipe up the rest of the pan juices. If you can't serve it immediately, put a lid on the pan, then reheat with just a few drops of water to loosen the sauce.

Serves 4

APPLES FOR SAM

A SMALL BUNCH OF PARSLEY, STALKS
  AS WELL AS LEAVES
5 OR 6 POTATOES, PEELED
7 PEPPERCORNS
5 TABLESPOONS OLIVE OIL
SALT

Boiled potatoes with parsley

These are simple boiled potatoes cooked with parsley stems and dressed later with olive oil. You can use any other herbs you like to just take the edge off plain boiled potatoes. Furthermore, these are good at room temperature, so you can prepare them beforehand for an outdoor occasion. They are lovely with barbecued meats, fish dishes, and stews and casseroles.

Bring a large pan of salted water to a boil and add the parsley, potatoes, and peppercorns (remembering exactly how many you put in so you can take them all out again and no one has to bite into one). Boil for about 20 minutes, or until the potatoes are soft and a little crumbly but not totally collapsing. Lift out with a slotted spoon to a serving dish. You can leave behind all the parsley, if you prefer, but I like it when some leaves cling to the potatoes.
    Check that you've left all the peppercorns in the water. Pour the olive oil over the potatoes, toss gently, and taste for salt. Serve warm, but even at room temperature they're good.

Serves 6 to 8

Remember how many peppercorns you put in
a dish so that you can remember to take them
all out again before you serve.
You might do seven—one for every day of
the week; three—for the number of children
in your family; four—how many times you've
been to France . . .

4 TABLESPOONS OLIVE OIL
8 FRESH BAY LEAVES
25 JUNIPER BERRIES
1 CHICKEN, CUT INTO 10 PIECES, SKIN REMOVED
SALT AND FRESHLY GROUND BLACK PEPPER
3 TABLESPOONS HOT WATER
½ CUP WHITE WINE

Sautéed chicken with bay leaves and juniper berries

My friend Francesca, a great and creative cook, taught me this. The fresh bay leaves give a wonderful flavor and smell. With a simple pan of boiled potatoes with parsley (page 233) and green vegetables sautéed in olive oil and garlic, this is the kind of thing I would present to my family on a cool autumn night.

Put the oil, bay leaves, and juniper berries in a large nonstick frying pan or flameproof casserole. Put the chicken on the bay leaves, turn the heat to medium, and put the lid on the casserole. Cook until the underside of the chicken is lightly golden and the top is white. Turn over and salt and pepper the done side. Add 2 or 3 tablespoons of hot water if the chicken looks like it's sticking, then cover and cook until the juices have all evaporated. Turn again and salt and pepper lightly.
     Squash the juniper berries with a fork to release the flavor, but still keep them fairly intact. Pour in the wine and cook uncovered until the wine has evaporated and the chicken is deep golden on all sides. When there is very little liquid in the pan, and even the bay leaves seem covered by some crusty sauce, turn off the heat, cover, and leave to stand for 10 minutes or so before serving.

Serves 4

1 CHICKEN (ABOUT 3½ POUNDS)
SALT
4 CLOVES GARLIC, PEELED BUT LEFT WHOLE
ABOUT 10 THYME SPRIGS
3 BAY LEAVES (FRESH, IF POSSIBLE)
6 OR 7 POTATOES, PEELED AND CUT
   INTO CHUNKS
JUICE OF 2 LEMONS
4½ TABLESPOONS BUTTER, SOFTENED
1 CUP WATER, PLUS 4 TO 5 TABLESPOONS
4 TABLESPOONS HEAVY WHIPPING CREAM

Roast chicken and potatoes with thyme, lemon, and garlic

This is a lovely roast chicken . . . with just a dash of cream to bring everything and everyone together. You will need to use a roasting pan that can also be put on the stovetop to heat up the sauce. If you don't have anything suitable, you can transfer all the chicken juices to a small saucepan.

Preheat the oven to 400°F. Wipe the chicken with paper towels and put breast-side-down in a large roasting pan. Put a little salt, a garlic clove, 3 of the thyme sprigs, and 1 of the bay leaves in the cavity of the chicken. Place the potatoes and remaining garlic around and pour the lemon juice over the top. Rub the skin of the chicken with some of the butter and dot the rest over the potatoes. Bury the rest of the thyme sprigs under the potatoes, then sprinkle salt over the potatoes and the chicken. Pour 1 cup of water around the edge of the pan.

Roast for about 1 hour or until the chicken is nicely golden, then turn it over and shuffle the potatoes around. Spoon the pan juices over the top of the chicken and potatoes and sprinkle some salt over the new top of the chicken. Roast for about 30 minutes, shuffling the potatoes around again halfway through without breaking them up too much, or until the chicken is deep golden and crispy and its juices run clear. Transfer the chicken to a generous serving platter with a bit of a raised edge and arrange the potatoes around the chicken. Keep warm.

Put the roasting pan of cooking juices over medium heat on the stovetop. Using a wooden spoon, scrape up all the golden bits from the sides and bottom of the pan. If there isn't much liquid, add 4 to 5 tablespoons of water. Bring to a boil and cook until slightly thickened. Stir the cream through and let it all bubble up, whisking so it all comes together as one. Pour over the chicken on the platter and serve immediately.

Serves 4

1 SMALL CARROT, PEELED AND HALVED
A SMALL PIECE OF LEAFY CELERY STALK
1 SLICE OF LEMON, 1/2 INCH THICK
4 PEPPERCORNS
A HANDFUL OF PARSLEY STALKS
1 TEASPOON SALT
6-OUNCE SEABASS OR COD, OR OTHER FIRM WHITEFISH FILLET
4-OUNCE BONELESS SALMON FILLET
4-OUNCE BONELESS WHTEFISH FILLET
4 MEDIUM POTATOES, PEELED AND CHOPPED
1 1/2 TABLESPOONS OLIVE OIL
2 EGGS
1 TEASPOON SWEET PAPRIKA
4 TABLESPOONS CHOPPED FRESH PARSLEY
2 1/2 TABLESPOONS DICED SCALLIONS
FRESHLY GROUND BLACK PEPPER
LIGHT OLIVE OIL, FOR FRYING
ABOUT 1 CUP DRY BREAD CRUMBS
LEMON WEDGES, TO SERVE

Fish cakes

These are complete on their own with a squeeze of lemon juice and a side salad, but wonderful with fries and homemade mayonnaise (page 240). Small helpers might enjoy squishing the mixture into patties with their hands—my daughter loved this part and wasn't at all worried about the fish and potato flecks that were taking off out of the bowl.

Put a pan of water on to boil and add the carrot, celery, lemon, peppercorns, half the parsley stalks, and a teaspoon of salt. Simmer over medium-low heat for about 10 minutes, then add all the fish. Simmer for 10 to 15 minutes, until the fish is soft, but not collapsing, and flakes easily. Turn off the heat and leave the fish to cool in the broth. Drain and flake the fish into a bowl, removing any little bones.

Meanwhile, simmer the potatoes and the rest of the parsley stalks in salted water for 15 minutes or so, until the potatoes are soft. Drain and mash.

Heat a dash of the olive oil in a nonstick frying pan and sauté the scallions until soft and slightly golden. Mash the fish with a potato masher and then add the potatoes. Squish the mixture through your fingers, like playing with sand on a beach, and pick out any bones or skin that you might have previously missed.

Whip the eggs and remaining olive oil in a small bowl and then add to the fish mixture with the paprika, chopped parsley, and scallions. Mix through well, still with your hands. Add salt or pepper, if needed. Form the mixture into balls about the size of an egg, then flatten slightly into patties. Put the bread crumbs on a plate and pat the fish cakes into them, coating them all over. Put the fish cakes on a clean plate, cover with plastic wrap, and chill for an hour.

Heat about 1 inch of oil in a large nonstick frying pan. Fry the fish cakes in batches, turning them gently with a spatula until they are golden on both sides. Lift them out onto a plate lined with paper towels to absorb the excess oil.

Serve warm with lemon wedges and a little extra salt, if you like. Leftovers can be pressed into sandwiches with some shredded lettuce and mayonnaise.

Makes 12 to 15

4 MEDIUM POTATOES
LIGHT OLIVE OIL, FOR FRYING
SALT

Very thin fries

You can cut your potatoes in all sorts of different ways. I remember that
crinkle-cut ones made a good impression, but you need a special cutter. If
you have a mandoline cutter, cut thin fries on it—first one way and then
the other—to get gridded potato-crisp style chips, and then fry them.

Peel the potatoes and cut them into slices about 1/4 inch thick, keeping them long.
Cut these into 1/4-inch sticks. Rinse under cold water and dry thoroughly on
paper towels.

Pour about 2 inches of oil into a pan that is suitable for deep-frying. Place over
medium-high heat until the oil is hot. You might need to fry the potatoes in
batches, depending on the size of your pan. Just a minute or so after you have put
the fries in the oil, give them a stir with a wooden spoon to make sure none are
stuck at the bottom. Leave them for a minute or two to crisp up and then give
another stir. Let them fry until they are nice and crisp and then lift them out into
a bowl lined with paper towels to absorb the excess oil. Transfer them to a clean
bowl, scatter with salt, and serve at once.

Serves 4

---

1 1/4 CUPS SOYBEAN OR CORN OIL
1/2 CUP LIGHT OLIVE OIL
1 CLOVE GARLIC, PEELED AND SQUASHED A BIT
3 EGGS
1 TEASPOON DIJON MUSTARD
1 TABLESPOON BALSAMIC VINEGAR
JUICE OF 1 LEMON
1/2 TEASPOON SALT
FRESHLY GROUND BLACK PEPPER

Mayonnaise

This is beautiful with some freshly chopped herbs stirred through before
serving. The garlic here is just to flavor the oil, so you can remove it
before it slides into the mayonnaise. This is good with fish cakes, and also
with fries for dunking. It is rich, so just a dollop is best, depending on your
personal taste, though. For something like this that uses uncooked eggs,
make sure your eggs come from a very reliable, very natural source.

Put the oils in a bowl with the garlic clove and leave for 15 minutes or so to infuse. Remove the garlic clove and throw it away.

In a small processor or with a handheld blender, whiz the eggs until they become very thick. Add the mustard, vinegar, lemon juice, and 1/2 teaspoon of salt and whiz together. With the motor running, add the oil drop by drop, and continue mixing until all the oil has been added and the mixture is thick and fluffy. Taste for salt and pepper. Cover the bowl and keep in the fridge. This is nice after it has been chilled for a couple of hours and it keeps for a few days in the fridge if well covered.

Makes 2 cups

----

1 SMALL CAULIFLOWER, TRIMMED
4 TABLESPOONS OLIVE OIL
2 CLOVES GARLIC, PEELED AND SQUASHED A BIT
SALT

Sautéed cauliflower

A simple preparation like this softens the cauliflower but lets it keep its flavor and natural sweetness. Adults might appreciate some anchovies, chopped up and added to the pan while the cauliflower is sautéing, and some baby capers, too, with perhaps a splattering of chile oil. You could also add some pine nuts and freshly chopped parsley to the pan—or anything else you think your family might like.

Break off the cauliflower leaves and cut them into thick chunks. Break or cut off the florets and slice the stem into chunks. Bring a large saucepan of salted water to a boil and add all the cauliflower pieces. Simmer until tender and then drain well.

Put the olive oil, garlic cloves, and cauliflower in a large nonstick frying pan and sauté over medium heat until the pieces are golden. This will take longer than you would think. Turn the pieces over from time to time so that they color all over. Taste for salt and lower the heat. Continue sautéing until the pieces are crusty here and there and crunchy, but not falling apart. Serve warm with bread or to accompany a main course.

Serves 6

7 OR 8 SMALL POTATOES, PEELED AND HALVED
   (OR CUT INTO LARGE CHUNKS)
OLIVE OIL, FOR FRYING
1 TEASPOON SALT
1/2 TEASPOON DRIED OREGANO

Fried potato halves with oregano

It is best to use new potatoes that can be halved or even left whole if they are small enough. When fried in this manner, they become almost just a crisp shell and are great with the oregano.

Bring a large pan of salted water to a boil and add the potatoes. Boil for about 25 minutes, until they are quite soft but not falling apart. Lift them out with a slotted spoon and put them in a large bowl (the heat will steam the excess water away). Use a skewer to poke almost right through each piece in a couple of places so that they fry right through.

    In a wide pan, heat enough oil to completely submerge the potatoes. When it is hot, carefully add the potatoes, stirring to make sure they don't stick. Cook over fairly high heat at first, then lower it a little and continue cooking until the potatoes have become deep golden crusty shells.

    Lift out the potatoes with a slotted spoon onto a plate lined with paper towels to soak up the oil and then move them to a clean plate. Toss the salt and oregano together, crushing the oregano between your fingers as you mix. Sprinkle the mixture over the potatoes and serve immediately.

Serves 4

6 OR 7 POTATOES
OLIVE OIL
1 CLOVE GARLIC, PEELED AND SQUASHED A BIT
1 ROSEMARY SPRIG
1 SAGE SPRIG
SALT

Pan-fried potatoes with rosemary and sage

This is a nice and simple version of fries for kids. They are a little more elegant than ordinary fries, and you don't have to use much oil and have a smell of frying hanging around your house for a couple of days, which is sometimes a good option.

Peel the potatoes and cut them into fat slices, then into chunks of about 1 1/2 inches. If you do this in advance, remember to keep them in a bowl of cold water with a splash of milk so that they don't darken. Drain and dry them well with paper towels.

Heat enough oil in a large wide frying pan to generously cover the bottom. Add the potatoes in a single layer and fry them over medium heat, shuffling them after a while when they are golden, and shaking the pan to turn them around so that they cook evenly. You might need to adjust the heat so that they don't brown before cooking through. When they are lightly golden all over, add the garlic clove and rosemary and sage sprigs, making sure they are in the oil. Continue cooking and shuffling the potatoes until they are golden brown, sitting the herbs and garlic on top of the potatoes if they look like they're burning. Lift out the potatoes with a slotted spoon to a wide serving bowl, scatter with salt, and shake them around again so it distributes. Serve now!

Serves 4

1 LOAF WHITE BREAD, UNSLICED
5½ TABLESPOONS BUTTER, MELTED
⅓ CUP RUNNY HONEY
1 TABLESPOON LIGHT BROWN SUGAR
½ CUP CHOPPED PECANS

White loaf with honey, butter, and pecans

I use a homemade white loaf (page 263) to make this. If you prefer, you can use an unsliced bought one—white sourdough is good. My friend Sue taught me how to make this. I think it's fantastic—especially for a picnic.

Preheat the oven to 350°F and line a baking sheet with parchment paper. Remove the crusts from the bread and cut it in half horizontally to give two layers (if your loaf is extra high, you can make three layers). Put the pieces on the sheet.

Mix the butter, honey, sugar, and pecans to get a gooey mixture. Pour and spread over the tops of the two bread halves. Bake for about 30 minutes, until the bread is crusty and golden on top (don't burn it or the nuts will be bitter). Let it cool a little, then cut into thick fingers. It will crisp up and become crunchier.

Makes about 16 fingers

¼ CUP FIRMLY PACKED BROWN SUGAR
1½ TABLESPOONS BUTTER
1½ TABLESPOONS MAPLE SYRUP
4 OR 5 DROPS OF VANILLA EXTRACT
½ CUP HEAVY WHIPPING CREAM

Toffee sauce

This is good warm, drizzled over an ice cream sundae or a bowl of Greek-style yogurt with some chunks of apple. You can leave it to cool in the pan and warm it up just slightly to serve.

Put the sugar, butter, syrup, and vanilla in a small pan and cook over very low heat for a few minutes until it all turns a good, deep toffee color. Add the cream, drop by drop at first, mixing it in with a wooden spoon. Cook until the sauce is bubbling up and has a lovely color. Be careful not to burn yourself while you're tasting it.

Makes ½ cup

1/4 POUND PLUS 5 TABLESPOONS BUTTER,
   SOFTENED
2/3 CUP SUPERFINE SUGAR, PLUS
   2 TABLESPOONS FOR THE TOP
1 TEASPOON VANILLA EXTRACT
1 TEASPOON FINELY GRATED LEMON RIND
A GOOD PINCH OF GROUND CARDAMOM
A LARGE PINCH OF NUTMEG
3 EGGS
1 3/4 CUPS ALL-PURPOSE FLOUR
1 1/2 TEASPOONS BAKING POWDER
1/2 CUP HALF-AND-HALF
4 SMALL RIPE PEARS

Pear butter cake

This is rich and delicious, and you can use just about any fruit you like. Serve it in a bowl with a bit of warm custard or a dollop of thick cream —or the way I like it, which is completely on its own. You can use buttermilk instead of the half-and-half or just milk. Omit the spices if you like something plainer, or add a little more if you prefer your cake spicier.

Preheat the oven to 350°F and grease a 9 1/2-inch springform cake pan.

Beat the butter and sugar together until creamy. Add the vanilla, lemon rind, cardamom, and nutmeg, and then add the eggs one by one, beating well after each one. Add the sifted flour and baking powder alternately with the half-and-half, and mix until you have a smooth batter.

Scrape out every drop into the cake pan. You don't need to be particular about leveling the surface because it will spread evenly during the baking. Bake for about 20 minutes.

Meanwhile, peel, quarter, and core the pears. Take the cake from the oven and quickly scatter the pears over the top. Sprinkle with the 2 tablespoons of sugar. Return to the oven and bake for another 45 minutes or so more, until the pears are lovely and golden in places, the cake is crusty, and a skewer poked into the middle comes out clean.

Cool slightly before cutting and serving warm or at room temperature. Keep the cake covered tightly with aluminum foil so that it doesn't harden and you can then warm it through to serve.

Serves 10 to 12

CARAMEL:
1/2 CUP SUPERFINE SUGAR
2 TO 3 TABLESPOONS WATER

2 3/4 CUPS MILK
1 CINNAMON STICK
3/4 CUP FINE SEMOLINA
1/4 CUP SUPERFINE SUGAR
1/2 TEASPOON VANILLA EXTRACT
1 EGG

Semolina puddings with caramel

Make these in little individual pudding molds—they look like tiny creme caramels. If you are up in time, they make a wonderful breakfast.

Preheat the oven to 325°F and butter six 1/2-cup ovenproof molds.

For the caramel, put the sugar and 2 to 3 teaspoons of water in a nonstick heavy-bottomed pan over medium heat. Heat it up until the sugar starts to melt, then tilt the pan to swirl it around—don't stir or the sugar will crystallize. Carry on heating and swirling a few times until all the sugar has melted and turned golden caramel brown. Pour about 1 1/2 tablespoons into the bottom of each mold, swirling the mold at the same time so that the caramel covers the bottom evenly.

Put the milk and cinnamon stick in a large heavy bottomed saucepan over medium heat. Just before it comes to a boil, whisk in the semolina in a thin steady stream so that no lumps form. Lower the heat and simmer, whisking all the time, for around 8 minutes, or until the milk has absorbed all the semolina. Stir in the sugar and vanilla, and remove from the heat. Sit the saucepan in a sink of cold water for 15 minutes to cool it down a little.

Whip the egg lightly in a bowl and then whisk it into the semolina. Spoon over the caramel in the molds, smoothing the top with the back of your spoon. Put all the molds in a roasting pan and pour enough hot water into the pan to come halfway up the side of the molds. Carefully move the pan to the oven and bake for about 45 minutes, until the puddings look set, golden, and slightly puffed up. Take the molds out of the pan and leave them to cool a little.

Upturn the molds and turn the puddings out onto individual plates. If you sit the bottoms of the empty molds in boiling water for a few minutes you'll be able to get more caramel out of them. The puddings are best served warm, with as much caramel as possible drizzled over them.

Serves 6

1 ½ TABLESPOONS SUPERFINE SUGAR
1 EGG
A FEW DROPS OF VANILLA EXTRACT
1 ½ TABLESPOONS BUTTER, MELTED
1 CUP ALL-PURPOSE FLOUR
1 TEASPOON BAKING POWDER
½ CUP MILK
BUTTER, FOR FRYING

Pancakes

These are good and quick for breakfast or an afternoon snack. I remember them fondly from when I was young. This small amount is just sufficient, I find, for my family, as they need to be served immediately. It's easy enough to double the quantities if you're serving a crowd, just make sure everyone is waiting at their plate to drizzle their pancake with honey or spread with jam and cream. Actually, I remember pancakes as ESPECIALLY good with a little drizzle of honey or syrup and a small dollop of vanilla ice cream.

Whisk together the sugar, egg, and vanilla until foamy. Whisk in the melted butter and then add the flour and baking powder. Pour in the milk, whisking it all together to make a smooth, thick batter.

Melt a little butter in a nonstick frying pan—just enough to coat the bottom. When it is sizzling, drop in tablespoons of batter, allowing enough room between them so that you can turn them over easily. Fry over medium heat until air bubbles appear on the surface and the bottoms are golden and set. Flip them over with a spatula and fry the other side. When the new undersides are golden brown, lift them onto a plate with your spatula and cook the rest of the batter, adding more butter to the pan as it is needed. Make sure that the pan keeps a steady heat and doesn't get too hot. Serve immediately.

Makes 20

2 EGGS, SEPARATED
1/3 CUP SUPERFINE SUGAR
1/2 TEASPOON VANILLA EXTRACT
4 1/2 TABLESPOONS BUTTER, MELTED
1 1/2 CUPS ALL-PURPOSE FLOUR
1/2 TEASPOON BAKING POWDER
3/4 CUP MILK

Waffles

Ideally, you need a waffle iron to make these. If you are lucky enough to have one—great. If not, you can make them in a frying pan as below, or you could even just fry little spoonfuls, flick your wrist a bit here and there and serve up crisp little make-believe waffles. And if you're really pushed for time, you can just mix all the ingredients together without even whisking the egg whites, although your waffles won't be quite so light and cloud-like. I like to serve these with cranberry syrup (page 15), filling up all the holes of the waffles. Otherwise, butter and jam, or honey, maple syrup, and a blob of whipped cream, or chocolate sauce are all fantastic . . . you decide.

Whisk the egg whites until they are fluffy and just holding soft peaks. In a larger bowl, whisk the egg yolks with the sugar and vanilla until creamy. Whisk in the butter, then the flour and baking powder. Add the milk, then fold in the egg whites.

Heat a waffle iron or a nonstick frying pan and brush with a little butter. If you're using a waffle iron, add about 5 tablespoons of batter into each space and close the machine. Cook, following the manufacturer's instructions, until the waffles are golden brown.

If you're using a frying pan, ladle about 5 tablespoons of mixture into the middle of the pan. Cook over medium heat until the underside is golden and the top has formed air holes. Flip over and cook the other side. When the waffle is deep golden and crispy in places, lift it out onto a plate and keep warm while you make the rest. Serve hot.

Makes 10 to 12

2 EGGS
1/2 TEASPOON VANILLA EXTRACT
1 1/2 TABLESPOONS SUPERFINE SUGAR
1 SCANT CUP ALL-PURPOSE FLOUR
1 TEASPOON BAKING POWDER
1 CUP MILK
BUTTER, FOR FRYING

TO SERVE:
FRESHLY WHIPPED CREAM
SUPERFINE SUGAR
LEMON WEDGES
MAPLE SYRUP
GROUND CINNAMON

Sweet crepes

I use a small nonstick frying pan about 8 inches in diameter for these. The batter makes about 10 to 12 crepes, which are not huge, and if your frying pan is bigger, you'll get fewer. This makes just enough for our family of four (allowing for one or two leftovers), with two each being just about perfect for the children. We often have our first one with lemon juice and a scattering of cinnamon sugar and our second with maple syrup and whipped cream. If we make it to the third one, then that's nice with a dollop of homemade jam. Often, if I make the pancakes for dinner, I put a little leftover batter in the fridge for the next morning, when I make a couple for the kids with jam. If the batter looks a bit thick after a night in the fridge, just thin it down with a little milk. A pinch or two of ground aniseed in the batter is a nice addition that even children seem to like.

Whip together the eggs, vanilla, and sugar. Add the flour and baking powder alternately with the milk, whisking well until it's smooth. Cover and leave to stand at room temperature for at least half an hour.

Melt a little butter in a nonstick frying pan—just enough to coat the bottom. When it's sizzling, add a small ladleful of batter. Tilt the pan so that the batter swirls out and around to thinly cover the bottom, mingling with some of the butter. Fry over medium heat until the underside is nicely golden, using a spatula to lift up the edge to check. Loosen the side with the spatula and flip the crepe over. Fry until the new underside is lightly golden, then slide out of the pan onto a plate and keep warm while you cook the rest of the batter, adding more butter when you need it. The first crepe is often not so great, but once you've got the hang of it and have got the pan temperature perfect, they'll work well.

Put out bowls of whipped cream, superfine sugar, lemon wedges, maple syrup, and enough cinnamon for everyone to help themselves to their own favorite topping. Make cinnamon sugar by mixing 1 tablespoon of sugar with 1 teaspoon of cinnamon, and that's lovely with a squeeze of lemon juice over the top.

Makes 12 crepes

white

Granola
Leek and potato soup
Semolina soup with butter and sage
White milk bread or rolls
Thin pizza with stracchino cheese
Ricotta gnocchi
Tomato pesto
White risotto in spinach broth
Pasta with cheese
Potato and yogurt salad
Baked fish parcels
Vanilla cake
Honey cake
Vanilla yogurt ice cream
Lemon rice pudding with roasted peaches
Baked cinnamon apples with buttermilk
  ice cream

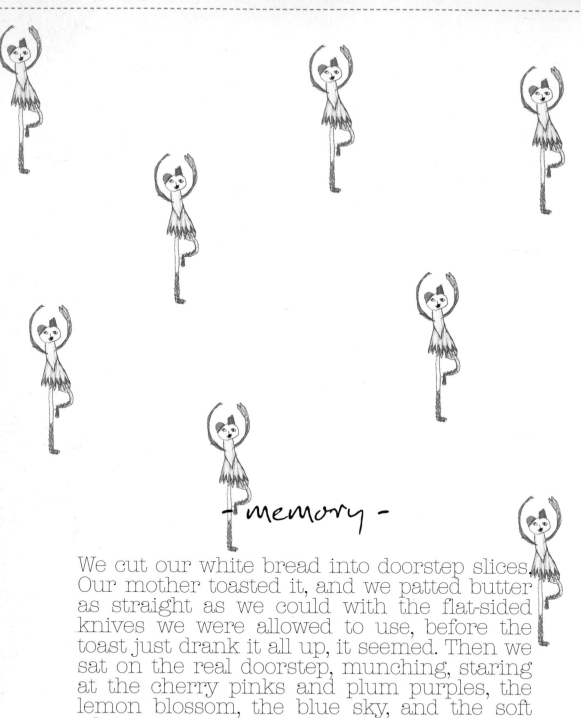

- memory -

We cut our white bread into doorstep slices, Our mother toasted it, and we patted butter as straight as we could with the flat-sided knives we were allowed to use, before the toast just drank it all up, it seemed. Then we sat on the real doorstep, munching, staring at the cherry pinks and plum purples, the lemon blossom, the blue sky, and the soft whipped cream white of the clouds.

1 CUP QUICK-COOKING OATS
5 TABLESPOONS SUNFLOWER SEEDS
3 TABLESPOONS SESAME SEEDS
1/2 CUP CHOPPED WALNUTS
1/2 TEASPOON GROUND CINNAMON OR ALLSPICE
1/3 CUP FIRMLY PACKED LIGHT BROWN SUGAR
1/2 CUP RUNNY HONEY
3 TABLESPOONS BUTTER

Granola

This is a healthy breakfast topped with some thick plain yogurt and fresh sliced fruit, and is always good splashed with cold milk. It is great to have at home and even serves as an emergency snack. You can use any nuts in place of the walnuts here, and add other ingredients or vary these to your liking. You can make more than the amounts given here and keep it in an airtight container or glass jar—but remember before baking it that it needs to be spread out in a flat, fairly thin layer in your pans.

Preheat the oven to 325°F and grease two large baking pans. Put the oats, sunflower seeds, sesame seeds, walnuts, and cinnamon in a bowl. Put the sugar, honey, and butter in a pan, and heat, stirring, until the butter has melted. Pour over the oat mixture in the bowl and mix well. (I like to do this with my hands and then get the children to take over, but you can mash it around with a wooden spoon, if you like, until it feels like wet sticky sand.)

Put half the mixture in each baking pan, spreading it out and then pressing it into a thin layer. Put both pans in the oven and bake for about 20 minutes. Turn the mixture over with a spoon and return the pans to the oven, the bottom one now on the top. Bake for another 15 to 20 minutes, or just until the granola is deep golden, turning it again during this time to give it an even color and break it up slightly (although it's nice if a few clustery bits remain). Take care not to overcook it, as just a bit past perfect can make it taste bitter. Turn off the oven and leave it in for another 10 minutes or so, then get it out of the oven, and leave it to cool completely in the pans. Once cool, this keeps very well in a cookie jar or something else airtight.

Makes 4 cups

6 LEEKS
3 TABLESPOONS BUTTER
2 CLOVES GARLIC, PEELED BUT LEFT WHOLE
2 TEASPOONS BRANDY
4 MEDIUM POTATOES, PEELED AND CUT
   INTO CHUNKS
SALT
6 CUPS HOT WATER
FRESHLY GRATED NUTMEG
½ CUP HEAVY WHIPPING CREAM
GRATED PARMESAN, TO SERVE

Leek and potato soup

This lovely warm soup is a simple classic combination, but one might not imagine that children could eat leeks so readily. You can add depth here by using chicken stock instead of water, or adding a few basic vegetables to the pan, but I like the purity of this recipe. Follow with a sautéed chicken breast with a couple of drops of white wine, or a simple fish fillet in herbs.

Trim the leeks and cut off the harder ends. Slice the leeks quite finely—you'll need about 4 cups—and put them in the sink with cold water. Swish them around with your hands to get rid of any dirt. Scoop them up into a colander to drain and wash them again if they are still sandy.

Melt the butter in a fairly large pan. Add the leeks and garlic, and sauté over medium-low heat until all the water has evaporated and the leeks are soft and faintly golden. Add the brandy and carry on cooking until it has evaporated. Add the potatoes and season well with salt. Add 6 cups of hot water and bring to a boil. Turn down the heat slightly, cover with a lid, and simmer for about 45 minutes, or until the leeks and potatoes are very soft. Grate in a little nutmeg. Purée the soup until it is totally smooth. If it is too thick for your taste, add a little hot water. If it seems too thin, return it to the pan and cook uncovered until it has thickened a bit. Taste for seasoning and add salt if necessary. Add the cream, heat through, and serve with a good tablespoon of Parmesan sprinkled over each serve.

Adults should grind pepper over theirs and, ideally, top with a few very fine slices of truffle!

Serves 6

5 CUPS MEAT, CHICKEN, OR VEGETABLE
  BROTH
1¼ CUPS FINE SEMOLINA
7 TABLESPOONS BUTTER
6 OR 7 SAGE LEAVES
3 TABLESPOONS GRATED PARMESAN CHEESE,
  PLUS MORE, TO SERVE
SALT

Semolina soup with butter and sage

This is a great emergency meal—ready in a few moments. If you use broth (meat, vegetable, or chicken), you will have a more profound tasting bowl of semolina, but if you don't have any at hand, you can use a bouillon cube, as I sometimes do, from a health food shop, with no additives. Like this, it is simple, quite delicious, and just easy to eat. The semolina can be made to any consistency you like: thicker or thinner and more soupy than this version. This is a simple Italian standard that I have seen served to children, elderly folk, and even invalids—whenever easy eating is required —and just with lashings of olive oil and Parmesan instead of the golden butter and sage. The pan will clean easily if you fill it with hot soapy water and leave it to soak for a while.

Put the broth in a large saucepan and bring to a boil (if you are using water, add 1½ teaspoons of salt). Pour in the semolina in a thin and steady stream, mixing with a wooden spoon and continuing to stir while it thickens. Lower the heat slightly so that it doesn't splutter up, and then cook for a few minutes, stirring all the time.

Take half the butter and melt a little knob of it in a small frying pan and then fry the sage leaves over medium heat until they crisp up. As the butter starts to turn golden, keep adding more, bit by bit, to slow down the cooking and burning process. Remove from the heat when the leaves are crisp and you have used up half of the butter. Keep the pan to one side.

Keep stirring the semolina so that there are no lumps and nothing gets stuck. Simmer gently for about 10 minutes, until there are air bubbles glooping on the surface. Stir in the 3 tablespoons of Parmesan and the other half of the butter. If it is too thick for your taste, stir in hot water as needed. Taste for salt.

Ladle into bowls, drizzle a little sage butter into each and add a sage leaf or two and another scattering of grated Parmesan. Adults can add a good grind of pepper. Eat immediately.

Serves 4

1 CUP WARM (COMFORTABLE TO YOUR
  FINGERS) MILK
1 (1/2-OUNCE) CAKE FRESH YEAST, CRUMBLED,
  OR 1 (1/4-OUNCE) PACKAGE ACTIVE DRY
  YEAST
1 TEASPOON HONEY
3 2/3 CUPS BREAD FLOUR
1/2 TEASPOON SALT
1 EGG, LIGHTLY BEATEN
3 TABLESPOONS BUTTER, MELTED

White milk bread or rolls

You can make this as one loaf or shape into smaller rolls. Children love small soft white rolls, it seems. Naturally, you can make different sizes or a different shape—long is nice for hot dogs. You can easily make a batch and freeze them in small bags, a few together, to whip out at almost the last moment of need. My kids like these with butter spread so thickly that they can see their teeth marks.

Put the milk, yeast, and honey in a small bowl, and stir until the honey melts. Leave it for about 10 minutes, or until it begins to froth a bit. Put the flour and 1/2 teaspoon of salt into a larger bowl. Add the yeast mixture, the egg, and butter, and mix through well. Knead for 10 minutes or so and, if it seems sticky, just hold the bowl firmly and move the dough around with your hand, rather than add more flour. Cover the bowl with a cloth and leave in a warm, draft-free place to rise for 1 1/2 to 2 hours, or until it has puffed up well.

   Lightly grease a 12 by 4-inch loaf pan and dust it with flour. Punch down the dough to flatten it and shape it into a rough loaf of a size to fit the pan. Cover with a cloth and leave in the warm place for another 45 to 60 minutes, or until it puffs right up in the pan. Meanwhile, preheat the oven to 375°F.

   Put the pan in the oven and bake for about 25 minutes, or until the top is firm and crusty and the loaf sounds hollow when tapped. Remove from the oven, knock the loaf out of the pan, and cool on a rack in a fly-free zone.

   This is best sliced warm and spread with butter, but you can keep the loaf for a few days in an airtight container (not a plastic bag) for excellent toast.

Makes 1 loaf or about 18 small rolls

DOUGH:
¾ CUP WARM (COMFORTABLE TO YOUR
   FINGERS) WATER
1 (½-OUNCE) CAKE FRESH YEAST, CRUMBLED, OR
   1 (¼-OUNCE) PACKAGE ACTIVE DRY YEAST
½ TEASPOON HONEY
2 TEASPOONS OLIVE OIL
2½ CUPS BREAD FLOUR
½ TEASPOON SALT

TOPPING:
9 OUNCES FRESH STRACCHINO, TALEGGIO,
   OR BEL PAESE CHEESE
⅔ CUP MILK
1½ TABLESPOONS OLIVE OIL

Thin pizza with stracchino cheese

My friend Julia showed me this. This amount of dough will make you two pizza crusts—you can freeze the unused half of dough once it has been punched down. Stracchino is a sour creamy cheese.

For the dough, put the water, yeast, honey, and oil in a large bowl with a fistful of the flour. Mix with an electric beater until smooth. Cover and leave for 30 minutes or so until it all froths up and looks foamy on the top. Add the rest of the flour and ½ teaspoon of salt. Mix well with your hands—it will be very soft, but try to work it without adding more flour. If it's too soft to knead, just slap it around in the bowl for a few minutes until it starts to feel elastic. Cover the bowl with a couple of cloths and leave it in a warm and draft-free place for about 1½ hours, or until the dough has puffed up well.

Preheat the oven to 450°F. Lightly brush a 12-inch round, square, or rectangular baking pan with olive oil. Punch down the dough to flatten it and divide it in half to make two crusts, or freeze half.

Spread the dough out gently in the pan to give a thin, even crust. If it won't stretch easily, leave it to relax for 5 minutes, and then gently stretch it out with the palms of your hands, starting from the center.

For the topping, put the cheese, milk, and oil in a blender or processor and pulse until smooth. Gently spread over the top of the dough, almost to the edge but leaving a small border. Turn this border in and over the cheese topping. Bake for 20 to 25 minutes, until the top is quite deep golden in various places. Remove and cool for a few minutes before cutting into squares. Eat warm.

Serves 8 to 10

2 CUPS GOOD-QUALITY RICOTTA CHEESE
3 TABLESPOONS GRATED PARMESAN CHEESE
1 SCANT CUP ALL-PURPOSE FLOUR
SALT
TOMATO PESTO (BELOW), TO SERVE
BUTTER, TO SERVE
GRATED PARMESAN CHEESE, TO SERVE

Ricotta gnocchi

I learned these from Giacomo, one of my brothers-in-law. They are palest white, cloud-soft, and delicate, and need to be served the minute they are cooked. We normally have these with the tomato pesto, below, but they are also great with just butter, sage, and Parmesan.

If you are serving these with tomato pesto, make sure it is ready before you cook the gnocchi.

Bring a large pan of salted water to a boil. Mix together the ricotta, Parmesan, flour, and a pinch of salt in a large bowl. With lightly floured hands, roll out the dough into thin sausages (about 5/8 inch thick). Try to avoid adding extra flour or your gnocchi will be tough. Cut with a sharp knife into little dumplings about 3/4 inch long.

Drop the gnocchi into the boiling water and cook for about 45 seconds, until they float to the surface. As they bob up, lift them out with a slotted spoon and put them into warmed serving bowls. If you need to, stir a couple of tablespoons of the cooking water through the pesto to give a good coating consistency, and spoon a dollop over each serve. Add a little butter and grated Parmesan and serve at once.

Serves 4

1/3 CUP OLIVE OIL
2 CLOVES GARLIC, PEELED
1 (14-OUNCE) CAN DICED TOMATOES
SALT
1/2 CUP BASIL LEAVES, TORN
4 TABLESPOONS PINE NUTS
1/3 CUP GRATED PARMESAN CHEESE

Tomato pesto

Heat 3 tablespoons of the olive oil in a saucepan with one of the garlic cloves. When it sizzles, add the tomato and season with salt. Simmer over medium heat for about 15 minutes, until the tomato thickens and becomes smooth, crushing it up with a wooden spoon from time to time.

Finely chop the other garlic clove and put it in a small processor or blender with the basil leaves and pine nuts. Pulse until finely chopped. Add the remaining olive oil and the Parmesan, and pulse just long enough to combine. Stir into the tomato sauce and heat for about 20 to 30 seconds. Remove the whole garlic clove before serving.

Note: if you are making the tomato pesto in advance, keep the pesto separate and add to the heated tomato sauce just before serving.

Serves 4

----

4 CUPS SPINACH COOKING WATER
4 TABLESPOONS OLIVE OIL
1 SMALL RED ONION, PEELED BUT LEFT WHOLE
1 1/3 CUPS RISOTTO RICE
SALT
1/2 CUP GRATED PARMESAN CHEESE
2 TABLESPOONS BUTTER
A LITTLE FRESHLY GRATED NUTMEG
GRATED PARMESAN CHEESE, TO SERVE
FRESHLY GROUND BLACK PEPPER, TO SERVE

White risotto in spinach broth

Just a suggestion for what to do with your spinach cooking water. My children's favorite food is white rice or pasta with parmesan and olive oil or butter. Boiling the pasta with a spinach or other vegetable broth, I feel, makes it more tasty and healthy. So next time you boil broccoli or spinach, save the cooking water. I often boil the spinach quickly to fill an omelette as a second course, then cook rice in the water for a first-course risotto.

Put the spinach broth in a large pan and bring to a boil, then reduce the heat to keep it at a slow simmer. Heat the oil in another large saucepan. Add the onion and rice, and cook over medium-high heat for about 30 seconds, stirring to coat the rice with oil. Reduce the heat to low and stir in a ladleful of hot broth. Season with salt (depending on whether your broth is already seasoned) and, when the broth has been absorbed, stir in another ladleful.

Continue in this way for about 20 minutes, until the broth has been used up and the rice is soft but still a little bit firm in the center. If you run out of spinach broth before the rice is tender just carry on with boiling water. This risotto is best when it's left a little liquidy, like a thick soup. Check for salt, remove the onion, and stir in the Parmesan, butter, and nutmeg. When the butter has melted, ladle the risotto into serving bowls and serve immediately with extra Parmesan and black pepper for whoever wants it.

Serves 4

3³/4 CUPS PASTA (I LIKE PENNE OR RIGATONI)
1²/3 CUPS SMOOTH SHEEPS' MILK RICOTTA
ABOUT ²/3 CUP MILK
³/4 CUP GRATED PARMESAN OR PECORINO
    CHEESE
FRESHLY GRATED NUTMEG
¹/2 TEASPOON SALT
GRATED PARMESAN CHEESE, TO SERVE
FRESHLY GROUND BLACK PEPPER, TO SERVE

Pasta with cheese

My kids just love anything that looks quite white and simple, so this is a very basic recipe that you can build on, even adding some cooked peas or zucchini. You can add any cheese you like to the basic ricotta mixture: mascarpone, mozzarella, pecorino, Parmesan . . . Adults might like some gorgonzola or similar added to theirs. My friend Caterina used a mature pecorino, which was stunning.

Bring a large pan of salted water to a boil and cook the pasta, following the instructions on the package.

Put the ricotta in a large serving bowl, add the milk, and whisk the two together with a fork. Add the Parmesan or pecorino, a good grind of nutmeg, and about ¹/2 teaspoon of salt, tasting to see if it needs more. Whisk well.

Drain the pasta, saving a few tablespoons of the water, and put with the ricotta mixture in the serving bowl. Toss through well, adding a little of the cooking water if it seems very dry. Serve immediately, with some extra Parmesan and a few twists of black pepper for the adults.

Serves 4

4 OR 5 MEDIUM POTATOES
2 CUPS PLAIN YOGURT
½ TEASPOON GROUND CUMIN
½ TEASPOON DRIED MINT
SALT AND FRESHLY GROUND BLACK
  PEPPER
½ RED OR YELLOW BELL PEPPER,
  CHOPPED
1 SMALL SHALLOT, FINELY CHOPPED

Potato and yogurt salad

I love this with schnitzelly things, but it's also good for barbecues and picnics. This is the kind of salad I ate so many times when I was young, only with mayonnaise. I make it often with yogurt now, as it's lighter. You can add anything else that you feel may be appreciated—some boiled carrots or peas, green beans, parsley, or chopped boiled egg.

Bring a pan of salted water to a boil and cook the potatoes until they are tender. Drain, leave them to cool a bit, and then peel. When they have completely cooled, cut them into small blocks.

Mix the yogurt, cumin, and mint in a large serving bowl and season to taste with salt and pepper. Add the potatoes, pepper, and shallot, and mix through well, taking care not to mash up the potatoes.

Serves 6

The girl across the road from us had a TV when they had just come out. We sat on the open porch with the TV moved out almost into the garden, eating a boiled potato salad that had many—too many, now that I think about it—spoonfuls of mayonnaise. We sat there for ages watching everything and anything in black and white.

WHITE

ABOUT ½ CUP DRY BREAD CRUMBS
4 THICK FIRM WHITEFISH FILLETS (ABOUT
  4 OUNCES EACH), BONES REMOVED
SALT
4 THICK SLICES OF LEMON, RIND REMOVED
½ CUP OLIVE OIL
2 LARGE CLOVES GARLIC, PEELED AND HALVED
8 SMALL THYME SPRIGS
5 TABLESPOONS RED WINE

Baked
fish parcels

This is really an example rather than a recipe, because once you have
made these a couple of times, you'll find it easy to go off and add your own
choice of the herbs and spices that you know will be loved in your own
household. I like this with plain boiled potatoes with parsley (page 233).
Try it with salmon instead of whitefish.

Preheat the oven to 400°F. Cut four pieces of aluminum foil or parchment paper,
quite a bit larger than your fish fillets. Put the bread crumbs on a plate and pat the
fish in them to coat both sides. Sprinkle the fish lightly with salt and put each fillet
on a separate piece of foil. Put a lemon slice on top, drizzle with a tablespoon of oil,
and put a garlic clove half and 2 thyme sprigs on each.
    Close up the parcels so that you will be able to open them easily: Hold the top
sides of the foil up and then fold or roll them down. Fold in the ends to seal them.
Drizzle the rest of the oil over the bottom of your oven dish. Put the fish parcels in
the dish and bake for about 20 minutes. You should be able to smell the cooked
fish, but I usually gently open one parcel with a fork and spoon, just to check that
it is cooked, and then seal it up again. Wait for 3 to 4 minutes (so that the oil
doesn't spit), then drizzle the wine into the dish and put it back into the oven.
When you start to hear activity from the oil, in about 3 or 4 minutes, remove the
dish from the oven again. The wine will have reduced to almost nothing, but adds a
lovely perfume to the fish. Serve the parcels immediately, unopened, helping
children to open their packages and not get too close to the steam.

Serves 4

½ POUND PLUS 2 TABLESPOONS (2¼ STICKS)
    BUTTER, SOFTENED
1 CUP PLUS 1 TABLESPOON SUPERFINE SUGAR
3 EGGS
1 TEASPOON VANILLA EXTRACT
2¼ CUPS ALL-PURPOSE FLOUR
1½ TEASPOONS BAKING POWDER
¾ CUP HALF-AND-HALF, OR MILK

FROSTING:
7 TABLESPOONS BUTTER, SOFTENED
1⅔ CUPS CONFECTIONERS' SUGAR
1 TEASPOON VANILLA EXTRACT
ABOUT 4 TABLESPOONS MILK

Vanilla cake

I love this soft cake. Here it is plain with a beautiful white frosting, but on occasion you could slice it in half through its equator and fill it with some whipped cream and a layer of not-too-sweet jam. The kids appreciate it when I stick candy all over the frosting. Or you could make a chocolate frosting and stick raspberries into that.

Preheat the oven to 350°F and grease a 9½-inch springform cake pan.
    Beat the butter and sugar together very well in a large bowl. Add the eggs one at a time, beating well after each one goes in. Add the vanilla and then sift in the flour and baking powder. Beat well, adding the half-and-half or milk a little at a time. You will have a thick and creamy batter. Scrape it out into the cake pan and bake for about 45 minutes, or until a skewer poked into the center comes out clean. Leave to cool completely before filling and frosting.
    For the frosting, put the butter into a bowl and gradually beat in the confectioners' sugar. Add the vanilla and 3 tablespoons of milk and beat well, then slowly beat in the rest of the milk, stopping when you have a smooth but fairly stiff frosting. Gently spread it all over the cake—it doesn't have to be perfect.

Cuts into 10 to 12 slices

1/4 POUND PLUS 3 TABLESPOONS BUTTER
1/2 CUP DARK BROWN SUGAR
1/3 CUP HONEY
1 1/2 TABLESPOONS WATER
1 2/3 CUPS ALL-PURPOSE FLOUR
1 1/2 TEASPOONS BAKING POWDER
1/2 TEASPOON GROUND CINNAMON
1 TABLESPOON FINELY CHOPPED ROSEMARY LEAVES
2 EGGS, BEATEN

LEMON FROSTING:
2 CUPS CONFECTIONERS' SUGAR
7 TABLESPOONS BUTTER, SOFTENED
1 TEASPOON GRATED LEMON ZEST
1 1/2 TABLESPOONS WATER
3 TABLESPOONS FRESHLY SQUEEZED LEMON JUICE

Honey cake

I love the idea of children having honey cakes—like Winnie the Pooh. I hope you are lucky enough to have tiny purple flowers on your rosemary when you make this, so you can scatter them over the finished cake.

Grease and line the bottom of an 8 1/2-inch springform pan. Put the butter, brown sugar, and honey in a small saucepan and add 1 1/2 tablespoons of water. Heat gently, stirring once or twice, until the butter melts and the sugar dissolves. Leave to cool for 15 minutes. Preheat the oven to 350°F.

Sift the flour, baking powder, and cinnamon into a bowl and add the rosemary. Add the honey mixture and eggs and beat until smooth.

Pour into the pan and bake for 35 to 40 minutes, or until a skewer comes out clean when you poke it into the center. Leave in the pan to cool completely.

To make the lemon frosting, sift the confectioners' sugar into a bowl. Add the butter, lemon zest and juice, and 1 1/2 tablespoons of water, and beat until smooth. You might like to add a few more drops of lemon juice after tasting it. Spread over the top and sides of the cake. The cake softens as it sits and will keep well for up to a week in a covered container.

Cuts into 8 to 10 slices

1 CUP HEAVY WHIPPING CREAM
1 SCANT CUP SUPERFINE SUGAR
1 TEASPOON VANILLA EXTRACT
2 CUPS GREEK-STYLE PLAIN YOGURT

Vanilla yogurt
ice cream

This is lovely—not too sweet—as it just really tastes like frozen yogurt. It's beautiful served with poached fruit or with a fresh fruit sauce, like apricot or raspberry (pages 107 and 54), dribbled over the top. You could even add a couple of cookies to the side of the plate, or sprinkle a fistful of granola over the top.

Whisk the cream with the sugar and vanilla until all the sugar has dissolved and the cream starts to thicken. Add the yogurt, whisking it in to incorporate and then pour into a bowl or container that has a lid. Put the lid on and put in the freezer. After an hour, give the mixture an energetic whisk with a hand whisk or an electric mixer. Put it back in the freezer and then whisk again after another couple of hours. When the ice cream is nearly firm, give one last whisk and put it back in the freezer to set.

Alternatively, pour into your ice cream machine and churn, following the manufacturer's instructions.

Makes 6 cups

Sometimes I watch them and see that they are counting between each bite to make their ice cream or fries last as long as possible. And they separate the food up into groups on their plates and save, just like I did, the best for last.

3 TABLESPOONS OLIVE OIL
1 SCANT CUP SHORT-GRAIN RICE
6 CUPS MILK
1 CUP HEAVY WHIPPING CREAM
1 TEASPOON FINELY GRATED LEMON ZEST
1/2 VANILLA BEAN, SPLIT IN HALF
FRESHLY GRATED NUTMEG
1/4 CUP SUPERFINE SUGAR, PLUS
  A LITTLE EXTRA FOR THE PISTACHIOS
1/2 CUP PISTACHIOS, SKINS REMOVED
SOFT DARK BROWN SUGAR, FOR SPRINKLING
3 PEACHES, PITTED AND HALVED
6 SMALL BLOBS OF BUTTER

Lemon rice pudding with roasted peaches

My friend Jo—a wonderful cook—gave me this. You can use nectarines, if you prefer them to peaches, and it is also nice with plums. If you have any rice pudding left over, whisk an egg white into it, shape it into little balls, and pan-fry them in butter. Sprinkle them with a little sugar and serve warm.

Preheat the oven to 500°F. Heat the olive oil in a heavy-bottomed pan, add the rice, and stir gently to warm it. Add the milk, cream, lemon zest, vanilla bean, and nutmeg, and bring to a boil. Lower the heat and simmer steadily for about 10 minutes, stirring quite often to make sure it doesn't stick. Add the superfine sugar and simmer for another 10 minutes, stirring as before.

Meanwhile, toss the pistachios with a dash of the brown sugar in a small pan and roast in the oven until they are just crisp in places.

Put the peaches in a baking dish, cut side up. Sprinkle about 2 teaspoons of brown sugar over each peach half and top with a small blob of butter. Roast without turning until the tops are golden brown and the peaches are still in shape but with some juices bubbling.

Just as the rice is tender and creamy, but with quite a bit of milky liquid left, remove it from the heat and serve in flat bowls. Serve with one or two peach halves with a little juice drizzled here and there and a small pile of sugared pistachios. This is good warm or cold.

Serves 6

BUTTERMILK ICE CREAM:
1 CUP HEAVY WHIPPING CREAM
1 SCANT CUP SUPERFINE SUGAR
1 TEASPOON VANILLA EXTRACT
2 CUPS BUTTERMILK

$3^{1}/_{2}$ TABLESPOONS BUTTER
4 LOVELY APPLES, CORED, AND HALVED
$^{1}/_{3}$ CUP FIRMLY PACKED LIGHT BROWN SUGAR
1 TEASPOON GROUND CINNAMON
3 TABLESPOONS MARSALA OR PORT
$^{1}/_{2}$ CUP WATER, PLUS $^{1}/_{2}$ CUP HOT WATER

Baked cinnamon apples with buttermilk ice cream

This is the sort of thing I like to eat on Christmas Eve—quite healthy and homely and just delicious. We eat it with teaspoons, scraping the soft apple out of the skins and eating it with the juice and ice cream. You could also fold a slightly sweetened fruit purée into the ice cream before churning it. You'll need an ovenproof dish that's about 10 by 8 inches and just large enough to take the eight apple halves compactly. You could bake the apples in advance, cover them with aluminum foil and then just heat them up a bit before serving.

For the ice cream, whisk the cream with the sugar and vanilla until all the sugar has dissolved and the cream starts to thicken. Add the buttermilk, whisking it in to incorporate, and then pour into a bowl or container that has a lid. Put the lid on and put in the freezer. After an hour give the mixture an energetic whisk with a hand whisk or an electric mixer. Put it back in the freezer, and then whisk again after another couple of hours. When the ice cream is nearly firm, give one last whisk and put it back in the freezer to set.

Alternatively, pour into your ice cream machine and churn, following the manufacturer's instructions.

Preheat the oven to 350°F and use some of the butter to grease a shallow ovenproof dish, just large enough to fit all 8 apple halves quite compactly. Halve the apples and neatly core them, making sure you don't pierce the skin. Arrange them in the baking dish, cut side up. Mix the sugar and cinnamon, and sprinkle over the apples. Put a blob of butter on each apple, sprinkle the marsala over the top, and dribble $^{1}/_{2}$ cup of water around the dish.

Bake for about 30 minutes, then dribble the pan juices over the apples, and add another $^{1}/_{2}$ cup of hot water to the dish. Bake for another 30 minutes or so, or until the apples are soft inside and golden on top but still have their shape. Serve warm or at room temperature, with some sauce spooned over the apples and a scoop or two of the ice cream.

Serves 4 (although there will be ice cream left over for another time)

Our dog, named "pulcino" chicken

Brown

Chocolate loaf
Mixed brown bread
Spaghetti with ground beef
Spelt and cranberry bean soup
Lentil soup
Lentil rice
Lentils and sausages
Brown rice risotto with butter and Parmesan
Pot-roasted veal with sage and garlic
Grilled beef and bread kebabs
Hamburgers
Brown bread and butter ice cream
Chocolate pannacotta
Chocolate cake with frosting
Brownies
Hot chocolate
Hazelnut chocolate balls
Chocolate bread custard
Milky Way bar sauce
Chocolate fudge sauce

- memory -

On April Fools' Day once we went to the local shop and asked for two bags of 1-cent candies. When poor old George had finally counted out the 200 we flew out of the shop, chorusing "April Fool." This is the same café where we bought our ice creams. Our mother would sometimes let us take an ice cream as we walked to school with our ribbons and braids and other girly hairstyles, and I loved that. Past the other silky pinks, colorful floral and checked ribbons, class dunces, older gangs, and fears accumulated on the sidewalk, waiting for the bell.

We loved the secret meetings in candy stores, and looking for small spaces outside to sit and eat, hiccuping our way home afterward.

I wanted to toast marshmallows on fires but didn't really enjoy children's camping where the oatmeal looked like homesickness in the smallest portion I had requested. I wanted to find my way with a flashlight through a clearing and eat brownies with the Brownies and Girl Scouts and drink bright berried drinks and roll chocolate through my hands, hopping with a messy face to the beat of the birds.

1 (½-OUNCE) CAKE FRESH YEAST
2 TABLESPOONS SUPERFINE SUGAR
1¼ CUPS MILK
3⅓ CUPS BREAD FLOUR OR
   ALL-PURPOSE FLOUR
⅓ CUP UNSWEETENED COCOA POWDER
3 TABLESPOONS BUTTER, MELTED
SALT

Chocolate loaf

This is a wonderful addition to your breakfast table. Despite its looks, it is definitely a bread and is quite a surprise, so you might need to prepare people who are expecting it to be cake. It is beautiful plain, or toasted with butter or homemade mandarin orange or strawberry jam (pages 106 and 68).

Crumble the yeast into a large bowl and add the sugar. Gently heat the milk in a small pan until it feels just a bit hotter than your finger, then add it to the yeast. Stir through and leave for 10 minutes or so, until the surface starts to turn spongy. Add the flour, cocoa powder, butter, and a pinch of salt, and mix in well. Knead with your hands for about 6 minutes until the dough is smooth and elastic with no lumps. If your dough is very soft, leave it in the bowl and just punch it around and squeeze it with one hand, holding the bowl with the other. Cover the bowl with a heavy dish towel and leave it in a warm, draft-free place for 1½ to 2 hours until it has puffed right up. Butter and flour a 12 by 4-inch loaf pan.

Knock the dough down to flatten it and shape it to the size of the pan. Drop it in, cover the pan with the dish towel, and leave it again in a warm place for anywhere between 30 minutes and an hour, until the dough has puffed up over the rim of the pan. While the dough is rising, preheat the oven to 350°F.

Remove the dish towel and bake the loaf for about 25 minutes, or until the top is firm and the bread sounds hollow when tapped on the bottom. Tip out onto a rack to cool. Once it has cooled down completely, this loaf can be frozen (even just a chunk of it) in a plastic bag and saved for another moment in time.

Makes 1 loaf

ABOUT 1½ CUPS WARM (COMFORTABLE TO
    YOUR FINGERS) WATER
1 (¾-OUNCE) CAKE FRESH YEAST, CRUMBLED, OR
    1 (¼-OUNCE) PACKAGE ACTIVE DRY YEAST
2 TEASPOONS HONEY
1½ TABLESPOONS OLIVE OIL
1 CUP SPELT FLOUR
¾ CUP BUCKWHEAT FLOUR
¾ CUP RYE FLOUR
⅔ CUP WHOLE WHEAT FLOUR
¾ CUP BREAD FLOUR
1 TABLESPOON FLAXSEED
1 TEASPOON SALT
¼ CUP SESAME SEEDS
½ CUP SUNFLOWER SEEDS

Mixed brown bread

I love going to the healthfood store and coming out with the various brown paper bags with all the different goods in to make this bread. It really makes me feel like I'm doing well when my kids have this for their school sandwiches. Apart from its healthy aspect, this is just simply lovely—nice for sandwiches or toasted with butter or jam. You might like to try other flours or combinations, too. This makes one large loaf or two smaller ones, and if you like, you can easily freeze one and keep it for another moment.

Put the water in a smallish bowl and add the yeast, honey, and oil. Stir until the honey melts and then leave it for 10 minutes or so, until it begins to froth up a bit.

Put the spelt, buckwheat, rye, whole wheat, and bread flours in a fairly large wide bowl, and add the flaxseed and 1 teaspoon of salt. Toast the sesame and sunflower seeds lightly in a dry frying pan and stir them into the flours.

Add the yeast mixture to the flours, and mix through well, kneading it in the bowl for at least 5 minutes until it is elastic. It may still be a little sticky, but only add more bread flour if you can't knead it because it's sticking to your hands. Cover the bowl with a couple of cloths and leave it in a warm and draft-free place for about 1½ hours, or until it has puffed up well. Punch down the dough to flatten it, divide it in half, and dust a large baking sheet with flour. Shape the dough into two longish loaves and sit them on the sheet, leaving space between as they will rise. Make a few slashes on their tops and cover with a cloth, making sure it loops in the middle of the two loaves. Leave it in the same draft-free spot for another 45 minutes or so, until the dough has puffed right up again.

Meanwhile, preheat the oven to 400°F. Remove the cloth and bake for about 25 minutes, until the bread is golden and crusty all over and sounds hollow when you tap it. Remove from the oven and cool a bit before serving. Best warm or at room temperature.

Makes 2 loaves

½ CUP OLIVE OIL
3 ONIONS, CHOPPED
SALT
2 CLOVES GARLIC, FINELY CHOPPED
2¼ POUNDS GROUND BEEF
2 BAY LEAVES
1 CINNAMON STICK
3 TABLESPOONS WORCESTERSHIRE SAUCE
1 TEASPOON DRIED MINT
2 TEASPOONS SWEET PAPRIKA
4 TABLESPOONS (½ STICK) BUTTER
1½ CUPS WHITE WINE
1 (28-OUNCE) CAN DICED TOMATOES
3 CUPS WATER
1 SMALL BUNCH PARSLEY, CHOPPED
1¼ (16-OUNCE) PACKAGES SPAGHETTI
GRATED PARMESAN, TO SERVE

Spaghetti with ground beef

This is exactly how my sister makes her meat sauce. The pasta will serve five or six people, but you should have about half the sauce left over. I always make my meat sauce in double quantities . . . leftovers can be frozen in small portions for quick dinners. It's great on toast with some parmesan sprinkled over the top, dolloped into mashed potatoes, or over gnocchi. And, of course, you can use it for making lasagne. If you are suspicious of your saucepan (that the meat might burn while you're browning it), then sauté the meat and onions in a nonstick frying pan and tip everything into the larger pan for cooking.

Heat the olive oil in a large pan. Sauté the onions with a pinch of salt over medium heat, stirring often until they are quite golden, soft, and sticky. Add the garlic, cook for a minute, and then add the beef. Mix it in with the onions, breaking up any lumps with a wooden spoon. Add the bay leaves, cinnamon stick, Worcestershire sauce, mint, and paprika, and sauté over high heat for 8 to 10 minutes, until the meat loses its moisture and starts sizzling. Add 1½ tablespoons of the butter and continue frying for about 10 minutes, until the meat changes color. Stir often, to prevent sticking and to brown all the meat.

Add the wine and cook for about 5 minutes until it has evaporated. Add the tomatoes, let them melt down for a bit, and then add 3 cups of water. Season with salt. Bring to a boil, lower the heat, and simmer uncovered for about 50 minutes, until it looks like a good, not-too-dry sauce. Add the parsley and simmer for another 10 minutes.

Cook the pasta in boiling salted water, following the package instructions. Drain and serve with a good dollop of meat sauce, a sprinkling of Parmesan, and a small blob of the remaining butter on each serving.

Serves 5 to 6

1 CUP DRIED CRANBERRY BEANS, SOAKED
   OVERNIGHT IN COLD WATER
SALT
4 TABLESPOONS OLIVE OIL
1 SMALL ONION, CHOPPED
1 CLOVE GARLIC, CHOPPED
1 CELERY STALK, CHOPPED
3 OUNCES UNSMOKED PANCETTA
1 CUP SPELT GRAIN, SOAKED OVERNIGHT
   IN COLD WATER
1/2 CUP CANNED TOMATO SAUCE
2 SAGE LEAVES
6 CUPS WATER
OLIVE OIL, TO SERVE

Spelt and cranberry bean soup

This is a good soup to try on children in winter: rich in iron and vitamins.
You will have to check the type of spelt you have as to whether it requires
soaking or not. It should be available in healthfood stores, if not at the
supermarket. Pearl barley can be used instead, if you like.

Drain the beans, put them in a large saucepan, and cover abundantly with cold
water. Bring to a boil and then skim the surface. Lower the heat slightly, and cook
for 1 to 1 1/2 hours, until the beans are soft but not mushy. Top up with a little hot
water when necessary during the cooking time. Season with salt toward the end.

Heat the olive oil in a large pan and sauté the onion over medium heat until
softened and very lightly golden. Add the garlic, celery, and pancetta, and sauté for
a few minutes more. Drain the spelt and add it to the pan with the tomato sauce,
sage leaves, and salt to taste. Stir through well and then add 6 cups of water. Bring
to a boil, lower the heat and cook uncovered for about an hour, or until the spelt
is soft. There should be enough liquid to be able to stir the spelt loosely with a
wooden spoon.

Drain the beans, keeping the cooking water. Purée the beans with just enough
of their water to keep the purée moist. Add to the spelt pan and stir in about
1 cup of the bean cooking water, or enough to make a thick soup. Cook for a couple
of minutes for the flavors to mingle, adjust the seasoning, and serve with a good
drizzle of olive oil. Adults might like to stir some freshly chopped chile into theirs.

Serves 6

1 1/3 CUPS BROWN OR GREEN LENTILS
1 LEAFY CELERY STALK, CHOPPED
2 CARROTS, PEELED AND CHOPPED
1/4 RED BELL PEPPER, SEEDED AND CHOPPED
1 SMALL RED ONION, CHOPPED
1/2 CUP CANNED TOMATO SAUCE
SALT
5 CUPS COLD WATER
2/3 CUP SHELLED PEAS
2 1/2 CUPS COARSELY CHOPPED SPINACH LEAVES
1 1/3 CUPS CHOPPED CABBAGE
OLIVE OIL, TO SERVE
FRESHLY GROUND BLACK PEPPER, TO SERVE

Lentil soup

Sometimes I just open the fridge and, having completely forgotten that I had bought some or other vegetable, I put together a soup like this. This makes a nice big stockpot, so you'll have leftovers for the next day. I like to serve this with toasted bread and a faint drizzle of balsamic vinegar with the olive oil on top—vinegar over lentil soup is quite Greek. Or I cook up some small pasta in a separate pan and add a little to each serving.

Rinse the lentils, getting rid of any hard stony bits. Put them in a large pan and add the celery, carrots, red pepper, onion, and tomato sauce, and season with salt.

Cover with about 5 cups of cold water and bring to a boil. Put the lid on the pan, lower the heat, and simmer for about 1 hour. Add the peas, spinach, and cabbage, and cook for another 15 to 20 minutes. Taste for salt. Serve with a good drizzling of olive oil and a few grinds of black pepper for adults.

Serves 5

Sometimes, if you didn't make it to the bathroom on time, they would give you a long aprony dress to wear while your clothes dried. That way everyone knew that you'd wet yourself. So the next couple of hours were horrid— and you still had to go to the enormous ancient dining room that smelled of wood and old cherries.

5 TABLESPOONS OLIVE OIL
1 LARGE RED ONION, FINELY CHOPPED
2 CLOVES GARLIC, PEELED AND FINELY CHOPPED
1/4 TEASPOON GROUND CINNAMON
1/4 TEASPOON SWEET PAPRIKA
1/4 TEASPOON GROUND CORIANDER
1 1/3 CUPS BROWN OR GREEN LENTILS, RINSED
    AND PICKED OVER
4 CUPS WATER, PLUS 1 CUP
SALT
1 CUP LONG-GRAIN RICE, RINSED WELL
2 TABLESPOONS BUTTER
5 TABLESPOONS CHOPPED FRESH PARSLEY

Lentil rice

My kids love a bowl of lentils with rice, so I make this in some form or another once or twice a week. Some nice bread and a ripe tomato salad make it a complete, not-too-heavy meal, although I think it would be nice, too, with a roast chicken or meat dish. I like this with some chile oil and a few drops of lemon juice sprinkled over the top, and the children enjoy it with quite a few spoonfuls of thick plain yogurt.

Heat the oil in a frying pan and fry the onion over medium–low heat, stirring often, until it is golden and sticky looking. Add the garlic, cinnamon, paprika, and coriander, and stir until you can smell the garlic. Remove from the heat.

    Meanwhile, put the lentils in a large pan, cover with 4 cups of water, and bring to a boil. Skim the surface and then simmer for 30 minutes, adding some salt halfway through.

    Scrape the onion mixture into the lentil pan and add the rice, butter, half the parsley, 1 cup of water, and a dash more salt. Stir well and bring back to a boil. Cover, turn the heat as low as possible, and cook for 15 minutes or so, until all the water has been absorbed and the rice is cooked through.

    Remove from the heat and fluff up. Cover the top of the pan with a clean dish towel, put the lid back on, and leave it for about 10 minutes. Add the remaining parsley and fluff it up again before serving.

Serves 4

I can still picture those ladies, round and bursting out of their checkered uniforms, serving up soupy plates of lentils and dribbling some vinegar over the top so that it sat like a still pool. They would be swinging their way in and out of those slatted kitchen doors as though they were barn dancing.

1 1/3 CUPS SMALL GREEN LENTILS
ABOUT 8 TABLESPOONS OLIVE OIL
1 SMALL RED ONION, FINELY CHOPPED
1 SMALL CARROT, PEELED AND CHOPPED
1/2 CELERY STALK, CHOPPED
1 CLOVE GARLIC, PEELED BUT LEFT WHOLE
4 CUPS HOT WATER
SALT
4 ITALIAN SAUSAGES
3 TABLESPOONS CHOPPED FRESH PARSLEY
OLIVE OIL OR CHILE OIL, TO SERVE

Lentils
and sausages

This is also lovely, especially on a wintry evening, with some mashed potatoes or the boiled potatoes with parsley (page 233). Or better still, add into the oil in your cooked sausage pan a whole clove of garlic and an extra tablespoon or two of olive oil. Add about 2 cups of blanched and chopped spinach and sauté until it has picked up the flavors of the pan.

Rinse the lentils very well to remove any grit. Heat half the olive oil in a heavy-bottomed pan and sauté the onion over medium-low heat for a few minutes until it is lightly golden and softened. Add the carrot, celery, and garlic, and sauté for another couple of minutes to soften them all. Add the lentils, turning them through the mixture to coat well and then add 4 cups of hot water. Season with salt and bring to a boil, then lower the heat slightly. Cook uncovered for about 40 minutes, until the lentils are soft and there is very little liquid left in the pan.
　　Meanwhile, prick the sausages here and there. Fry them in 1 1/2 tablespoons of oil in a nonstick frying pan until they are golden brown on all sides, adding more oil if it's needed. Make sure they are cooked through. When the lentils are done, stir in the parsley and add the sausages. Taste for salt, heat through for a minute or two, and then serve with a drizzle of olive oil over the lentils. Some adults may like a drizzling of chile oil over theirs.

Serves 4

6 CUPS VEGETABLE COOKING WATER
4 TABLESPOONS OLIVE OIL
2 CLOVES GARLIC, PEELED BUT LEFT WHOLE
1 1/2 CUPS BROWN RICE
SALT
1/2 CUP GRATED PARMESAN CHEESE, PLUS
   MORE TO SERVE
2 TABLESPOONS BUTTER
FRESHLY GROUND BLACK PEPPER, TO SERVE

Brown rice risotto with butter and Parmesan

I make this often. Instead of water, I often use the liquid saved from when I've boiled vegetables. The water used for cooking broccoli for the gratinéed broccoli or sautéed broccoli with tomato (pages 203 and 200) is perfect to use here, or use a vegetable bouillon cube with no additives from the healthfood store.

Put the vegetable broth in a large pan and bring to a boil, then reduce the heat to keep it at a slow simmer. Heat the oil in another large saucepan. Add the garlic and rice, and cook over medium-high heat for about 30 seconds, stirring to coat the rice with oil. Reduce the heat to low and stir in a ladleful of hot broth. Season with salt (depending on whether your broth is already seasoned) and, when the broth has been absorbed, stir in another ladleful.

Continue in this way for about 1 hour, until the broth is used up and the rice is softened but still a little bit firm in the center. If you run out of vegetable broth before the rice is tender just carry on with boiling water. This risotto is best when it's left a little liquidy, like a thick soup. Remove the garlic cloves and stir in the Parmesan and butter. Check the seasoning and, when the butter has melted, ladle into serving bowls and serve immediately with extra Parmesan and black pepper for whoever wants it.

Serves 4

½ CUP OLIVE OIL
ABOUT 1½ POUNDS YOUNG VEAL LEG,
    OR ROUND ROAST, ABOUT 4 INCHES
    IN DIAMETER
2 CLOVES GARLIC, UNPEELED
1 SAGE SPRIG
SALT
½ CUP WHITE WINE
4 TO 6 TABLESPOONS WATER

Pot-roasted veal with sage and garlic

At first glance, this might not seem like a recipe that kids would love, but it is a great dish that I learned from my mother-in-law. Giovanni remembers the way the juices looked on his plate when he was a child—the way they separated deliciously into two colors. Serve with buttered noodles, your favorite potatoes, or just sautéed greens. If you have leftovers, slice the meat thinly and use it to fill bread rolls, with a bit of sauce spooned in, too.

Heat the oil in a casserole that will just accommodate the meat. Add the meat, garlic, and sage, and brown the meat on all sides over medium heat, turning it carefully with a pair of tongs. Take care not to pierce the meat so that the juices stay inside. Sprinkle the browned top with a fair amount of salt, let it soak in for a bit, then turn it over and salt the new top. If the garlic and sage are looking too dark, sit them on top of the meat.

Add the wine and leave it to bubble up for a few minutes. Add 4 to 5 tablespoons of water and reduce the heat to low. Cover the casserole and simmer for 15 minutes or so, until the meat is still soft but is lightly cooked all the way through. Overcooking will dry it out, so check it now and then. The exact cooking time will depend on the heat and the size of your meat. Turn it over a couple of times while it's cooking and add a little water if necessary; there should be a good amount of sauce to serve with the meat. Turn off the heat and leave the casserole with the lid on for at least 15 minutes before serving.

Serve the veal in thin slices with the sauce spooned over the top, warm or at room temperature.

Serves 5 to 6

1 1/4 POUNDS BEEF TENDERLOIN SLICES
2 TO 3 THYME SPRIGS
2 ROSEMARY SPRIGS
2 CLOVES GARLIC, PEELED AND SQUASHED
  A BIT
1/2 CUP OLIVE OIL
SALT
ABOUT 4 SLICES (1/2 INCH THICK) DAY-OLD
  WHITE BREAD
LEMON WEDGES, TO SERVE
OLIVE OIL, TO SERVE

Grilled beef and bread kebabs

These are very small and easy-to-eat skewers with soft cubes of beef tenderloin alternating with tiny blocks of bread—rather like antipasto for adults, and a perfect size for kids. Keeping the meat and bread pieces small is important, as they must be cooked really quickly on all sides so that the bread toasts beautifully rather than burns. I like to make them into about 1/2-inch cubes but, if you like, you can make them a bit bigger. You will need to marinate the meat in the herbs and oil for a few hours before you grill them. Adults can add some ground dried chile to their marinade. If you're using bamboo skewers, remember to soak them in water first so that they don't catch fire on the grill. I love to serve this with a handful of homemade salted fries and a butter lettuce salad. If you don't have time to make your own fries, even just a few packaged chips is nice.

Trim away any fat from the beef and cut it into 1/2-inch cubes. Put them in a bowl with the thyme, rosemary, garlic, and olive oil, and add a small scattering of salt. Turn everything over to coat the beef well, cover the bowl, and leave it in the fridge or a cool place for a few hours. Turn the beef over a few times while it's marinating so that the flavors mingle. Take out of the fridge 30 minutes or so before cooking.

For the bread, blocks that have some crust attached are needed here, so cut the crusts off the bread by slicing 1/2 inch in. Keep the bread centers to make fresh bread crumbs or to feed to the ducks. Cut along the crusts to make 1/2-inch blocks. Thread the skewers alternately with beef and bread, starting and finishing with a piece of beef.

Preheat the barbecue or grill. Cook the skewers about 2 inches away from the embers, using the rosemary and thyme sprigs to brush on the marinade and turning the skewers over quite quickly so that the bread doesn't burn. They must be seared golden on all sides and dark with flavor in some parts. Sprinkle with a little salt and serve immediately, drizzled with a squeeze of lemon juice and some olive oil.

Makes 10 skewers

PINK SAUCE:
½ CUP BEST-QUALITY TOMATO KETCHUP
3 TABLESPOONS MAYONNAISE
2 TABLESPOONS LEMON JUICE
1 ½ TEASPOONS WORCESTERSHIRE SAUCE
1 TEASPOON SWEET PAPRIKA
SALT AND FRESHLY GROUND BLACK
    PEPPER

ABOUT 5 TABLESPOONS OLIVE OIL
2 LARGE RED ONIONS, THINLY SLICED
3 THYME SPRIGS
SALT
1 ¾ POUNDS GROUND BEEF
3 TABLESPOONS CHOPPED FRESH PARSLEY
1 EGG, LIGHTLY BEATEN
FRESHLY GROUND BLACK PEPPER
6 SLICES GOUDA CHEESE (SOME MAY LIKE
    GORGONZOLA)
2 JUICY TOMATOES, SLICED
ABOUT 1 CUP TENDER BUT CRISP INNER
    BUTTER LETTUCE LEAVES
ABOUT 4 PICKLED CUCUMBERS, THINLY
    SLICED DIAGONALLY
6 SESAME BUNS, HALVED

Hamburgers

We all love these, especially all the fiddling around with so many small and different bowls in the middle of the table, and being able to choose our own fillings. Kids might even like the onions and pickles, when they're choosing for themselves. You can decide if you want to make the meat patties bigger or smaller, depending on who you will be serving. Your ground beef will need some fat in it so that it stays moist and quite juicy after cooking. Make sure not to overcook the patties and dry them out— they should be just nicely charred here and there for flavor. This might seem like a lot of fuss, but it is all work done beforehand and, hopefully, there might even be someone who will take over the fire and cooking part for you. I usually serve these with pan-fried potatoes with rosemary and sage (page 245) or just a handful of packaged potato chips.

For the pink sauce, put the tomato ketchup, mayonnaise, lemon juice, Worcestershire sauce, and paprika in a serving bowl and season with some salt and pepper. Mix with a fork until smooth.

Heat 4 tablespoons of the oil in a nonstick frying pan and add the onions. Fry over low heat until they are golden and sticky, but take care that they don't burn. Add the thyme sprigs and a pinch of salt, and continue frying the onions, stirring with a wooden spoon, for about 15 minutes, until they get a little crisp.

Meanwhile, put the beef, parsley, and egg in a bowl, and season with some salt and black pepper. Mix well with your hands and then shape into six large flat patties. They should be about 4 inches in diameter and not more than 3/4 inch thick, so squeeze them between your palms and shape them with your fingers. Preheat a barbecue or grill pan and brush it lightly with oil.

Grill the patties over a medium-high flame until they are nicely browned and charred in a couple of places. Make sure they don't get smoked and don't fry them slowly or they will just become hard. They should be cooked through but moist and juicy inside, and should ooze a little cooked meat juice onto your bun. Cover the patties with a slice of cheese and let it just melt (if it seems necessary, cover it loosely with a square of aluminum foil).

Put the tomatoes, lettuce, pickles, and warm onions out on the table in separate bowls. Heat the bun halves on the barbecue for a couple of seconds and then put the patties inside and serve immediately, letting everyone make their own by adding sauce, tomatoes, lettuce, pickles, and onions as they like. Serve with fries, baked potatoes, or just a green salad.

Makes 6

We saved our chip packages and then we'd lay them on a baking sheet and slow-roast them in the oven to shrink them down to miniatures, turning out their corners carefully while they were still hot to keep their shapes. We loved to glue pins on the back and wear them as brooches.

3 SLICES BROWN BREAD, TORN INTO CHUNKS
1/2 CUP LIGHTLY PACKED BROWN SUGAR
4 1/2 TABLESPOONS BUTTER
2 EGGS
1 TEASPOON VANILLA EXTRACT
1/2 CUP MILK
1 1/2 CUPS HEAVY WHIPPING CREAM

Brown bread and butter ice cream

I was most excited when I first heard about this. I thought, how great for kids, but adults love it, too. I added the butter and I love it sometimes with a faint drizzling of not-too-rich toffee sauce. I make this when I have some leftovers from the mixed brown bread loaf (page 291) but, of course, you don't have to make your own bread especially for this ice cream. I love to serve this as an afternoon snack. The crumbs have to be caramelized and hardened so that they taste like praline in the ice cream.

Preheat the oven to 400°F. In a processor, pulse the bread into crumbs. Grease a large baking pan with a little butter and sprinkle the crumbs and the sugar over it, then mix together with your hands. Bake for about 12 minutes until the crumbs are golden and crisp, turning them over twice during this time. Watch that the crumbs don't burn and become bitter. Leave the crumbs to cool, then break up any clumps with your hands.

Melt the butter in a small pan until it starts to turn a little golden and smells good. Pour into a bowl to cool.

Meanwhile, whisk the eggs with the vanilla. Heat the milk with 1/2 cup of the cream in a pan over medium-low heat until almost boiling. Whisk a ladleful into the eggs, mixing constantly to prevent them from scrambling. Gradually pour in the rest of the liquid, whisking all the time. Pour it all back into the saucepan, lower the heat to minimum, and heat for a few minutes, whisking all the time, to cook the eggs and thicken the mixture a bit. Remove from the heat and cool for 10 to 15 minutes, whisking now and then. Stir in the remaining cream, the melted butter, and the sugary crumbs, and pour into a bowl or container that has a lid. Put the lid on and leave in the fridge until totally cool.

Put the bowl in the freezer. After an hour give the mixture an energetic whisk with a hand whisk. Put it back in the freezer and then whisk again after another couple of hours. When the ice cream is nearly firm, give one last whisk and put it back in the freezer to set.

Alternatively, pour into your ice cream machine and churn, following the manufacturer's instructions.

Makes 4 cups

1/8 OUNCE (2 SHEETS) LEAF GELATIN, OR
   2 TEASPOONS POWDERED GELATIN
1 CUP MILK
2 CUPS HEAVY WHIPPING CREAM
4 TABLESPOONS SUPERFINE SUGAR
1/2 CUP CHOPPED SEMISWEET CHOCOLATE
1 TABLESPOON UNSWEETENED COCOA POWDER,
   SIFTED

Chocolate pannacotta

These are light and creamy, soft, and chocolaty. They are lovely just on their own, eaten straight out of their molds but, if you want to be a bit dressy, you could serve them with white chocolate sauce or surrounded by a bright ring of cranberries and a blob of cream. Or perhaps some sautéed quinces, nectarines, or peaches.

Put the gelatin leaves in a bowl of cold water to soften them. If you're using powdered gelatin, put 4 tablespoons of the milk in a small bowl and stir in the gelatin. Leave for a minute or two until it dissolves and swells a bit.

Meanwhile, put the milk, cream, sugar, chocolate, and cocoa in a saucepan over low heat. Stir it with a wooden spoon as it heats so that it becomes completely smooth and nothing sticks to the bottom. Turn off the heat just before it reaches boiling point.

Squeeze the water out of the softened gelatin leaves and stir them into the hot chocolate milk. If you're using powdered gelatin, stir some of the hot chocolate milk into it to soften, then stir it all back into the saucepan and carry on stirring until it's completely smooth. Leave it to cool, whisking now and then to make sure the gelatin has dissolved.

Pour the mixture into six 1/2-cup pudding or pannacotta molds and then cover them with plastic wrap. Put in the fridge overnight or until set.

To unmold, loosen the top edges gently with your fingers. Dip the bottom of the molds into hot water for just a couple of seconds (any longer might turn your pannacotta to liquid again) and tip out onto serving plates.

Makes 6

1/4 POUND PLUS 5 TABLESPOONS BUTTER
1/3 CUP CHOPPED SEMISWEET CHOCOLATE
1/4 CUP UNSWEETENED COCOA POWDER
3 EGGS, SEPARATED
3/4 CUP SUPERFINE SUGAR
1 CUP ALL-PURPOSE FLOUR
1 1/2 TEASPOONS BAKING POWDER
4 TABLESPOONS MILK

FROSTING:
5 1/2 TABLESPOONS BUTTER, SOFTENED
1/2 CUP CONFECTIONERS' SUGAR
1/4 CUP UNSWEETENED COCOA POWDER
3 TABLESPOONS MILK
2 GENEROUS TEASPOONS HONEY

Chocolate cake with frosting

This is exactly the kind of chocolate cake I loved as a child. Sometimes I make this just chocolate, sometimes halved and filled with not-too-sweet raspberry or strawberry jam, or with purée and a few dollops of cream (and then I don't frost it). If you like, you might also add some chopped nuts in with the flour or scatter some over the top.

Preheat the oven to 350°F. Butter and flour a 9 1/2-inch springform pan. Melt the butter in a small saucepan over low heat, then add the chocolate and cocoa, and stir until melted. Remove from the heat. Whisk the egg whites in a bowl until they are creamy and stiff. In another bowl, whisk the egg yolks until they are foamy, then beat in the sugar. Add the chocolate mixture, a bit at a time initially to acclimatize the eggs. Next, sift in the flour and baking powder and mix well. Add the milk and mix until smooth.

Carefully fold in the beaten whites, trying not to deflate them, and gently mix until they are completely incorporated into a fluffy but dense mixture. Scrape out into the pan and bake for about 30 to 35 minutes. Remove from the oven and cool completely in the pan before moving to a serving plate.

For the frosting, whip the butter with the confectioners' sugar until fluffy. Whisk in the cocoa a bit at a time so that it doesn't fly everywhere. When it is completely incorporated, add the milk and honey, and whisk until very smooth. Spread it over the top of the cake with a spatula, using swift smooth strokes. I like it not completely smooth but in chocolate waves.

Cuts into 10 to 12 slices

3/4 POUND (3 STICKS) BUTTER
2 CUPS CHOPPED SEMISWEET CHOCOLATE
1/2 CUP UNSWEETENED COCOA POWDER, SIFTED
6 EGGS, SEPARATED
1 1/2 CUPS SUPERFINE SUGAR
1 TEASPOON VANILLA EXTRACT
1 2/3 CUPS ALL-PURPOSE FLOUR

FILLING:
1 1/2 CUPS HEAVY WHIPPING CREAM
2 TEASPOONS CONFECTIONERS' SUGAR
FEW DROPS OF VANILLA EXTRACT
2 CUPS STRAWBERRIES, HULLED AND HALVED IF LARGE

ICING:
1 CUP CHOPPED SEMISWEET CHOCOLATE
1/3 CUP HEAVY WHIPPING CREAM

Brownies

Toward the middle of the baking, this has the most gorgeous smell, which runs like streamers through your home when you take the brownies out of the oven. This is my friend Artemis's recipe. She makes them so often that this is the most familiar smell from her kitchen. She likes them with whipped, unsweetened cream. You can add some toasted nuts, apple, or pear chunks, or anything else you think might go well. Serve these on their own in squares to nibble on, or slightly warm with a dribbling of chocolate sauce and a scoop of vanilla ice cream. They also freeze well so I like to make up this big batch and freeze a few for an emergency snack, but you could also make half the amount in a smaller pan (6 by 8 inches). I sometimes make this large quantity (in my big rectangular pan) and then cut it in half into two squares once it's cooled. Layered with strawberries and whipped cream, it makes a beautiful cake. It's a bit messy maybe to cut and serve, but I have noticed all the kids eyeing this at our parties. Use really good quality chocolate.

Preheat the oven to 350°F. Butter and flour an 11 1/2 by 15 1/2-inch baking pan that is at least 1 1/4 inches deep. Put the butter in a medium-size pan over low heat. When it begins to melt a little, add the chocolate. Stir frequently with a wooden spoon until all the chocolate has melted and the mixture is smooth. Don't overheat it or the chocolate might seize up. Remove from the heat and whisk in the cocoa powder, then leave it to cool a bit.

In a clean bowl, whisk the egg whites until soft peaks form. In another large bowl, whisk the egg yolks with the sugar and vanilla until creamy, then fold in the flour. Add the cooled chocolate and butter, mixing well, and then fold in the whites until everything is thoroughly mixed.

Scrape out every drop into your pan and put in the oven for about 25 minutes, or until a skewer poked into the center comes out clean. Don't overcook it though; the brownie should be quite moist in the center with a crusty top and edges. Leave it to cool completely.

If you are going to fill and ice the brownie, cut it in half across the long side. Whip the cream, confectioners' sugar, and vanilla together until firm peaks form, and spread it over the top of one piece. Sprinkle the strawberries over it, and then put the other piece of cake on top to make a sandwich.

For the icing, gently melt the chocolate and cream together in a small saucepan, stirring all the time. As soon as it is smooth, take from the heat. Add a few more drops of cream, if needed, so that it will drip onto the cake. Spread the icing all over the top of the cake, letting some dribble over the edges. Wait for the icing to set before cutting.

For brownies, cut the cake into 2-inch squares. If you are not going to eat them immediately, let them cool completely and then store in a sealed container or well covered with plastic wrap so that they don't dry out. Leftover brownies can be broken up into bits and sprinkled into just-about-set vanilla ice cream.

Makes about 48 brownies or 1 cake

2/3 CUP CHOPPED BEST-QUALITY SEMISWEET CHOCOLATE
2 CUPS MILK
1/2 CUP HEAVY WHIPPING CREAM
1 TEASPOON CONFECTIONERS' SUGAR
UNSWEETENED COCOA POWDER OR GROUND CINNAMON, TO SERVE

Hot chocolate

This is lovely and wintry and makes a nice start to a birthday, a special day, a Sunday, the New Year, or just any old day. It also looks beautiful in small glasses and you can make mocha chocolate by replacing 1/2 cup of the milk with freshly made, very strong espresso coffee.

Heat the chocolate and milk in a heavy-bottomed saucepan over medium heat, stirring constantly with a wooden spoon so it doesn't catch. Bring it to just below boiling point and whisk with a wire whisk to make sure it is completely smooth.

Meanwhile, whisk together the cream and confectioners' sugar until quite thick but not stiff—just dense enough to sit on top of the hot chocolate.

Pour the hot chocolate into cups and gently spoon the cream over the top, dropping it first onto the back of a spoon and letting it slide onto the top of the chocolate. Sieve a tiny amount of cocoa powder or cinnamon over the top and serve at once. This can be drunk as it is so that the chocolate streams through the cream, or the cream can be stirred through first.

Serves 2

3 HAZELNUT WAFER COOKIES
2 CUPS FINELY CHOPPED, ROASTED, PEELED
    HAZELNUTS
ABOUT ⅔ CUP CHOCOLATE HAZELNUT SPREAD
1⅔ CUP CHOPPED SEMISWEET CHOCOLATE

Hazelnut chocolate balls

My kids absolutely love to help me roll these in their small sweet palms—although it is difficult for them to try not to lick all the mixture off their hands. These are from a friend of Giovanni—he tasted them at work and spoke about them in such very descriptive terms that I made him hound her until she finally gave me the recipe.

Crumble the cookies into a bowl and add the hazelnuts and about two-thirds of the hazelnut spread to start with. Mix together until it all looks a bit like mud cake. Try rolling a small portion into a ball—if it breaks up, mix in more chocolate hazelnut spread until it will hold a shape. If the weather is hot, put the mixture into the fridge for a while before rolling.

Line a baking sheet or large flat plate with aluminum foil. Roll slightly heaping teaspoonfuls of mixture between your cool palms into compact little balls. Put them on the sheet and into the fridge for an hour or so to firm up.

Melt the chocolate in the top of a double boiler, making sure that the water doesn't touch the top bowl. Remove from the heat and let the chocolate cool for a few minutes. Drop the balls in one by one, turning them around so that they are completely covered. Return them to the sheet, where they will flatten a bit on the bottom. Let them set completely, even in the fridge for the first half hour or so if the weather's hot. Bring them out to room temperature and store in a jar in a cool dark place (or in the fridge in hot weather). They will keep for a couple of weeks.

Makes about 30

5½ TABLESPOONS BUTTER
1 CUP CHOPPED SEMISWEET CHOCOLATE
½ CUP SUPERFINE SUGAR
¼ CUP HEAVY WHIPPING CREAM
4 EGGS
14 TO 15 SLICES SANDWICH BREAD,
    CRUSTS REMOVED

Chocolate bread custard

This is quick, good, and really easy, and it produces a lovely soft chocolate custard with a crusty top. You can use any bread you like here—I just use plain ready-sliced sandwich bread, which leaves just a whisper of salt on the tongue. You can use brown, white, or any other bread. You could also use a homemade white loaf (page 263). I make this in a round dish that's about 8 inches wide and about 3 inches high and can be taken straight to the table.

Preheat the oven to 350°F and butter a shallow 4-cup ovenproof dish.

Melt the butter, chocolate, and sugar together in the top of a double boiler, stirring toward the end with a wooden spoon so that it is all smooth. Remove from the heat, stir in the cream, and leave to cool slightly.

Beat the eggs until they are creamy. Gradually add the chocolate mixture, starting with just a little and eventually mixing it all in to make a smooth custard.

Cut each slice of bread in half diagonally. Use half the slices to make an overlapping layer in the bottom of the dish. Pour over just less than half of the custard, making sure that all the bread is coated. Leave for 5 minutes for the bread to soak up some custard, then layer on the rest of the bread. Pour over the remaining custard and rock the dish so that all the bread is covered with chocolate custard. Leave for 5 minutes.

Put the dish in a larger baking pan and pour in enough hot water to come halfway up the sides of the custard dish. Put in the oven for about 30 minutes, until the custard is set and the top is crusty.

Serve warm, in wedges or spoonfuls, with thick cream or ice cream.

Serves 6

1 CUP HEAVY WHIPPING CREAM
5 (2-OUNCE) MILKY WAY MIDNIGHT BARS

Milky Way bar sauce

This is wonderfully rich and good—and really quick to make in an emergency. We like it dribbled down the side of a milkshake or slightly warm over ice cream, so that the cold makes the caramel set just slightly. When the pan is left covered on the stove or in the fridge, everyone goes with a teaspoon and takes out a healthy scoop, and the marks of the diggers clearly remain.

Pour half the cream into a heavy-bottomed pan and heat gently. Coarsely chop the Milky Way bars and add to the pan, stirring all the time with a wooden spoon, until they are completely melted. Make sure that the cream is not too hot and that nothing gets stuck on the bottom of the pan, which would ruin your chocolate. When everything is nearly all melted together, add the rest of the cream, and whisk to break up the soft lumps. Remove from the heat and carry on whisking until the sauce is completely smooth. Cover when it has cooled a bit. Serve warm or even at room temperature, but store in the fridge if you don't finish it all. Even a teaspoon of it cold or at room temperature is great for lifting the spirits.

Makes 2 cups

---

4 1/2 TABLESPOONS BUTTER
1/3 CUP SUPERFINE SUGAR
1/3 CUP FIRMLY PACKED DARK BROWN SUGAR
1/2 CUP HEAVY WHIPPING CREAM
1/2 CUP UNSWEETENED COCOA POWDER, SIFTED

Chocolate fudge sauce

This is ideal for making ice cream sundaes, or just pouring over vanilla ice cream or warm brownies.

Put the butter, sugars, and cream in a pan, and heat gently, stirring a few times, until the butter has melted. Add the cocoa and cook, stirring all the time now until the sauce is smooth and glossy. Use hot, warm, or at room temperature. You can keep this in a covered container in the fridge for a couple of weeks.

Makes 1 1/3 cups

Monochrome

Fish soup with poached fish to follow
Chicken broth
Pasta in chicken broth
Bread dumplings in chicken broth
Chicken croquettes
Chicken soup
Vegetable broth
Meat broth
Cottage pie
Fish pie
Pork schnitzels
Pan-fried breaded lamb rib chops
Fried fish fillets
Baked fish fillets
Potato and chickpea mash
Zucchini bread
Banana bread
Apple bread with sugar and cinnamon topping
Oat cookies
Maple syrup and vanilla ice cream
Pecan butter cookies
Gingerbread cookies

- memory -

Christmas was my best time, probably. It seemed like I hardly ever slept a wink the night before, wondering how and where he would actually come into the house, and if we'd left the milk and cookies in an obvious enough place. And there was all that anticipation of whether or not our lists would come true. So we would rise with the sun and mess around making as much softly deliberate noise as possible until our mother got up. She was normally the first up in the house. But we still had to wait for our father, so he could see the gifts that had come in the night, and he had a habit of sleeping in on Sundays and days like these. That was solid torture. It seemed as if he would go on sleeping forever, through any amount of noise. And then, at last, we would get into the actual gifts room—I will always remember the beautiful boxes everywhere, mountains of things from grandfathers and cousins, flowing almost out of the room like a wild, rushing and very alive river. We might have nibbled on the gingerbread cookies and other goodies, cross-legged on the floor with cups of warm milk and still in our pajamas. We could linger that day, much longer than usual, in our pajamas.

LEMON OIL:
ABOUT 5 TABLESPOONS OLIVE OIL
JUICE OF HALF A LEMON
SALT
SMALL SPRINKLING OF CRUMBLED DRIED OREGANO,
   OR CHOPPED FRESH PARSLEY

2 SHALLOTS, PEELED BUT LEFT WHOLE
2 CLOVES GARLIC, PEELED BUT LEFT WHOLE
2 LARGE CARROTS, PEELED AND CUT INTO CHUNKS
1 LARGE ZUCCHINI
7 SMALL POTATOES, SCRUBBED
2 SMALL LEAFY CELERY STALKS, HALVED
4 TO 5 WHOLE PARSLEY STEMS
7 PEPPERCORNS
1 BAY LEAF (FRESH IF POSSIBLE)
SALT
10 CUPS WATER
1 (8-OUNCE) SALMON FILLET, SKINNED
1 (10-OUNCE) OCEAN PERCH FILLET
1/2 CUP LONG-GRAIN RICE
2 EGGS
JUICE OF 2 LEMONS

Fish soup with poached fish to follow

This is a light soup and not too fishy, finished with an egg and lemon sauce. The poached fish is served as a second course with lemon oil or mayonnaise. I prefer not to use whole fish if I'm making this for children. Whatever you use, make sure there are no bones and strain the broth well. I often make a chicken soup in the same way, boiling the whole chicken for a little longer in slightly more water.

For the lemon oil, whisk the oil, lemon juice, herbs, and a little salt until fairly thick. Taste and add more salt, or pepper if you like.

   Put the shallots, garlic, carrots, zucchini, potatoes, celery, parsley, peppercorns, the bay leaf, if it is dried, and some salt in a large pan with about 10 cups of water. Bring to a boil, lower the heat to a high simmer, and cook, uncovered, for about 25 minutes. The zucchini should be nice and soft, so remove it with a slotted spoon to a plate. Remove the carrots and the potatoes, too, if they are soft. If not, they can be left for a few more minutes. Simmer the broth for another 15 minutes, then add the fish and the bay leaf, if it is fresh. Gently simmer for 10 minutes, or until the fish is cooked through. Carefully lift out the fish, shallots, and celery onto a platter and keep warm.

Strain the broth into a clean pan, discarding the peppercorns and herbs. Bring the broth to a boil, add the rice, and simmer for about 20 minutes until it is cooked.

Meanwhile, whisk the eggs until they are foamy and then mix in the lemon juice. Whisk in a ladleful of hot broth and, when that is combined, whisk in another ladleful. Take the pan of broth from the heat and stir the egg mixture into it. Return to very low heat for just a few moments to warm through, but don't let it get too hot or the eggs will scramble. Taste for salt and then serve immediately, with a good grinding of back pepper for those who'd like it.

Serve the platter of fish, shallots, carrots, potatoes, zucchini, and celery as a second course. Everyone can choose what they want, dousing the fish with the lemon oil, or some mayonnaise, or both.

Serves 4

---

1 CHICKEN (ABOUT 2³/4 POUNDS), SUITABLE
   FOR BOILING
2 CARROTS, PEELED AND HALVED
2 LEAFY CELERY STALKS
SMALL HANDFUL OF PARSLEY STALKS
7 BLACK PEPPERCORNS
3 SMALL SHALLOTS, PEELED BUT LEFT WHOLE
1 CLOVE GARLIC, PEELED BUT LEFT WHOLE
10 CUPS WATER
1 TEASPOON SALT

Chicken broth

You could add some extra herbs to direct the flavors in other directions here—maybe some thyme, bay leaf, or lemon grass. This is a simple and wholesome broth and a good basis for so many meals—boil some pasta in it for a first course, or try it with very small dumplings (page 329). I often make chicken croquettes with the boiled chicken (page 330).

Put the chicken into your largest stockpot and add the carrots, celery, parsley, peppercorns, shallots, and garlic. Add 10 cups of water and 1 teaspoon of salt and bring to a boil. Lower the heat and put the lid on the pan, leaving just a little gap for the steam to escape. Simmer for 1¹/2 hours, skimming now and then.

Turn off the heat and leave the broth until it's cool enough to handle. Carefully take out the chicken. Strain what's left, keeping the broth to use for pasta or dumplings. You decide if you'd like to save the carrots to eat later on.

Makes 8 cups

8 CUPS CHICKEN BROTH (PAGE 327)
⅓ (16-OUNCE) PACKAGE SPAGHETTINI, OR
1⅔ CUPS OTHER TINY PASTA
GRATED PARMESAN CHEESE, TO SERVE

Pasta in chicken broth

This is so quick to make and I don't think any child would ever turn it down. You just drop pasta into boiling broth while shouting for everyone to get their hands washed and be seated. Add an extra dash of salt to the broth now that you will be cooking pasta in it.

Bring the broth to a boil in a large pan. Break up the pasta into shorter lengths and add to the broth. Bring back to a boil, stir a couple of times, and then cook the pasta according to the package instructions. The pasta will absorb some of the broth as it cooks. Serve immediately, diving down with your ladle to the bottom of the pan to make sure that everyone has a fair share of pasta and broth. Top each serving with a heap of grated Parmesan.

Serves 4

APPLES FOR SAM

2 TO 3 SLICES DAY-OLD WHITE BREAD, CRUSTS CUT OFF
2/3 CUP MILK
1 1/2 TABLESPOONS BUTTER
1 SHALLOT, FINELY CHOPPED
1 CLOVE GARLIC, CHOPPED
4 OUNCES UNSMOKED PANCETTA, FINELY CHOPPED
1 EGG, LIGHTLY BEATEN
3 TABLESPOONS CHOPPED FRESH PARSLEY
3 TABLESPOONS GRATED PARMESAN CHEESE
FRESHLY GRATED NUTMEG
SALT AND FRESHLY GROUND BLACK PEPPER
8 CUPS CHICKEN BROTH (PAGE 327)

Bread dumplings in chicken broth

This is the sort of dish all kids remember having at their grandmother's. I think it's wholesome and warming to poach the dumplings in the broth, but you will find that they give off little bits of parsley and bread that make your broth a bit cloudy. If you prefer to keep your broth clear, cook the dumplings separately in boiling salted water and add them to the broth to serve.

Tear up the bread and put it in a bowl with the milk. Leave it to soak for about 20 minutes. Melt the butter in a frying pan and sauté the shallot over medium-low heat for a few minutes until it is golden. Add the garlic and pancetta, and sauté until lightly browned. Cool a little and then add to the bread mixture. Add the egg, parsley, Parmesan, a couple of grinds of nutmeg, and salt and pepper to taste. Squash it all together with your hands. Dampen your hands with warm water and roll little balls of mixture the size of small walnuts (you should get 20 to 25 dumplings). Put the dumplings on a plate, cover with plastic wrap, and refrigerate for 30 minutes or so.

Bring the broth to a boil in a large saucepan. Add the dumplings, give them a stir, and then simmer for 8 to 10 minutes. Ladle the broth into serving bowls, giving everyone four or five dumplings each.

Serves 5

1 BOILED CHICKEN (PAGE 327)
3 TABLESPOONS BUTTER
1 SMALL RED ONION, FINELY CHOPPED
1 1/2 TABLESPOONS CHOPPED CELERY LEAVES
1 1/2 TABLESPOONS CHOPPED FRESH PARSLEY
2 SMALL CLOVES GARLIC, FINELY CHOPPED
1 RIPE TOMATO, PEELED AND CHOPPED
1 1/2 TABLESPOONS ALL-PURPOSE FLOUR
1 CUP CHICKEN BROTH (PAGE 327)
1 EGG, LIGHTLY BEATEN
SALT
DRY BREAD CRUMBS, FOR COATING
LIGHT OLIVE OIL, FOR FRYING
LEMON WEDGES, TO SERVE

Chicken croquettes

This is what I like to make with the chicken that has been boiled for broth. I love serving meals like this—meals that fit together like the pieces of a puzzle—so a small bowl of pasta in broth can be followed by chicken croquettes with a simple green salad.

Pick all the chicken meat off the bones and throw away all the skin, bones, and bits you don't want. Chop up the chicken finely, and put it in a bowl.

Melt half the butter in a small pan, and sauté the onion over medium-low heat until it is soft and lightly golden. Add the celery, parsley, and garlic, and when you can smell the garlic, add the tomato. Simmer until it has totally melted, squashing it with a wooden spoon now and then as you stir.

Meanwhile, melt the rest of the butter in another small pan over medium heat, and then stir in the flour. Whisk in the broth, and let it cook for a few minutes until it is bubbling up nicely. Whisk well to make sure it is totally smooth. Pour into the bowl of chicken and add the tomato mixture, too. Add the egg, and mix everything together well. Taste for salt, adding a little extra if you think it's needed.

Put the bowl in the fridge for half an hour or so, so that you are able to roll out the croquettes more easily.

Take scoops of the mixture, more or less the size of eggs, and shape them into croquettes. Put the bread crumbs on a plate and lightly roll the croquettes in them.

Pour about 3/4 inch of oil into a large nonstick frying pan and put over high heat. When the oil is hot, add enough of the croquettes to fit comfortably in the pan. Fry until they are deep golden brown all over, turning them gently with tongs. Lift them out onto a plate lined with paper towels to absorb as much of the oil as possible while you fry the rest. Put them onto a clean platter to serve, with lemon wedges, if you like.

Makes about 25 croquettes

1 CHICKEN (ABOUT 2³/4 POUNDS)
1 LEAFY CELERY STALK, ROUGHLY CHOPPED
2 SMALL CARROTS, PEELED AND HALVED
1 SMALL LEEK, TRIMMED AND HALVED
ABOUT 12 BLACK PEPPERCORNS
12 CUPS WATER
3¹/2 TABLESPOONS BUTTER
1/4 CUP ALL-PURPOSE FLOUR
3 TABLESPOONS MARSALA OR PORT
1 EGG
FRESHLY GRATED PARMESAN OR PECORINO CHEESE,
  TO SERVE

Chicken
soup

When I asked Giovanni about his childhood food memories, he said there
was a chicken soup so velvety and creamy that he can never forget it.
Here is my father-in-law Mario's chicken soup that all generations love.
It has a very thick, almost oatmeal, consistency—if you prefer, you can cut
all the chicken into strips instead of puréeing it and save the leftovers
for sandwiches.

Put the chicken in a large stockpot with the celery, carrot, leek, and peppercorns.
Add about 12 cups of water and some salt and bring to a boil. (If the water doesn't
all fit in your stockpot, put in as much as you can and add the rest when it has
reduced.) Skim the surface with a slotted spoon, lower the heat, and simmer for
1 1/2 hours. Lift the chicken out onto a plate to cool and strain the broth into a
clean pan.

Pick all the chicken meat from the bones. Chop about 1 cup of the chicken meat
into longish strips and put the rest of it into a blender. Chop until it is almost a
purée and keep on one side for now.

Melt the butter in a smallish pan, then add the flour and stir with a wooden
spoon for a few minutes until it begins to turn golden. Add a ladleful of hot broth
and mix in well and, when the flour has absorbed this, whisk in another ladleful of
broth. Simmer for about 10 minutes, whisking every now and then so that it is
very smooth. Add the Marsala and then pour it all back into the large broth pan
together with all the chicken meat. Simmer for another 10 minutes.

Whip the egg in a small bowl. Add a ladleful of the hot broth to the egg,
whisking to avoid scrambling it, and then mix this back into the broth. Return the
pan to the lowest possible heat and stir with a wooden spoon for a minute or so to
just cook the egg through.

Serve immediately, scattering a heaping tablespoon of Parmesan or pecorino
over each bowl.

Serves 8 or more

3 CARROTS, PEELED AND HALVED
2 ZUCCHINI
2 SCALLIONS, TRIMMED
2 LEAFY INNER CELERY STALKS
3 RIPE CHERRY TOMATOES, HALVED
2 CLOVES GARLIC, PEELED BUT LEFT
  WHOLE
A SMALL HANDFUL OF PARSLEY
7 PEPPERCORNS
1 TEASPOON SALT
10 CUPS COLD WATER

Vegetable broth

This is so quick and easy and is, I feel, an essential dish when you're cooking for children. It can be used for cooking a white risotto, a ladleful will add depth to a casserole or stew, or it can just be drunk from a cup. You can add anything you fancy to flavor this broth in another way. Sometimes I put in a piece of red pepper, just for extra and new vitamins. And you could add some stronger herbs—a bay leaf or some basil. Make sure your vegetables are top quality though, not those that are left over and exhausted in the bottom of the fridge.

Put all the ingredients in a very large pan with 1 teaspoon of salt and 10 cups of cold water. Bring to a boil and then lower the heat to simmer. Put the lid on the pan, and continue cooking for about $1\frac{1}{2}$ hours, until the vegetables have surrendered all their goodness and flavor into the broth. Taste for salt and add more if necessary.

Strain through cheesecloth or a fine sieve. (Don't throw the vegetables away; someone might like to eat them with a little olive oil and a few slices of leftover roast meat.) The broth will keep in the fridge for a couple of days and can also be frozen.

Makes 8 cups

ABOUT 1 1/2 POUNDS BEEF ON THE BONE, SUITABLE
FOR BOILING, FAT REMOVED
10 CUPS WATER, PLUS 1 TO 2 CUPS HOT WATER
2 MEDIUM CARROTS, PEELED
2 LEAFY INNER CELERY STALKS
A SMALL HANDFUL OF PARSLEY
2 RIPE TOMATOES, QUARTERED
1 LARGE CLOVE GARLIC, PEELED BUT LEFT
WHOLE
ABOUT 7 BLACK PEPPERCORNS
1 TEASPOON SALT
2 CHICKEN LEGS
1 RED ONION, OR 2 SHALLOTS, PEELED
BUT LEFT WHOLE

Meat broth

I love to serve broth in a tazza (a large tea cup) just before a meal, like they do in the old-style Florentine restaurants. Or you could make this a full meal with tortellini or other pasta, dumplings, or plain rice for a "risotto in bianco" with grated parmesan or grana. I make this with two chicken legs (the whole legs with thighs, not just the drumsticks) and some meat suitable for boiling so that it isn't too strong and meaty for the kids, but you can do all meat if you prefer a stronger broth. You can leave a bit of fat on the meat, but I prefer to remove that heavier layer. Try making meat and chicken croquettes from the meat if your family isn't wild about eating plain boiled meat.

Put the beef in a large stockpot with 10 cups of water. Add the carrots, celery, parsley, tomatoes, and garlic, and bring to a boil. Skim the surface, and then add the peppercorns and a teaspoon of salt. Lower the heat and simmer uncovered for about half an hour. Add the chicken and bring back to a boil. Lower the heat and simmer, covered, for 1 1/2 hours. Add 1 1/2 to 2 cups of hot water after 45 minutes or so to maintain the level.

Turn off the heat and leave with the lid on for 15 minutes to cool down a bit. Carefully remove the beef and any bits that you'd like to keep, then strain the liquid into a clean pan or a bowl, depending on what you are going to do with it.

Makes 8 cups

5 TABLESPOONS OLIVE OIL
1³/4 POUNDS GROUND BEEF
4 TABLESPOONS DRY WHITE WINE
1 LARGE ONION, CHOPPED
2 CLOVES GARLIC, FINELY CHOPPED
1 LARGE CARROT, CHOPPED
1 (14-OUNCE) CAN TOMATO SAUCE
SALT
1 BAY LEAF
2 ALLSPICE BERRIES
4 BASIL LEAVES, TORN
3 TABLESPOONS CHOPPED FRESH
   PARSLEY
3 CUPS HOT WATER
²/3 CUP SHELLED PEAS
7 TO 8 MEDIUM POTATOES, SCRUBBED BUT
   NOT PEELED
3 TABLESPOONS BUTTER
²/3 CUP MILK
A LITTLE FRESHLY GRATED NUTMEG

Cottage pie

You can make one large pie here or use small dishes for individual servings. Just remember how many allspice berries you put in so you can count them out again once the sauce is ready. If you prefer not to use wine in your cooking, you could always add some unsweetened grape juice (red or white) instead.

Heat half the oil in a nonstick frying pan and fry the ground beef over fairly high heat for about 10 minutes until it is golden brown, stirring often and breaking up any clusters with a wooden spoon. Pour in the wine and scrape up any bits that are stuck to the bottom of the pan. When the wine has evaporated, remove the pan from the heat.

   Meanwhile, heat the remaining oil in a large saucepan. Sauté the onion for 5 minutes or so over low-medium heat until it is lightly golden and a bit sticky. Add the garlic and carrot, and sauté for a few minutes more so that the carrot looks a bit caramelized. Add the tomato sauce and cook for a couple of minutes, then add the browned beef. Season well with salt and add the bay leaf, allspice berries, basil, and parsley. Stir in 2 cups of hot water. Bring to a boil and then turn the heat to low, cover the pan, and cook for 30 minutes. Add the peas and 1 cup of hot water, and simmer uncovered for another 30 minutes. Add a little water if the meat sauce seems very dry; it should neither be runny nor too stiff. Check the seasoning and try to find all the allspice berries.

Preheat the oven to 350°F. Meanwhile, boil the potatoes in salted water for about 30 minutes (depending on their size) until they are soft enough to mash. Drain, and when they're cool enough to handle, peel and mash, or pass through a food mill. In a small saucepan, heat the butter and milk and, when the butter has melted, add to the potatoes. Add the nutmeg, taste for salt, and mix to a soft and fluffy mash (add a little more butter or milk if it seems too stiff).

Butter a 10-cup ovenproof dish or 6 to 8 individual dishes. Spoon in the meat sauce, smoothing the surface, and then spoon mashed potato over the top, spreading it very gently to completely cover the sauce. Roughen the mash with a fork here and there so you get some crispy bits. Bake for 30 minutes, until the top is softly crusted and golden in places.

Serves 6 to 8

. . . and at night, once they are sound asleep, there are opened tubs of yogurt here and there, and not-even-half-eaten apples and strawberries. And still bits of chewed-up liver or other meat they tossed to their friend—the dog.

SAUCE:
2 TABLESPOONS BUTTER
1/4 CUP ALL-PURPOSE FLOUR
1 1/4 CUPS VEGETABLE BROTH (PAGE 334), WARMED
1/2 CUP HEAVY WHIPPING CREAM
SALT AND FRESHLY GROUND BLACK PEPPER

4 TABLESPOONS BUTTER
1 CLOVE GARLIC, PEELED AND SQUASHED A BIT
2 1/4 CUPS SLICED BUTTON MUSHROOMS
SALT
3 TABLESPOONS WHITE WINE
FRESHLY GROUND BLACK PEPPER
1 1/4 POUNDS SKINLESS HALIBUT, COD, OR SNAPPER FILLETS
1 POUND RAW SHRIMP, PEELED AND DEVEINED
3 TABLESPOONS CHOPPED FRESH PARSLEY
6 TO 7 MEDIUM POTATOES, PEELED AND CUT INTO CHUNKS
3/4 CUP MILK, WARMED
LEMON WEDGES, TO SERVE

Fish pie

This is Harriet's—my mom's friend in Finland—a wonderful, stylish lady and cook. I tasted this many years ago and have always remembered it. Her original recipe uses perch fillets, but you can use any fish fillets you like, just make sure they have no bones. In this pie, the mashed potatoes are only around the rim, not covering the whole thing, and it is important to use a dish that is no deeper than 2 1/2 inches. Maybe make a few smoked salmon crostini for an appetizer and serve a green salad and bread with your pie, and that really is a complete family dinner, I feel.

For the sauce, melt the butter in a smallish saucepan and then stir in the flour. Cook for a minute or so over medium heat and then add the broth, whisking well to make a smooth sauce. Let it bubble up for a few minutes and then stir in the cream. Taste for salt and pepper (your broth will probably be seasoned already).

Preheat the oven to 400°F and butter a 13 by 9 by 2 1/2-inch ovenproof dish. Heat 1 1/2 tablespoons of the butter and the garlic in a frying pan and, when it is sizzling, add the mushrooms and a little salt. Sauté over high heat, shifting the mushrooms around with a wooden spoon until all the juices have evaporated and they turn golden. Add the wine and some pepper and cook until the wine has evaporated. Remove from the heat.

Cut the fish into large chunks of about 2 inches and put in the bottom of your dish. Scrape the mushrooms out over the fish, then add the shrimp. Scatter with the parsley and a few grinds of pepper. Pour the sauce over the top. Bake for about 20 minutes or until the sauce is bubbling and a bit golden here and there.

Meanwhile, boil the potatoes in salted water until soft. Heat the remaining butter in the milk. Drain the potatoes and mash them, or pass them through a food mill into a bowl. Beat in the rest of the butter and the warm milk and season.

Arrange the mashed potatoes in dollops just around the rim of the dish, then bake the pie for another 10 minutes or so, or until the mash is a little golden in places. Leave it to stand for 5 or 10 minutes before serving with lemon wedges.

Serves 5

1 THICK PORK FILLET, ABOUT
   1 1/4 POUNDS, TRIMMED OF ALL FAT
2 LARGE EGGS
2 CLOVES GARLIC, VERY FINELY CHOPPED
3 TABLESPOONS CHOPPED FRESH
   PARSLEY
SALT AND FRESHLY GROUND BLACK
   PEPPER
ABOUT 1 CUP DRY BREAD CRUMBS
LIGHT OLIVE OIL, FOR FRYING
LEMON WEDGES, TO SERVE

Pork schnitzels

My mother always made piles of these. You can also use veal, if you like. These, with bread and some pan-fried potatoes scattered with fresh herbs, are a dream meal—and one that would have made me sing as a child. Lemon veal or this were my best. If there are any at all left the next day, they are lovely in a roll with a few green salad leaves, a squeeze of lemon or lime and, if you like, a small dollop of mayonnaise. Great for a picnic.

Slice the pork into 3/4-inch pieces and then pound the slices flat with a meat mallet to about 1/16 inch thick. Cut these in half so that they are about 2 inches square, and then put them in a flattish dish.

   Whisk the eggs, garlic, and parsley together in a small bowl, and season lightly with salt and pepper. Pour over the pork and turn it over with your hands so that all the pieces are coated with egg. Cover with plastic wrap and set aside for about 30 minutes.

   Put the bread crumbs on a plate. Lift the pork out of the egg mixture with a fork and pat both sides into the crumbs, pressing them down with your palms so they stick. Pour enough oil into a large nonstick frying pan to shallow-fry the pork in batches over medium heat until golden and crisp on both sides. (If any crumbs burn in the oil, wipe out the pan and pour in fresh oil.) Lift out onto paper towels to drain and then put on a clean platter. Serve with lemon and an extra sprinkling of salt. Good served warm or at room temperature, or even cold from the fridge.

Serves 6

4 TO 5 SLICES SOFT WHITE BREAD, CRUSTS
CUT OFF
1 EGG
2 TEASPOONS GRATED PARMESAN CHEESE
SALT AND FRESHLY GROUND BLACK
PEPPER
4 LAMB RIB CHOPS, TRIMMED
3 TABLESPOONS LIGHT OLIVE OIL
2½ TABLESPOONS BUTTER
LEMON WEDGES, TO SERVE

Pan-fried breaded lamb rib chops

This is just lovely with handmade fries and ripe tomato salad (page 47) or some sliced bright red tomatoes. You could do as my friend Julia might: Start with a big bowl of minestrone, then serve these chops. She taught me this way of breading the lamb, and that's all you need for a meal, I feel. You could also use thin veal rib chops here—they tend to be much larger, so just make sure they are completely cooked through.

Put the bread in a blender or processor and pulse to make coarse crumbs. Tip them out onto a flat plate. Whisk the egg and Parmesan together and season with salt and pepper if you like. Pour into a flattish bowl.

Gently pound the chops to flatten the meat to about ¼ inch thick. Wipe them with a paper towel to get rid of any stray pieces of bone. Dip them in the egg, making sure they are well covered everywhere. Shake off the excess egg and then pat them firmly on both sides in the bread crumbs.

Heat the oil and butter in a large nonstick frying pan (the exact amount you will need for frying will depend on the size of your pan). Add the rib chops and fry over medium-high heat until they are golden on both sides. Lift them out onto a plate lined with paper towels to absorb the excess oil. Serve immediately, with a sprinkling of salt and the lemon wedges.

Serves 2

I loved those Italian restaurants as a child . . . where they bring you a white plate with a schnitzel, a bit flattened so it almost takes up the whole plate, and a plain lemony-yellow lemon unfancily cut next to it.

2 EGGS
GRATED RIND OF 1 SMALL LEMON
1 CUP ALL-PURPOSE FLOUR
1 TEASPOON BAKING POWDER
1 TEASPOON SWEET PAPRIKA
SALT AND FRESHLY GROUND BLACK
  PEPPER
1/2 CUP COLD SPARKLING WATER
LIGHT OLIVE OIL, FOR FRYING
1 1/4 POUNDS COD OR OTHER FIRM
  WHITEFISH FILLETS, CUT INTO STRIPS
LEMON WEDGES, TO SERVE

Fried fish fillets

You can serve these on their own or with some vegetables that have also been cut into thick sticks, dipped in the batter, and fried. Zucchini, green beans, artichokes, and cauliflower are all lovely like this. I like to serve a bowl of thin fries alongside as well.

Whisk the eggs and lemon rind in a bowl. Sift in the flour, baking powder, and paprika, and add some salt and pepper. Whisk in the water, and continue whisking until the batter is smooth—it will be a fairly thick batter.

Pour about 1 1/2 inches of oil into a large frying pan, and heat it up enough for shallow-frying.

Dip the strips of fish in the batter, shake off the excess, and fry for a few minutes on each side until they are crisp and golden. Pat dry on paper towels, and then serve at once, with lemon juice squeezed over the top and some extra salt.

Serves 4

APPLES FOR SAM

ABOUT 1/2 CUP ALL-PURPOSE FLOUR
ABOUT 3/4 CUP DRY BREAD CRUMBS
2 SMALL EGGS
1 1/2 TABLESPOONS CHOPPED FRESH
   PARSLEY
SALT
1 1/4 POUNDS FISH FILLETS, CUT INTO
   CHUNKS
4 TO 5 TABLESPOONS OLIVE OIL
LEMON WEDGES, TO SERVE

Baked
fish fillets

Here is a nice and healthy way to cook your fish, in case you worry about frying in batter too often.

Preheat the oven 425°F. Spread the flour on one flattish plate and the bread crumbs on another one.

Whisk the eggs and parsley together in a shallow bowl and add some salt. Sprinkle the fish with some salt, too.

Pat the fish chunks in the flour first, then in the egg, and finally in the bread crumbs, turning to coat them thoroughly each time. Put the fish in a baking pan and drizzle with a little of the oil. Turn the fish over and drizzle a little more oil over the top.

Bake the fish in the oven for 10 minutes, then turn the pieces over and bake for another 5 minutes or so until they are golden and crisp. Serve with an extra scattering of salt and some lemon juice squeezed over the top.

Serves 4

3 MEDIUM POTATOES, PEELED AND CUT
   INTO CHUNKS
1 CUP MILK
2 TABLESPOONS BUTTER
2½ TABLESPOONS OLIVE OIL
2 CLOVES GARLIC, PEELED BUT LEFT WHOLE
1 SMALL SAGE SPRIG
1 CUP COOKED OR CANNED CHICKPEAS,
   DRAINED
SALT

Potato and chickpea mash

If you have some cooked chickpeas left over from something else, this is a great nutritious way to serve them to the small ones of our world. If you need to be a bit more spontaneous, just use canned chickpeas. You can serve this with an extra drizzle or so of olive oil, if you like.

Boil the potatoes for 20 to 25 minutes in salted water until they are soft. Heat the milk and butter in a small pan until the butter melts. Heat the olive oil, garlic, and sage in a saucepan over medium heat until you can smell the garlic. Add the chickpeas, and sauté for a few minutes so that the flavors of the garlic and sage mingle with the chickpeas. Remove the garlic and sage. Purée the chickpeas with a handheld blender until they are completely smooth and silky, adding a little of the milk and butter mixture if necessary.

Mash the potatoes or pass through a food mill into a wide bowl that you can eventually use for serving. Add the remaining milk and butter mixture, and mix it in well. Fold in the chickpea purée and taste for salt. Serve warm or at room temperature, drizzled with extra virgin olive oil if you like.

Serves 6

2/3 CUP PECANS
1 CUP SUPERFINE SUGAR
3/4 CUP LIGHT OLIVE OIL
1 TEASPOON VANILLA EXTRACT
3 EGGS
2 1/4 CUPS ALL-PURPOSE FLOUR
1 1/2 TEASPOONS BAKING POWDER
1/2 TEASPOON BAKING SODA
1/2 TEASPOON GROUND CINNAMON
PINCH OF GROUND NUTMEG
SALT
ABOUT 3 ZUCCHINI, COARSELY GRATED
FRESHLY GROUND BLACK PEPPER
2 TEASPOONS GRATED LEMON ZEST

Zucchini bread

You can't really tell that there is a vegetable in here. This is a lovely bread to make in the summer when there is an abundance of zucchini, and it will keep moist for a few days if you wrap it well. I find a slice makes a great snack, even in times of predinner emergency.

Preheat the oven to 350°F. Butter and flour a 12 by 4-inch loaf pan. Spread the pecans in a baking pan and toast them in the oven until they are just crisp and lightly roasted (keep a close eye on them so that they don't burn), then remove the pan from the oven and leave them to cool.

Beat the sugar with the oil and vanilla until smooth and then add the eggs one by one, beating well after each addition. Keep on beating until you have a thick, yet light and fluffy batter. Sift in the flour, baking powder, baking soda, cinnamon, and nutmeg. Add a pinch of salt, the zucchini, several good grinds of black pepper, and the lemon zest, and fold together well. Coarsely chop the pecans and gently stir through the batter.

Scrape the batter into the pan and bake for 55 to 60 minutes, or until a skewer poked into the middle of the loaf comes out clean. Leave the pan on a rack to cool for 10 minutes before turning the loaf out onto the rack to cool. Serve warm or at room temperature, buttered if you like. Well wrapped up, this stays moist and soft for days, and it toasts well even after it's lost its moistness.

Cuts into 10 to 12 slices

¼ POUND PLUS 1 TABLESPOON BUTTER
1 CUP FIRMLY PACKED DARK BROWN
    SUGAR
3 OR 4 MEDIUM RIPE BANANAS, MASHED
2 EGGS
1 TEASPOON VANILLA EXTRACT
1 TEASPOON GROUND CINNAMON
SALT
2 CUPS ALL-PURPOSE FLOUR
1 TEASPOON BAKING POWDER
¾ TEASPOON BAKING SODA
4 TABLESPOONS WARM MILK

Banana bread

This is my schoolfriend Alexia's recipe: Her mom was a fantastic cook and she always made this. It is a healthy snack or breakfast and an excellent way to use up bananas that otherwise might be on their way out. I always end up making this because bananas in my house just never keep the pale waxy complexion that they have in the shops. For some reason, they start deteriorating the minute they come home with me. You can add some chopped walnuts or hazelnuts, too, and some cinnamon. Serve it on its own, or even lightly buttered and with your favorite jam.

Preheat the oven to 350°F and butter a 12 by 4-inch loaf pan.

Cream the butter and sugar until smooth and then whisk in the mashed bananas. Add the eggs, vanilla, cinnamon, and a pinch of salt and whisk in well. Sieve in the flour and baking powder and beat until smooth. Mix the baking soda into the milk and stir into the batter.

Scrape the mixture into the pan and bake for about 50 minutes, until the bread is crusty on the top and a skewer poked into the middle comes out clean. Turn out onto a rack to cool.

Serve warm or cold, plain or toasted with butter, but allow to cool completely before storing in an airtight container, where it will keep well for several days.

Cuts into 10 to 12 slices

SCANT 3/4 CUP SUGAR
1/4 POUND PLUS 3 TABLESPOONS BUTTER,
   SOFTENED
2 EGGS
1 CUP ALL-PURPOSE FLOUR
1 TEASPOON BAKING SODA
1 TEASPOON BAKING POWDER
1/2 TEASPOON GROUND CARDAMOM
1/2 TEASPOON GROUND CINNAMON
SALT
ABOUT 2 APPLES, PEELED, CORED,
   AND COARSELY GRATED
2/3 CUP WALNUTS, LIGHTLY TOASTED AND
   COARSELY CHOPPED
1 TEASPOON VANILLA EXTRACT

TOPPING:
2/3 CUP WALNUTS, FINELY CHOPPED
1/3 CUP LIGHTLY PACKED BROWN SUGAR
1 TEASPOON GROUND CINNAMON

Apple bread with sugar and cinnamon topping

I love the name apple bread—it carries me off in my fantasy to some very green hills with chunky plates and bowls of fresh cream, with rosy-cheeked children skipping about here and there. It is perfect for snacks, breakfast, with a meal, or as a meal, with a few chunks of cheese. And maybe even a small pile of fresh blueberries and indeed another pile of fresh cream would be lovely with it. This keeps for several days, well wrapped up. I find it's an excellent healthy snack to have on hand to give to a suddenly starving child. I often send a bit for school snacks as well as banana bread.

Preheat the oven to 350°F. Butter and flour a 12 by 4-inch loaf pan. Beat together the sugar and butter until fluffy. Add the eggs, and beat them in well. Sift the flour, baking soda, baking powder, cardamom, and cinnamon in, and add a pinch of salt. Mix well. Add the apples, walnuts, and vanilla, and mix those through well. Scrape the mixture into the pan.

For the topping, mix together the walnuts, sugar, and cinnamon, and then scatter abundantly over the top of the batter. Bake for about 45 minutes, or until the top is crusty brown and a skewer poked into the middle comes out clean. Check after 30 minutes and cover the top with foil if it is already quite brown.

Cool slightly before turning out carefully. Do this over your serving plate so that you don't lose any topping. Serve slightly warm or at room temperature, on its own, with whipped cream, or with a simple vanilla ice cream.

Cuts into 10 to 12 slices

1 EGG
2/3 CUP LIGHTLY PACKED LIGHT BROWN
   SUGAR
1 TEASPOON VANILLA EXTRACT
5 1/2 TABLESPOONS BUTTER, SOFTENED
1/2 CUP ALL-PURPOSE FLOUR
1/3 CUP WHOLE WHEAT FLOUR
1 TEASPOON BAKING POWDER
SALT
1 CUP QUICK-COOKING OATS
1 1/2 TABLESPOONS MILK

Oat
cookies

These are plain, healthy, and good. You could serve them for breakfast instead of oatmeal sometimes, with a mug of warm milk.

Preheat the oven to 350°F and line a large baking sheet with parchment paper.
   Whip the egg, sugar, and vanilla together until the sugar has dissolved. Beat in the butter and then sift in the all-purpose and whole wheat flours and baking powder. Add a pinch of salt and the oats, and mix well with a wooden spoon. Stir in the milk. With lightly moistened hands, shape the dough into walnut-sized balls and put them, well spaced, on the baking sheet. Flatten them a bit so they look like mini hamburger patties. Bake for about 15 minutes until they are golden around the edges (they might still be a little soft on top). Cool on a wire rack and then keep in your cookie jar for up to 5 days.

Makes about 25 cookies

355

1 CUP HEAVY WHIPPING
    CREAM
½ CUP PURE MAPLE SYRUP
1 CUP MILK
1 TEASPOON VANILLA EXTRACT

Maple syrup and vanilla ice cream

I am crazy about this with the pecan butter cookies (page 358). You could also sauté some chopped walnuts or pecans in butter and then fold them through when the ice cream is just about ready. This will keep for up to a week in the freezer.

Mix together the cream and maple syrup in a bowl or container that has a lid. Whisk in the milk and vanilla. Put the lid on the bowl and put it in the freezer. After an hour give the mixture an energetic whisk with a hand whisk or an electric mixer. Put it back in the freezer and then whisk again after another couple of hours. When the ice cream is nearly firm, give one last whisk and put it back in the freezer to set.

Alternatively, pour into your ice cream machine and churn, following the manufacturer's instructions.

Serves 6 to 8

MONOCHROME

popsi then

1/2 POUND (2 STICKS) BUTTER, SOFTENED
1/3 CUP CONFECTIONERS' SUGAR, PLUS
   A LITTLE EXTRA FOR DUSTING
1 TEASPOON VANILLA EXTRACT
2 1/4 CUPS ALL-PURPOSE FLOUR
2/3 CUP PECANS, CHOPPED

FROSTING:
2 CUPS CONFECTIONERS' SUGAR
2 TABLESPOONS BUTTER, SOFTENED
1 TEASPOON VANILLA EXTRACT
3 TABLESPOONS MILK
A FEW DROPS OF FOOD COLORING

Pecan butter cookies

These are Stella's (Richard's mom), and I have been hooked since I first tasted them. Made without the frosting, they are gorgeous with maple syrup and vanilla ice cream (page 355). Although I love the pecans here, you might like to try it with another nut—perhaps walnuts or hazelnuts. This will give you about 40 cookies. You might like to frost yours with a soft creamy frosting tinted with your favorite color.

Preheat the oven to 375°F. Cream the butter with the confectioners' sugar and vanilla until it is smooth. Add the flour in four portions, mashing it in well with a wooden spoon after each addition. Mix the nuts through.

Divide the dough into quarters. Dip your fingers in confectioners' sugar and then, from each quarter of dough, roll 10 balls the size of cherry tomatoes. Put on two ungreased baking sheets, leaving some space between each ball. Flatten each one a bit, and then dip your thumb in confectioners' sugar and make an indent in each ball. The sugar will sit in here and, even if you're not frosting the cookies, it'll look good.

Bake one sheet at a time for about 15 minutes or until the cookies are firm and golden and slightly darker around the edges. Bake for a few more minutes, if necessary. They are delicate, so carefully lift them off the sheets and onto racks to cool. Wait until they are completely cold if you are going to frost them; otherwise, store them in a cookie jar.

To make the frosting, cream together the confectioners' sugar, butter, vanilla, and milk until completely smooth. You may need to use more or less milk to get a soft, buttery consistency. Add the food coloring, mixing it in well. If you are not ready to frost the cookies immediately, cover the bowl with a wet paper towel.

Use a small butter knife or a teaspoon to spread the frosting rustically into and over the indentations in the cookies. When the frosting has hardened a little, store the cookies in a jar. They will keep for up to a week at room temperature.

Makes 40

1/4 CUP MAPLE SYRUP
1/2 TEASPOON GROUND GINGER
1 TEASPOON GROUND CINNAMON
A PINCH OF GROUND CLOVES
1/2 TEASPOON GROUND CARDAMOM
1/2 CUP HEAVY WHIPPING CREAM
1/2 CUP SUPERFINE SUGAR
7 TABLESPOONS BUTTER, SOFTENED
1 EGG
2 CUPS ALL-PURPOSE FLOUR
1 TEASPOON BAKING POWDER

Gingerbread cookies

My mother's friend Iria gave me this recipe. It smells of Christmas and is typical in Finland, she says. You can make gingerbread men or any shapes you like (and there are many cutters available—trees, bells, hearts, birds, cows, flowers). I think these are lovely to dust with confectioners' sugar, wrap up, and put in a beautiful wrapped box for a gift. They are not too spicy—but very Christmassy. If you make holes in the cookies with a skewer when they have just come out of the oven, you can thread them with ribbon or string and hang them on your tree as decorations.

Put the maple syrup, ginger, cinnamon, cloves, and cardamom in a small saucepan over low heat, stirring to dissolve all the spices. Remove from the heat and allow to cool a bit, then stir in the cream with a wooden spoon. Mix well, making sure that nothing is left stuck on the bottom.

Beat the sugar and butter together for a minute or two, until the sugar dissolves. Add the egg. Mix in the flour and baking powder alternately with the maple syrup cream. Mix well with a wooden spoon until the mixture is thick and smooth. Cover the dough with plastic wrap and leave in the fridge for at least 3 hours or even overnight.

Preheat the oven to 375°F and line two baking sheets with parchment paper.

Take lumps of the dough and roll out on a floured surface with a floured rolling pin to about 1/4 inch thick. Add extra flour as you roll if you find the dough too soft to handle. (You can also make the cookies very thin if you prefer, and they will then need less time in the oven.) Cut out shapes with your cookie cutters. Put about half the shapes on the baking sheets, leaving just a little space between them for spreading. Bake one sheet at a time for 12 to 15 minutes, or until the cookies are golden with a deeper gold around the edges.

Lift them onto wire racks to cool and use the same sheets to bake the rest of the cookies. (If you are making holes to hang them from your Christmas tree, do that now, and then hang them when they harden.) These will keep in a cookie jar or plastic bag for up to 2 weeks.

Makes about 35 cookies, depending on the shapes

popsi now

stripes

Pot-roasted steak with spinach and omelette
Little spinach and carrot ramekins
Pomegranate and apple gelatin desserts
Vanilla ice cream
Chocolate ice cream
Ice cream sundaes
Chocolate and vanilla milkshakes and double thickshakes
Raspberry ripple ice cream
Chocolate and vanilla marble cake
Chocolate and vanilla cookies
Chocolate toffee nut squares

- memory -

I remember the ice cream man with the box on his bicycle, coming down the road and ringing his bell. The diagonal red and silver stripes in that milky sorbet. Such sweet, chocolaty music . . . I wish I could have that again. We did that once—got my father to take us up to the shop and bought 20 ice creams and attached them onto our bicycles somehow and rode down the road trying to sell them before they melted— then strewed them, like petals, to our neighbors. And once I took an ice cream to school in my small suitcase and thought to eat it at lunch break. There was such a mess and ripples of laughter from the other small childen.

1 SMALL CELERY STALK
1 SMALL CARROT, PEELED AND COARSELY
  CHOPPED
1 LARGE RED ONION, COARSELY CHOPPED
7 TABLESPOONS OLIVE OIL
1 (14-OUNCE) CAN DICED TOMATOES
4 TABLESPOONS CHOPPED FRESH PARSLEY
1 CUP HOT WATER
SALT
1 CLOVE GARLIC, PEELED AND SQUASHED A BIT
5 CUPS COARSELY CHOPPED SPINACH LEAVES
1 1/2 TABLESPOONS BUTTER
3 EGGS
3 TABLESPOONS GRATED PARMESAN CHEESE
1 1/4 POUNDS THICK SLICE OF RUMP STEAK
FRESHLY GROUND BLACK PEPPER
1/4 POUND THINLY SLICED HAM
1/2 CUP RED WINE

Pot-roasted steak with spinach and omelette

Ask your butcher to slice the meat in half horizontally, stopping just before he cuts all the way through so that the steak opens out like a book. I love to serve this with buttered noodles, and you might even like to add a few peas to the omelette for a spotted effect.

Put the celery, carrot, and onion in a processor and pulse until they are finely chopped, or do so by hand. Heat 4 tablespoons of the oil in a flameproof casserole and fry the chopped vegetables over medium heat until they are nicely golden. Add the tomatoes and parsley, and cook for about 5 minutes, until the tomatoes collapse and bubble up thickly. Add 1 cup of hot water, season with salt, and keep warm.

　Meanwhile, heat 2 tablespoons of oil and the garlic in an 11-inch nonstick frying pan and add the spinach. Cook over medium heat until the spinach wilts, turning it over often so that it cooks evenly. Remove from the pan and season with salt. Drain well.

Wipe out the pan with a paper towel. Add the butter and melt over medium-low heat. Beat the eggs, Parmesan, and a little salt together, and pour into the pan. Swirl the pan so that the egg reaches the side to make a flat omelette. Fry until it is just set, spiking it here and there if necessary so that the uncooked egg runs to the bottom. Remove from the heat.

Lay the steak out flat, and cover with a sheet of plastic wrap. Pound with a meat mallet until the steak is 1/8 inch thick all over. Remove the plastic, and season the meat with salt and pepper. Slide the omelette from its pan to cover the meat, then spread the spinach on top, and cover this with the ham slices. Roll up tightly and tie with string.

Heat the remaining oil in the frying pan, and brown the meat on all sides over medium heat, salting the browned parts as you go. Add the wine, and cook until it bubbles up, scraping the bits off the bottom of the pan. Put the meat and the wine juices in the casserole dish with the tomato sauce (if the sauce looks as if it needs more liquid, add a little more water), cover, and simmer over low heat for about 20 minutes, until the meat is cooked through but still tender. Remove from the heat, and leave with the lid on for another 15 minutes before slicing. Serve with the sauce spooned over. Nice with buttered noodles or mashed potatoes.

Serves 4

4 MEDIUM CARROTS, PEELED AND CHOPPED
5 CUPS LOOSELY PACKED SPINACH LEAVES

BÉCHAMEL SAUCE:
4$^{1}/_{2}$ TABLESPOONS BUTTER
$^{1}/_{3}$ CUP ALL-PURPOSE FLOUR
1$^{1}/_{3}$ CUPS MILK, WARMED
SALT AND FRESHLY GROUND BLACK PEPPER
FRESHLY GROUND NUTMEG

$^{3}/_{4}$ CUP GRATED PARMESAN CHEESE
2 EGGS, LIGHTLY BEATEN

Little spinach and carrot ramekins

I use little individual ramekins (about 2$^{1}/_{2}$ inches wide at the top, 1$^{1}/_{2}$ inches across the bottom, and 1$^{1}/_{2}$ inches high). They look good in this size and are perfect servings for all-size humans. These are baked in a bain marie so they stay beautifully moist.

Preheat the oven to 350°F and butter ten little $^{1}/_{2}$-cup ramekins. Cook the carrots in boiling salted water until they are soft. Lift them out with a slotted spoon, purée, and put into a bowl. Add the spinach to the boiling carrot water, and blanch for a few minutes until it is all wilted and soft. Drain, leave until it has cooled enough to handle, and then squeeze out all the excess water. Chop up finely and put in a separate bowl.

To make the béchamel, melt the butter in a small saucepan over low heat. Whisk in the flour and cook for a few minutes, stirring constantly, then begin adding the warm milk. It will be immediately absorbed, so work quickly, whisking with one hand while adding ladlefuls of milk with the other. When the sauce seems to be smooth and not too stiff, add salt, pepper, and a grating of nutmeg, and continue cooking, even after it comes to a boil, for 5 minutes or so, mixing all the time. It should be a very thick and smooth sauce.

Pour off any water that has collected in the bottom of the carrot bowl, then mix in 10 tablespoons of the béchamel along with half of the Parmesan. Stir the rest of the béchamel and Parmesan into the spinach. Taste each bowl, adding extra salt, pepper, or nutmeg if you think it's needed. Add half the beaten eggs to each bowl, and mix them in well.

Divide the spinach mixture among the ramekins. Rap them firmly on the table to flatten the mixture, then divide the carrot purée among the ramekins. The mixture should just fill the molds.

Put the ramekins in a roasting pan and add enough hot water to the pan to come halfway up the sides of the molds. Move the pan to the oven and bake for about 45 minutes, or until the molds are puffed, golden, and firm. Turn the oven off and leave the pan in the oven for about 10 minutes. Remove the ramekins from the pan, run a knife around the rims then turn them out onto plates.

Makes 10

VEGETABLE OIL, FOR GREASING
2/3 CUP POMEGRANATE JUICE (FROM
  2 LARGE POMEGRANATES)
3 TABLESPOONS FRESHLY SQUEEZED
  LEMON JUICE
1/3 CUP SUPERFINE SUGAR
8 TABLESPOONS WATER
1 (1-OUNCE) PACKAGE LEAF GELATIN, OR
  2 TABLESPOONS POWDERED GELATIN
2/3 CUP APPLE JUICE

Pomegranate and apple gelatin desserts

When I was a child, they recommended Jell-O and ice cream after tonsil operations because it goes down so well when you have a sore throat. I forget about Jell-O sometimes, and then, when I remember, I make it— because actually it's like giving your child a slice of pure fruit juice. I make it with a good pure-as-possible juice—you can use any flavor you like, but you do need color in your desserts. Serve the desserts plain, or with a small scoop of vanilla or buttermilk ice cream or even a little pile of the actual fruit, served on the side with a dusting of confectioners' sugar. You can make just three pomegranate and three apple desserts and forget about the stripes, if you're short of time.

Brush four 1-cup molds with vegetable oil and then wipe out the excess oil with a paper towel. If you're using leaf gelatin, put the pomegranate juice, 1 1/2 tablespoons of lemon juice, and 1/4 cup of sugar in a saucepan with 4 tablespoons of water. Heat gently, stirring until the sugar dissolves. Put half the gelatin leaves in a bowl of cold water to soften for a couple of minutes. Squeeze out the excess water and add the gelatin to the pan. Stir until it has completely dissolved. (If you're using powdered gelatin, don't put 4 tablespoons of water into the juice pan, but put it in a small bowl and sprinkle the gelatin over it. Leave for a minute or two until it softens and swells, and then stir it into the hot juice. Continue stirring until it is completely smooth.)

Put the apple juice in a small saucepan with the remaining lemon juice, remaining sugar, and 4 tablespoons of water. Heat gently, stirring until the sugar dissolves. Soak the remaining gelatin leaves in cold water for a couple of minutes and, when softened, squeeze them out. Add to the pan of apple juice and stir until the gelatin has completely dissolved. (Once again, you need to change the method slightly if you're using powdered gelatin.)

Divide half of the pomegranate mixture between two of the molds. Put the remaining mixture to one side, but do not refrigerate. Divide half of the apple mixture between the other two molds and put what's left aside.

Refrigerate the molds for about 3 hours, until the desserts are almost completely set. Now carefully spoon the rest of the apple mixture on top of the pomegranate mixture and vice versa, so that each dessert has two stripes. (If the gelatin mixture has already started to set in the pan, heat it up very slightly to just melt it, leave to cool completely, and then pour over the set layer.) Put the molds back in the fridge for at least 4 hours or overnight, until the desserts are set.

To serve, gently pull the desserts away from the sides of the molds with your fingers. Quickly dip each mold into a bowl of hot water twice (too long and your dessert will dissolve). Turn out onto a plate. If it doesn't want to come away, help it along by slipping your fingers down one side—the whole dessert should then plop onto your plate. Serve plain or with ice cream.

Serves 4

3 EGGS
½ CUP SUPERFINE SUGAR
1 TEASPOON VANILLA EXTRACT
1 CUP MILK
1 VANILLA BEAN
2 CUPS HEAVY WHIPPING
    CREAM

Vanilla ice cream

This is simple and quick to make and fairly essential for serving with a whole range of desserts. I also find just a scoop of vanilla ice cream alone is one of the cleanest and purest foods possible. If you don't have a vanilla bean, just use an extra teaspoon of good vanilla extract. The washed and dried vanilla bean can be popped into a jar of sugar to make vanilla sugar. So next time you need sugar and vanilla, use your vanilla sugar instead.

Whip together the eggs, sugar, and vanilla until smooth and creamy. Put the milk in a saucepan. Split the vanilla bean lengthwise, scrape the seeds into the milk with the tip of a teaspoon, and throw the bean in, too. Heat gently so that the vanilla bean and seeds flavor the milk. Just before the milk comes to a boil, remove it from the heat, and whisk a ladleful into the eggs to acclimatize them. Whisk in another ladleful and then tip the whole lot back into the saucepan with the milk. Put it over the lowest possible heat and cook for a minute or so, whisking all the time, just so that the eggs cook through. Remove from the heat, whisk in the cream, and pour into a bowl or container that has a lid. Leave to cool completely, whisking now and then while it cools so that you get the maximum flavor from the vanilla bean. Remove the vanilla bean and rinse and dry it for another use.

Put the lid on the bowl and put it in the freezer. After an hour give the mixture an energetic whisk with a hand whisk or an electric mixer. Put it back in the freezer and then whisk again after another couple of hours. When the ice cream is nearly firm, give one last whisk and put it back in the freezer to set.

Alternatively, pour into your ice cream machine and churn, following the manufacturer's instructions.

Makes 5 cups

1 ⅓ CUPS CHOPPED SEMISWEET CHOCOLATE
1 ½ CUPS MILK
3 EGG YOLKS
½ CUP SUPERFINE SUGAR
1 TEASPOON VANILLA EXTRACT
1 CUP HEAVY WHIPPING CREAM

Chocolate
ice cream

This is rich and beautiful. It makes me incredibly happy to have a scoop of beautiful chocolate and a scoop of beautiful vanilla next to each other. I don't like ice cream to be too sweet, and the chocolate you use will be important in determining the amount of sugar. Use the best-quality chocolate you can buy. You might even like to try this one day with a couple of spoonfuls of cocoa powder stirred in for an even richer hit of chocolate. Save the whites in the freezer for pavlova or meringues—you never know when you'll need them.

Put the chocolate and milk in a heavy-bottomed saucepan over low heat, whisking often until it has all melted together. Take care that it doesn't stick and burn. Meanwhile, whisk the egg yolks with the sugar and vanilla in a bowl until thick and creamy. Whisk in a ladleful of the warm chocolate milk to acclimatize the eggs. Whisk in another ladleful and then tip the whole lot back into the saucepan and put it over the lowest possible heat. Cook for a minute or so, whisking all the time, just so that the eggs cook through. Remove from the heat. Whisk in the cream and pour into a bowl or container that has a lid. Leave to cool completely and then put the lid on the bowl and put it in the freezer. After an hour give the mixture an energetic whisk with a hand whisk or an electric mixer. Put it back in the freezer and then whisk again after another couple of hours. When the ice cream is nearly firm, give one last whisk and put it back in the freezer to set.

    Alternatively, pour into your ice cream machine and churn, following the manufacturer's instructions.

Makes 5 cups

FOR EACH SUNDAE:
4 TABLESPOONS CRANBERRY SYRUP (PAGE 15),
  FRUIT SAUCE (PAGES 54 AND 107), OR
  CHOCOLATE OR TOFFEE SAUCE (PAGES 321
  AND 247)
2 SCOOPS ICE CREAM
4 TO 5 TABLESPOONS LIGHTLY WHIPPED CREAM

Ice cream sundaes

Once you know your family's favorite flavors, you can really have fun here. Serve these in a big bowl or glass for a very special treat, with your own homemade chocolate, toffee, or fruit sauce, and freshly whipped cream. One scoop chocolate, one scoop vanilla, one scoop maple syrup and vanilla ice cream (page 355) with chocolate sauce is also good. You can also make sorbet sundaes (mango, pomegranate, and strawberry) with a little whipped cream. And you can also scatter some chopped nuts over the cream and add chunks of fresh fruit, too. You can go quite over the top, as long as there are not too many kids seated and waiting.

Drizzle a little of the sauce or syrup around the side of a sundae bowl or dessert glass so that it sticks there. Put the ice cream in the bottom, top with the cream, and drizzle the syrup or sauce over the top. Leave it for a few minutes for the syrup to run down through the cream and ice cream, then serve before the ice cream melts too much.

Makes 1

My children like to have a scoop of chocolate and a scoop of vanilla. And I watch them stirring and staring into their bowls through the various stripes and streaks of brown and white that finally settle into beige soup. It flings me right back in time to my childhood.

FOR EACH MILKSHAKE:
2 SCOOPS CHOCOLATE OR VANILLA ICE CREAM
   (PAGES 376 AND 374)
1 CUP MILK
4 TABLESPOONS CHOCOLATE FUDGE SAUCE OR
   MILKY WAY BAR SAUCE (PAGE 321)

FOR EACH DOUBLE THICKSHAKE:
3 SCOOPS CHOCOLATE OR VANILLA ICE CREAM
   (PAGES 376 AND 374)
4 TABLESPOONS CHOCOLATE FUDGE SAUCE OR
   MILKY WAY BAR SAUCE (PAGE 321)

Chocolate and vanilla milkshakes and double thickshakes

I loved these when I was growing up. I like to make them chocolate or vanilla—both with some chocolate sauce drizzled so that it is stuck around the side of the glass and has to be scraped off with a spoon. Vanilla ice cream with some berry sauce (page 54) dribbled around the glass is also good, or strawberry sorbet (page 59) instead of vanilla ice cream.

If you don't have a special milkshake machine, move the ice cream from the freezer to the fridge 5 minutes or so beforehand so that it is slightly softened and easy to whisk.
   Whisk the ice cream in a bowl until it is soft and creamy. You can do this by hand or with a handheld blender. Add the milk and whisk until smooth and frothy.
   Trickle most of the sauce around a tall glass so that it clings to the side and then pour in the milkshake. Drizzle the last of the sauce on top and serve at once, with straws (everything always tastes delicious with straws).

Serves 1

DOUBLE THICKSHAKE: Whisk the softened ice cream with a handheld blender until it is soft and creamy.
   Trickle most of the sauce around a tall glass so that it clings to the side and then pour in the thickshake. Drizzle the last of the sauce on top and serve at once, with straws and a long teaspoon.

Serves 1

ICE CREAM:
1 CUP MILK
3 EGGS
1/2 CUP SUPERFINE SUGAR
1 TEASPOON VANILLA EXTRACT
2 CUPS HEAVY WHIPPING CREAM

RASPBERRY PUREE:
3 TABLESPOONS SUPERFINE SUGAR
JUICE OF HALF A LEMON
1/2 CUP WATER
2 CUPS RASPBERRIES

Raspberry ripple ice cream

Try to use fresh raspberries here, but frozen will do if you can't find any. Sometimes I love a tiny scoop of this with a tiny scoop of strawberry sorbet and a tiny scoop of vanilla ice cream. Just on its own, or with a couple of vanilla cookies on the side.

For the ice cream, heat the milk gently in a saucepan. Whisk the eggs, sugar, and vanilla extract together in a bowl until they are smooth and creamy. Just before the milk comes to a boil, remove it from the heat, and whisk a ladleful into the eggs to acclimatize them. Whisk in another ladleful and then pour the eggs and milk back into the saucepan. Turn down the heat to its lowest and cook for a minute or so, whisking all the time, just to cook the eggs through. Remove from the heat, whisk in the cream, and pour into a bowl that has a lid. Leave to cool completely, whisking now and then while it cools.

Put the lid on the bowl and put it in the freezer. After an hour, remove the bowl from the freezer and give the mix an energetic whisk with a hand whisk or an electric mixer and then put it back in the freezer. Whisk again after another couple of hours. Put it back in the freezer until it is nearly firm.

Meanwhile, make the raspberry purée. Put the sugar, lemon juice, and 1/2 cup of water in a small saucepan, and bring to a boil. Simmer over low heat for about 5 minutes until it has reduced a bit. Take it off the heat, add the raspberries, and then purée until smooth. Strain the purée through a fine sieve to catch all the seeds. Cool completely.

Swirl the purée through the ice cream with a spoon. Make a few more swirls, folds, and pirouettes, but not so many that the purée starts to blend in with the ice cream. Cover the bowl again and return to the freezer to set completely.

Alternatively, pour the ice cream mixture into an ice cream machine and churn following the manufacturer's instructions. When it is ready, transfer to a freezer container, and then add the raspberry purée and make your swirls.

Take out of the freezer a few minutes before serving so that it is not rock hard.

Makes 6 cups

1/2 POUND PLUS 2 TABLESPOONS (21/4 STICKS)
    BUTTER, SOFTENED
1 1/4 CUPS SUPERFINE SUGAR
4 EGGS
2 1/4 CUPS ALL-PURPOSE FLOUR
1 1/2 TEASPOONS BAKING POWDER
2/3 CUP HEAVY WHIPPING CREAM
1 TEASPOON VANILLA EXTRACT
2 1/2 TABLESPOONS UNSWEETENED COCOA POWDER

Chocolate and vanilla marble cake

This is a recipe from my mother's Finnish friend Iria. She and my mom say that every Finnish woman has her own recipe for a classic stripy "tiger cake." You can also make this with just vanilla and have a plain sponge cake—good for filling with jam and cream or covering with a chocolate frosting—but most people love to see the two different colors in the cake. Children enjoy helping with this—they love licking the beaters and the chocolate and vanilla bowls.

Preheat the oven to 350°F. Grease and flour a 9 1/2-inch springform cake pan or a small bundt pan.

    Beat the butter and sugar together until pale and creamy. Add the eggs one at a time, beating well after each one goes in. Sift in the flour and baking powder and beat well, then beat in the cream so that you have a fluffy mixture. Divide the batter between two bowls, putting more than half into one bowl. To this, add the vanilla, and beat it in well. Sift the cocoa into the other half, whisking it in completely.

    Dollop most of the vanilla batter into the greased pan (you don't have to entirely cover the bottom). Then dollop the chocolate batter in here and there, followed by the remaining few tablespoons of the vanilla batter. Use a skewer or the tip of a teaspoon to make a few swirls so that the two batters become a bit stripy. You don't want them mixing together, but distinct white and brown patches swirling into each other.

    Bake for 50 to 60 minutes, or until a skewer poked into the center comes out clean. Cool in the pan before turning out.

Makes one 9 1/2-inch cake

1/4 POUND PLUS 5 TABLESPOONS BUTTER,
 SOFTENED
2/3 CUP SUPERFINE SUGAR
SALT
1 EGG
1 TEASPOON VANILLA EXTRACT
2 CUPS ALL-PURPOSE FLOUR
1 1/2 TABLESPOONS UNSWEETENED COCOA POWDER

Chocolate and vanilla cookies

These are lovely and easy, and something that kids can make from beginning to end, as long as you don't worry too much how they turn out. They could also be good to use for making and shaping Christmas decorations—you could make white or brown faces with eyes, mouth, hair, even white and brown braids. . . . You might like to add some ground cinnamon, anise, cardamom, or other spices to the dough.

Mash together the butter and sugar in a bowl with a wooden spoon. Add a pinch of salt and all but 1 1/2 tablespoons of the flour, and work them in. Whisk the egg with the vanilla and add this to the bowl, mixing it all well. Now knead it quickly, gently, and thoroughly.

Divide the dough in half. Add the cocoa to one half, kneading it in thoroughly. Knead the remaining 1 1/2 tablespoons of flour into the other half. Pat both doughs down into flattish disks, cover separately with plastic wrap, and refrigerate for about 30 minutes.

Preheat the oven to 350°F.

On a lightly floured surface, roll out the doughs separately to a thickness of about 1/4 inch, depending on what you decide to make. You can cut out circles, squares, and Christmas shapes with a cookie cutter, cut free-form shapes with a small blunt knife, or make braids by folding strips of each color over each other and pressing the ends together. Put on baking sheets lined with parchment paper, allowing a little room for the cookies to spread. Bake for 12 to 15 minutes, or until they are crisp.

Makes plenty!

2¼ CUPS PECANS OR WALNUTS,
    COARSELY CHOPPED
1 POUND (4 STICKS) BUTTER
1 TEASPOON VANILLA EXTRACT
SALT
2½ TABLESPOONS WATER
2¼ CUPS SUGAR
1⅔ CUPS CHOPPED SEMISWEET CHOCOLATE

Chocolate toffee nut squares

These are my friend Toni's. She always arrives with a bagful for me and the kids, and so she finally showed me how to make them. You don't have to cut them into perfect squares—they are nice broken up into irregular bits. These are lovely wrapped up and taken to a friend as a gift—just as Toni did for me.

Line an 11 by 16 by 1-inch baking pan with a double thickness of parchment paper. Sprinkle the nuts in, and flatten them with the back of a wooden spoon to make a compact even layer.

Put the butter and vanilla in a heavy-bottomed saucepan and add a pinch of salt and 2½ tablespoons of water. Heat until the butter melts and just starts to bubble, then add the sugar. Cook over low heat, stirring almost continuously to prevent it sticking to the bottom, until you have a thick, rich toffee-colored mass that comes away from the side of the pan when stirred—if you have a candy thermometer, it will be at just below 300°F. It could take up to 20 minutes to get there, depending on your pan and the heat. If the toffee looks like it's separating at any point, take it off the heat and vigorously beat in 2½ tablespoons of hot water to bring it together again, taking care, as it may splash up.

Carefully pour the toffee over the nuts, pouring around the sides first, and working your way in to cover all the nuts. Sprinkle the chocolate as evenly as possible over the hot toffee, then leave it for 5 minutes to soften before spreading it evenly with a spatula. Leave to cool and set completely—in the fridge if the weather is very hot. Use the parchment paper to lift it out of the pan. Break up into pieces and keep in a cookie jar, or in the fridge if the weather's hot.

Makes about 20 squares

multicolor

Smoothies
Tiny savory tartlets
Raw vegetables with sauce for dunking
Meat and vegetable soup
Mixed vegetable risotto
Sausage and potato frittata
Meatloaf with roasted vegetables
Roasted zucchini and tomatoes with thyme
Pavlovas with oranges and cherries
Tiny sweet tartlets with crema and fruit
Pandoro birthday cake

- memory -

Our toys might come alive at night, we believed, just like in the stories they had read us. And so we tried not to fall asleep, fighting against our dragging lids, and crossing our hearts that we'd wake each other when the excitement began. We never saw that happen, but we could imagine it as we played the next day—skirts flapping, dusty shoes, and trying not to crumple the butterfly's wing that we had just saved.

We would sift through our dried flowers and want to help, now and then, in the house with the fun jobs, like snipping away the roses that had finished with their blossoming, or spilling more water or food into our dog's bowl. Washing up the dishes and mopping floors were among our very favorites, along with whisking anything cakey or cookie-like and licking the bowl afterwards, and washing our dolls' clothes in a big bowl of soapy water outside on the veranda. There were also some dull things that we sometimes got asked to do, but mostly we tried to shuffle away, pretending our ears were blocked. Laying the table was an in-between kind of job. But tidying up was our worst. We just couldn't see the point of that at all.

PEACH SMOOTHIE:
1 JUICY PEACH, PEELED, PITTED, AND SLICED
1/2 CUP GREEK-STYLE PLAIN YOGURT
1/2 CUP MILK
1 HEAPING TEASPOON HONEY

APRICOT SMOOTHIE:
4 APRICOTS, PEELED, PITTED, AND CUT INTO CHUNKS
1/2 CUP BUTTERMILK
1/2 CUP MILK
1 TEASPOON HONEY

STRAWBERRY SMOOTHIE:
3/4 CUP STRAWBERRIES, HULLED
1/2 CUP BUTTERMILK
1/2 CUP MILK
1 TEASPOON HONEY

BLUEBERRY AND RASPBERRY SMOOTHIE:
1/2 CUP BLUEBERRIES
1/2 CUP RASPBERRIES
1/2 CUP MILK
1/3 CUP GREEK-STYLE PLAIN YOGURT
1 TEASPOON MAPLE SYRUP

Smoothies

These are wonderful for breakfast or just as a snack. You can use pretty much any fruit you like. My kids love these and like to see a wedge of the fruit on the top of their smoothie glass. Use a nice creamy plain yogurt and make sure your fruit is ripe and cold before you make these.

Blend all the ingredients until very smooth and frothy, and add more honey or maple syrup if you prefer your smoothie sweeter.

All make 1 large glass

PASTRY SHELLS:
1/2 POUND PLUS 1 TABLESPOON BUTTER, CUT
    INTO CUBES
2 CUPS ALL-PURPOSE FLOUR
1/2 TEASPOON SALT
4 TABLESPOONS COLD WATER
2 TEASPOONS OLIVE OIL

Tiny savory tartlets

I always make these for birthdays. They are just the right size to pop into a child's mouth. Adults love them, too, and you can be as modern as you like with your fillings. The number of pastry shells you get will depend on the size of your molds. Mine are tiny individual ones, while some are punched into a pan of 12 or 24.

For the pastry, put the butter and flour in a bowl with 1/2 teaspoon of salt, and crumble with your fingers until it is like coarse sand. Add 4 tablespoons of cold water and the oil, and work into a loose dough. Knead quickly but gently until smooth, then flatten, cover with plastic wrap, and refrigerate for about an hour.

Preheat the oven to 350°F and have ready 45 tiny tart molds or mini-muffin pans that are 1 3/4 inches across the top and no more than 3/4 inch deep. They don't need to be greased (there is enough butter in the dough).

Break off small balls of pastry about the size of cherry tomatoes, and flatten into the molds with your thumb and forefinger, pressing to 1/8 inch thick. (If your molds are shallow, roll out the pastry first, then press into the molds and trim the excess pastry away.) Bake for about 20 minutes, or until golden, and then cool a bit in the molds before gently removing. Leave to cool completely before filling.

These can be made the day before and kept in an airtight container overnight.

Makes about 40 tartlet shells

FILLING IDEAS:
- soft-boiled eggs mashed with olive oil and chopped parsley;
- avocado mashed with lemon juice and paprika;
- an 11-ounce can of tuna in oil, mashed with 3 soft-boiled eggs, a chopped scallion, 2 tablespoon chopped parsley, 3 tablespoons mayonnaise, the juice of 1 lemon, a pinch of paprika, and 2 1/2 tablespoons light olive oil.

The tartlets are best with something creamy to balance the pastry. Any soft cheese like mozzarella works well, and sometimes I like to use 1 cup smooth ricotta mixed with 1/4 cup grated Parmesan, 1 tablespoon olive oil, the juice of half a lemon, and a little fresh thyme. I fill all the shells with this, then top with any of the following:
- roasted tomatoes, basil oil, Parmesan flakes;
- smoked salmon, dill sprigs, a drizzle of lemon juice;
- bresaola or prosciutto, torn basil leaves, Parmesan flakes.

7 TABLESPOONS OLIVE OIL
1 TEASPOON HONEY
1/2 TEASPOON DIJON MUSTARD
1 1/2 TABLESPOONS SESAME SEEDS
1 1/2 TABLESPOONS BALSAMIC VINEGAR
SALT
JUICE OF 1 LEMON
1 ROSEMARY SPRIG
1 CLOVE GARLIC, PEELED AND SQUASHED A BIT
1 RED BELL PEPPER, CUT INTO THICKISH CHUNKS
1 SMALL FENNEL BULB, TRIMMED, HALVED,
    AND CUT INTO SLICES
4 INNER CELERY STALKS, CUT INTO STICKS
FIRM INNER LEAVES OF A SMALL ROMAINE LETTUCE
4 TO 5 THICK SLICES BROWN BREAD, CUT
    INTO CHUNKS

Raw vegetables with sauce for dunking

Use the best-looking, healthiest, and most colorful vegetables you can find. You might like to make variations—some mashed avocado, or a soft creamy cheese for dipping as well. The sauce can be served in individual bowls or just one big communal bowl if it's family.

Put the oil, honey, mustard, sesame seeds, and vinegar in a bowl, and whisk together well with a fork. Add salt to taste. Squeeze in lemon juice, tasting as you go, and stop when you're happy with the flavor. Add the rosemary and garlic, and leave for the flavors to mingle while you prepare the vegetables.

Rinse the vegetables, drain, and pat dry. Stack in groups on a platter, and pile the bread on, too. Serve with the bowl of sauce and a pile of napkins.

Serves 4

1 ¼ POUNDS LEAN STEWING BEEF
10 CUPS COLD WATER
4 OR 5 VERY RIPE TOMATOES
2 LEAFY CELERY STALKS, CHOPPED
3 CARROTS, PEELED AND CHOPPED
1 HANDFUL PARSLEY, COARSELY CHOPPED
2 BAY LEAVES
5 ALLSPICE BERRIES
SALT
4 SMALLISH ZUCCHINI, CHOPPED
3 OR 4 MEDIUM POTATOES, PEELED AND CUT
  INTO SMALL CHUNKS
FRESHLY GROUND BLACK PEPPER
GRATED PARMESAN CHEESE, TO SERVE
OLIVE OIL, TO SERVE

Meat and vegetable soup

You'll need the largest stockpot you've got to make this nutritious and tasty soup. A bit of everything goes in here and you can take it straight to the table as a complete meal with your favorite bread. You could leave out the meat and use just vegetables, if you like, adding a couple more varieties. I use very lean beef here but, if you like the taste of the fat, make sure you buy a good piece of meat and don't trim it. Keep the cut-up potatoes in a bowl of cold water or cut them up later while the soup is cooking, as they only need to go in for the last 40 minutes. This is an abundant amount of soup that will serve many and still give you leftovers and enough time the next day to make a cake.

Cut up the meat into 1-inch cubes, or smaller if you would prefer to find them that way in your bowl later. Put them in a large stockpot and cover with about 10 cups of cold water. Bring to a boil, skimming the surface until it is clear. Simmer, covered, for about 30 minutes.

Meanwhile, cut the core out of each tomato and cut a cross on the bottom. Drop them into the boiling meat broth for about 20 seconds, until they wrinkle and the skin starts to come away. Lift them out with a slotted spoon, peel them, and chop them up. Add to the meat pan with the celery and carrots, and bring back to a boil, skimming the surface again if necessary. Add the parsley, bay leaves, and allspice berries, counting how many you put in so you know exactly how many to remove before serving. Season with salt, lower the heat, and simmer for about 1 ½ hours, uncovered at first until the liquid level reduces a bit, and then covered. Add the zucchini and potatoes about 40 minutes from the end. Taste that there is enough salt and add pepper, if you want. Check the liquid level, adding a little more water toward the end if you prefer it more soupy than stewy. Serve warm, with Parmesan and olive oil drizzled over the top of each serving.

Serves 6 to 8

4 TABLESPOONS OLIVE OIL
1 RED ONION, FINELY CHOPPED
1 LEAFY CELERY STALK, CUT INTO SMALL BLOCKS
2 SMALL CARROTS, PEELED AND CUT INTO
 SMALL BLOCKS
2 OR 3 SMALL ZUCCHINI, CUT INTO
 SMALL BLOCKS
2/3 CUP SLICED GREEN BEANS
1 LARGE RIPE TOMATO, PEELED, DESEEDED, AND
 CHOPPED
2 OR 3 BASIL LEAVES, TORN
1 SCANT CUP RISOTTO RICE
1/2 CUP WHITE WINE
5 CUPS HOT WATER
SALT AND FRESHLY GROUND BLACK PEPPER
2 TABLESPOONS CHOPPED FRESH PARSLEY
2 TABLESPOONS BUTTER
1/3 CUP GRATED PARMESAN CHEESE, PLUS
 EXTRA FOR SERVING

Mixed vegetable risotto

Sometimes I like to serve this a little more liquid than a normal risotto so that it's a bit soupy when I take it to the table but carries on absorbing liquid. You can add absolutely any other vegetables you like to this basic version. I give the children a large tea cup as well as their plate of risotto, then they can spoon tiny quantities of risotto into the cup, patting it around the edge, so that it cools quicker. Giovanni has always done this since he was a child, so that he doesn't have to wait for ages for his risotto to cool down.

Heat the oil in a wide heavy-bottomed pan suitable for making risotto. Sauté the onion, celery, and carrots over medium heat until they are lightly golden and softened. Add the zucchini, beans, tomato, and some of the basil, and sauté for another 5 minutes or so. Add the rice, sauté for a couple of minutes to coat it with oil, and then pour in the wine. Let it bubble up and then reduce. Add 4 cups of the hot water and some salt and pepper, and bring to a boil. Lower the heat and simmer for about 20 minutes, stirring now and then.

  Toward the end, when it looks like most of the liquid has been absorbed, add the remaining 1 cup of hot water. Taste to check that there is enough salt. The risotto is ready when the rice is cooked and the dish is still a bit liquid. Stir in the rest of the basil, the parsley, butter, and Parmesan, and leave with the lid on for a couple of minutes. Serve with extra Parmesan.

Serves 5 to 6

2 SMALL POTATOES, SCRUBBED
7 TABLESPOONS OLIVE OIL
ABOUT 3/4 POUND ITALIAN-STYLE SAUSAGES,
    SKINNED AND CRUMBLED
1 RED ONION, CHOPPED
1 CARROT, PEELED AND CHOPPED
1 CUP FINELY SLICED BUTTON MUSHROOMS
5 TABLESPOONS CHOPPED FRESH PARSLEY
6 EGGS, LIGHTLY BEATEN

Sausage and potato frittata

This is from Richard and Sue, my two American friends, and I like this for a Sunday breakfast, or supper with whole wheat bread. If you think your children won't enjoy the vegetables here, you could make it with just the sausage, potatoes, and parsley—or anything else you know will be appreciated.

Boil the potatoes in their skins in lightly salted water until they are tender but not breaking up. Drain, cool, and then cut into chunks, keeping the skins on. Put to one side for now.

Heat $2^{1/2}$ tablespoons of the oil in a $10^{1/2}$-inch nonstick frying pan over medium heat and fry the sausage meat until it is quite deeply golden, breaking up clusters with a wooden spoon. Lift out into a bowl with a slotted spoon. Add the onion to the pan and sauté until golden, then add the carrot. Sauté for 5 minutes or so, until both become soft and a bit gooey. Add another $1^{1/2}$ tablespoons of oil and the mushrooms, and sauté until the mushrooms have given up their water and turned golden. Season lightly if needed. Spoon the contents of the pan into the bowl with the sausage.

Preheat the broiler to medium-high.

Add the last of the oil to the pan and sauté the potatoes until they have a golden crust in some places. Stir in the parsley and the contents of the sausage bowl, and cook for a minute or two. Reduce the heat to medium-low and pour in the eggs, stirring everything with a wooden spoon so that the eggs leak under here and there. Once the bottom looks softly set, put the pan under the broiler so that the frittata sets just enough to be cut into slices. Don't overdo it though, as this is nice when it is still a little soft. Serve warm with your favorite bread.

Serves 6 to 8

ABOUT 4 SLICES WHITE BREAD, CRUSTS REMOVED
1/2 CUP MILK
2 LARGE CARROTS, PEELED
2 LARGE ZUCCHINI, TRIMMED
1 LARGE POTATO, PEELED
1 RED BELL PEPPER
1 1/4 POUNDS LEAN GROUND BEEF
3 TABLESPOONS CHOPPED FRESH PARSLEY
1 CLOVE GARLIC, FINELY CHOPPED, PLUS 2 CLOVES GARLIC, UNPEELED
2 TABLESPOONS GRATED PARMESAN CHEESE
1 EGG, LIGHTLY BEATEN
SALT
5 TABLESPOONS OLIVE OIL
4 OUNCES THINLY SLICED PANCETTA
2 SAGE SPRIGS
2 SMALL ROSEMARY SPRIGS
1 1/2 TABLESPOONS ALL-PURPOSE FLOUR
1/2 CUP WHITE WINE
1 CUP HOT WATER

Meatloaf with roasted vegetables

My friend Julia, who is a marvelous cook, showed me this. You could also make it with leftover roast meat—all pulsed up in a processor. Use a large baking pan so that your vegetables can sit quite flat and are not steaming on top of each other. If you prefer, leave out the sauce-making at the end and just serve this with tomato ketchup.

Preheat the oven to 350°F. Soak the bread in the milk for about 15 minutes, squashing it up with your hands so it collapses.

Cut the carrots in half lengthwise, then each half into four. Cut the zucchini in half lengthwise, then in half again to make chunks. Cut the potato into more or less the same shaped wedges, and the pepper into strips. Put to one side.

Put the ground beef in a bowl with the parsley, chopped garlic, Parmesan, egg, soaked bread, and a level teaspoon of salt. Mix together until smooth, then form a very large loaf like a giant egg.

Drizzle half the olive oil into a large flameproof baking pan, and put the meat-loaf on top. Cover with overlapping slices of pancetta, tucking them in at the bottom. Scatter the vegetables around, drizzle them with the remaining oil, and toss with some salt. Tuck the sage, rosemary, and garlic under the vegetables. Bake for about 1 1/4 hours, turning the vegetables halfway through. They should be crusty and golden and the pancetta crispy. Turn the oven off. Remove the meatloaf and vegetables to a platter, cover with foil, and put back in the oven to keep warm.

Put the baking pan on the stovetop over high heat and sprinkle in the flour. Cook, stirring constantly to scrape up all the bits and pieces from the bottom of the dish. Pour in the wine and stir until it has evaporated. Add 1 cup of hot water, season with salt, and cook until the sauce becomes smooth and thickens a bit. Serve with the meatloaf cut into thick slices and the vegetables.

Serves 6

7 OR 8 SMALL ZUCCHINI
ABOUT 3 OR 4 CARROTS, PEELED
ABOUT 6 TOMATOES
3 CLOVES GARLIC, FINELY CHOPPED
1 LEAFY CELERY STALK, HALVED LENGTHWISE
   AND THINLY SLICED
4 TABLESPOONS CHOPPED FRESH PARSLEY
8 TABLESPOONS OLIVE OIL
SALT AND FRESHLY GROUND BLACK PEPPER
6 THYME SPRIGS

Roasted zucchini and tomatoes with thyme

I love this—it is healthy and appetizing and tasty for a side dish or as a light meal on its own with some bread. It is important that your tomatoes are deep red and beautifully ripe. I particularly like this simple combination, but you can use other herbs instead—perhaps basil or rosemary—and you might like to include some other vegetables, depending on who you are serving and what they like. Red bell peppers, eggplant, and potatoes could all be cut up and included here. You'll need one large baking pan of about 10 by 14 inches where the vegetables can sit quite flat. If you aren't going to serve this immediately, switch off the oven when the vegetables are cooked, but leave the pan in there to cool down completely.

Preheat the oven to 400°F. Trim the zucchini and slice them diagonally into chunks of about 1 1/4 inches: Slice once in one direction, and then in the other direction, and so on. Put them in a large baking pan. Slice the carrots diagonally in one direction to give longish strips about 1/8 inch thick. Add to the pan. Cut the tomatoes into wedges (six or eight depending on the size of the tomato) from top to bottom. Put in the dish and add the garlic, celery, parsley, and oil. Season quite generously with salt and pepper, roll up your sleeves, and mix everything through with your hands. I love doing this, and so do my kids, but you can use a large spoon if you prefer. Bury the thyme sprigs underneath and put the pan in the oven. Bake, uncovered, for 30 minutes, turning the vegetables over once in this time.

Turn the vegetables again, lower the heat to 350°F, and cook for another 1 1/4 hours, or until the vegetables are golden roasted and moist and the natural sweetness of the tomatoes and carrots has come into being. Turn the vegetables once or twice more during this time, trying not to mash things up, but the tomatoes will invariably be melting and losing their shape. There should be very little liquid left, so you may have to add a few drops of water. Serve hot, or at room temperature.

Serves 6 to 8

MULTICOLOR

3 LARGE EGG WHITES, AT ROOM TEMPERATURE
1 TEASPOON CORNSTARCH
1 CUP SUPERFINE SUGAR
A FEW DROPS OF VANILLA EXTRACT
1/2 TEASPOON APPLE OR WHITE WINE VINEGAR

TO SERVE:
2 ORANGES
24 CHERRIES
1 CUP HEAVY WHIPPING CREAM
1 1/2 TABLESPOONS CONFECTIONERS' SUGAR,
    PLUS SOME FOR SERVING

Pavlovas with oranges and cherries

This makes eight small pavlovas, but if you want one big one, just double the amounts and extend the cooking time by 10 minutes. The egg yolks can be used for making egg custard (page 135), or chocolate ice cream (page 376), or they can be added to an omelette. If you are making a large pavlova, pile all the meringue into the center of your lined baking sheet and pat it out to about an 11-inch circle, smoothing the middle of the top where your cream and fruit will sit. If you want to make 16 small pavlovas, use two baking sheets and switch them around in the oven halfway through the baking time. And, if you want to, you can make them even smaller for children and get more out of the mixture. I like this with oranges and cherries, but you can put pretty much any fruit on top with the cream. A few chopped pistachios always look good, as well.

Preheat the oven to 300°F and line a large baking sheet with parchment paper. Whisk the egg whites in a large bowl and, once they form white peaks and start stiffening, add the cornstarch. Begin adding the sugar, sprinkling it in a bit at a time, and keep whisking until you have added it all and everything seems like it may climb out of the bowl on its own. Whisk in the vanilla and vinegar.

Use two tablespoons to form the meringues on the baking sheet—make eight rounded piles that are about 4 inches across, although you could make them a bit taller, slimmer, or more elegant if you like. Flatten the tops slightly so that your cream and fruit will have somewhere to sit, and smooth around the sides with the back of a teaspoon. Cook on the middle shelf of the oven for 40 minutes or so (check after 10 minutes and lower the temperature a little if the meringues are coloring). Switch off the oven, and leave the pavlovas in for 30 to 40 minutes to cool, then remove them from the oven to cool completely. You can then store them, sealed, at room temperature for up to 5 days until you are ready to serve them.

To serve, peel the oranges with a sharp knife, taking off all the pith. Cut out the segments by slicing down either side of the membranes. Halve the cherries and remove the pits. Whip the cream and confectioners' sugar until peaks form, spoon onto the pavlovas, and scatter with fruit. Dust with confectioners' sugar.

Serves 8

1/4 POUND PLUS 1 TABLESPOON BUTTER, CUT INTO CUBES
2 1/2 TABLESPOONS SUPERFINE SUGAR
2 CUPS ALL-PURPOSE FLOUR
SALT
4 TABLESPOONS COLD WATER
2 TEASPOONS OLIVE OIL

CREMA:
2 2/3 CUPS MILK
1/4 CUP ALL-PURPOSE FLOUR
1/4 CUP CORNSTARCH
1/2 CUP SUPERFINE SUGAR
3 EGG YOLKS
3 TABLESPOONS BUTTER
1 TEASPOON VANILLA EXTRACT
1/2 CUP HEAVY WHIPPING CREAM

Tiny sweet tartlets with crema and fruit

Top these with fresh fruit such as raspberries, grapes, pomegranate seeds, and wild strawberries. If you like, you can make the tart shells and crema the day before, but whisk the cream into the crema just before filling the shells. You will probably have some crema left over, so you could dollop it into pancakes, or eat it with cookies, or just straight off the spoon.

For the pastry, put the butter, sugar, and flour in a bowl with a small pinch of salt, and crumble with your fingers until it is like coarse sand. Add 4 tablespoons of cold water and the oil and work into a loose dough. Knead quickly but gently until smooth, then flatten, cover with plastic wrap, and refrigerate for about an hour.

Preheat the oven to 350°F and have ready 45 tiny tart molds or mini-muffin pans that are 1 3/4 inches across the top and no more than 3/4 inch deep. They don't need to be greased (there is enough butter in the dough).

Break off small balls of pastry about the size of cherry tomatoes and flatten into the molds with your thumb and forefinger, pressing to 1/8 inch thick. (If your molds are shallow, roll out the pastry first, then press into the molds and trim the tops.) Bake for about 20 minutes, or until golden, then cool a bit in the molds before gently removing. Leave to cool completely before filling.

For the crema, put 2 cups of the milk in a pan and warm it over low heat. Mix the flour, cornstarch, and sugar together in a bowl. Whisk the remaining milk with the egg yolks, add to the bowl, and whisk until smooth. Pour into a saucepan and put over medium-low heat. Gradually stir in the warm milk and keep stirring until it thickens. Add the butter and vanilla, and stir until smooth. Remove from the heat and allow to cool, stirring often. Cover and refrigerate until ready to use.

Just before filling the pastry shells, whip the cream to soft peaks. Give the crema an energetic whisk so there are no lumps, then fold the whipped cream through. Dollop a teaspoon or so into each shell and top with a bit of fruit. Keep in the fridge if you are not eating them straightaway.

Makes about 45

½ CUP MILK
½ TEASPOON ORANGE FOOD COLORING
4 CUPS COARSELY CHOPPED WHITE
    CHOCOLATE
1 PANDORO CAKE
SMALL COLORED CANDIES, LARGER
    CANDIES, AND SMALL LOLLIPOPS
BIRTHDAY CANDLES

Pandoro birthday cake

For this you will need one pandoro cake (from an Italian bakery) with its beautifully exaggerated form. In an emergency, once, I used this as a cake for Cassia's birthday. I iced it with bright orange chocolate that I dripped over the whole gorgeous pandoro, top and sides, and then stuck candy into. If you can't find bright orange chocolate, just use white chocolate mixed with orange food coloring. This cake will keep well for a couple of days, so you can make it in advance.

Put the milk and food coloring in a small saucepan and heat until hot but not boiling. Keep warm.

Put the chocolate in a large bowl over a saucepan of boiling water, making sure that the water doesn't touch the bottom of the bowl. Heat, stirring a few times, until the chocolate melts and is quite smooth. Stir in the hot colored milk and continue heating and stirring until it is all blended in and the chocolate is glossy and smooth.

Put the pandoro on a large serving plate. Quickly cover it with the chocolate, drizzling and spreading it with a spatula as you work. It doesn't have to be perfect —it is lovely exaggerated. Stick the candies on just before the chocolate sets, positioning the larger and heavier ones closer to the bottom so they don't slide down, and holding them in place until they take hold. Decorate with the lollipops and candles.

Serves many

It's the memories that really
make you rich . . .

I remember stepping out onto our school stage, searching for the faces of those I loved most among all the hundreds of others. The same faces that fed me first and tucked special things into small boxes for me to take to school.

Now, I will sew beads onto feathers for their concerts, encourage them when their tummies are sore from too much candy, and have them wake up to the smell of hot buttered toast.

They crawl along at the pace of tortoises, stopping to admire things I long ago lost time for, chattering in their squeaky notes. Those wonderful calm moments of no rivalry—just going along with the flow and the evergreen jigsaw-puzzling that keeps one family boat from sinking. For how can they all be allowed to row when they want to, and stop when they are tired?

I line them up at night among their dolls and toys and examine their perfect faces and fraying toenails. I love you, mice . . .

APPLES FOR SAM

D

Q

R

S

T

V

APPLES FOR SAM

from Tessa

Thank you Giovanni (Pepsi) for your love and trust, and to my mice Yasmine (Mini) and Cassia (Cha-cha)—the pearls in my life —and to cousins Anais and Daniel for the fun always. Thank you Tanja (Ludi) and Nicolas (Nin) for our colorful and varied childhood memories. To mom and dad for being the best.

To Kay for your insight and trust, to Jo and Jane for your incredible generosity in time and soul, and to Juliet and Diana, Sarah, Inca and all the team who helped to carry this book to the end of the rainbow. Thank you nonna Wilma and nonno Mario—I will always walk next to you with a basket to collect bits and pieces. To aunt Julietta and aunt Paola and all those who helped me to gather recipes, watered my ideas, gave me your own flowers and answered thousands of questions. I thank you for your enthusiasm: Richard, Sue, Lisa, Ella, Julia, Fabio, Luca, Luisa, Giacomo, Angela, Caterina, Paolo, Paola, Barbara, Andrea, Alessandro, Francesca, Anabelle, Adam, Peta, Artemis, Nikki, Anette, Kiki, Maria, Evelyn, Jem, Patrizia, Toni, Sylvana, Mariella, Agnese, Harriet, Iria, Alexia, Bernard, Alan, Gill, Kristen, Jo, Didi, Ioanna, and Nina.

And to my team—Michail, Manos, and Lisa. You are something magical. Thank you.